ROBESPIERRE

ROBESPIERRE

Portrait of a Revolutionary Democrat

———◆◆———

GEORGE RUDÉ

THE VIKING PRESS · NEW YORK

Published in 1976 by The Viking Press, Inc.
625 Madison Avenue, New York, N. Y. 10022

LIBRARY OF CONGRESS CATALOGING IN PUBLICATION DATA
    Rudé, George
        Robespierre : portrait of a Revolutionary Democrat.
        Bibliography: p.
        Includes index.
        1.   Robespierre, Maximilien Marie Isidore de, 1758-1794.
    DC146. R6R83 1975   944.04′1′0924[B]   75-2448
    ISBN 0-670-60128-4

Printed in U.S.A.

CONTENTS

Contents

ILLUSTRATIONS

INTRODUCTION

It is one of the hazards of the author of a book on the French Revolution that his intention to write something entirely fresh or original is liable to be overtaken by events. For the Revolution is one of those episodes in human history that offers an inexhaustible field for exploration; and, even today, after more than a century and a half of Revolutionary studies, as soon as one book appears on the publishers' lists at least another dozen – and I speak only of France, Britain and the U.S.A. – are already in the course of preparation. It is true that the hazard of having the ground cut from under his feet is not so great when an author chooses to focus on one single figure – even one as eminent as Robespierre – rather than on the Revolutionary period as a whole; and when, four years ago, I began to plan this book, I was comforted by the fact that no major study of him had appeared in English since J. M. Thompson wrote his great 2-volume biography over 35 years before. Yet fashions inevitably change and interest in Robespierre, for so many years at a low ebb in the English-speaking world, has revived, no doubt under the impact of recent world events; and, where the field was relatively open a couple of years ago, two biographies have now appeared in English, of which the first was published in 1972 and the second has been announced for publication this year.

Such a development, while it marks a welcome addition to Robespierrist studies, comes, of course, as a bit of a shock to an author who thought he had the field to himself. Yet I am a little reassured by the fact that mine is not, according to some definitions at least, a biography at all. It is not one, for example, in the sense recently given to the term by Mr John Brooke, who, in offering his own biography of George III to the public, writes that "the technique of the biographer is like that of the detective of fiction: no fact, however trivial, is without value in reconstructing the life of his subject". And, to illustrate the point, he proposes not merely to present his subject "warts and all", but to find answers to such questions as: what time did he get up in the morning? did he shave himself or was he shaved by his valet? what did he have for breakfast? how did he spend his day? what did he like for dinner? and when did he go to bed? As the reader will see, no more than a casual attention is paid to such matters in this volume; and while Mr Brooke may occasionally be thought to be over-zealous in pursuing his subject into the bed-chamber, my fault is no doubt the opposite one of leaving such intimacies almost strictly alone. I confess, too, that even on the subject of "warts" I have been what to some readers may appear unduly selective; for I have not been much concerned, as some earlier English historians and biographers of Robespierre appear to have been, whether he would have been an agreeable dinner-companion or a suitable match for my daughter. So, while not attempting to hide them, I have attached little importance to certain of his less attractive personal characteristics, such as his lack of a sense of humour, his priggishness and personal vanity, his "irascible sensitivity" (as a contemporary put it), and his indifference to, or contempt for, the common pleasures of life. Such a failing in social graces is not calculated to "make friends and influence people" and, as the reader will see in the second part of this book, they won him many enemies both in his lifetime and since; yet they have not seemed to me to be more than of marginal relevance to the study of a political leader and practitioner of revolution and of the impact he made on the history of his times.

This, in fact, is a political portrait rather than a personal biography, though the one does not always exclude the other. It is divided into four parts, of which the first is narrative-descriptive and the other three are thematic and analytical. In the first part, I have attempted to present Robespierre in the context of the major events of the pre-Revolutionary and Revolutionary years. This is intended to provide the non-specialist reader with a brief outline of the *facts* of the case, though he must not suppose that even such a bald presentation is entirely untouched by the author's personal prejudices, choices and whims.

In the second part, I have thought it useful to present the "changing image" of Robespierre as it has evolved, over the 180 years that have passed since his death, from the opinions expressed about him by succeeding generations of opponents and supporters. These are mainly historians; and the reader will note that while there have been wide divergences in the views of historians of every generation, there has been a distinct tendency for the *collective* opinion of posterity to change with the times and that the reputation of Robespierre today (for reasons that I have tried to explain) stands considerably higher in the Pantheon of Revolutionary leaders than it did in the generation following his death.

Parts III and IV fall into a somewhat different pattern. Unlike the first two, they are divided into chapters, and each chapter presents a different aspect of Robespierre as an "ideologue" or as a practitioner of revolution, whether as a political or social democrat, or as a politician, a popular leader or a leader of revolution. The intention here is to go over some of the earlier ground again from a different perspective and, it is hoped, to enable the reader to test the validity of the judgments of others and to arrive at some general conclusions of his own.

It will be seen, then, that this is more of a work of synthesis than one of basic, original research, though some of my own investigations into the Revolutionary crowd has gone into its preparation. But, as will be amply evident, I have drawn far more on the original work of others: on the biographies by J. M. Thompson in England and by Gérard Walter, Jean Massin and Marc Bouloiseau in France; on Albert Mathiez' numerous pieces on the Incorruptible, on Albert Soboul's great monograph on the popular movement in Paris, and – more generally – on the never-failing guidance to be found in the works of Georges Lefebvre. In addition to these, the real bricks and mortar of the book are provided by Robespierre's own speeches and writings, of which the most useful and complete edition is that published by the Société des Etudes Robespierristes in Paris.

PART I

The Man and the Events

Maximilien-François-Marie-Isidore de Robespierre was born at
Arras, the small provincial capital of Artois, in northern France, on
6 May 1758. It was within a year or two of the fall of Quebec, of
Rousseau's *Lettre à d'Alembert* and Voltaire's *Essai sur les moeurs* and the
year that Damiens was torn apart on the Place de Grève for stabbing
Louis XV with a pocket-knife. His father, Maximilien-Barthélemy
François, was a lawyer and the son and grandson of lawyers, who had
been admitted to the bar at Arras in 1756 and had married Jacqueline-
Marguerite Carraut, the daughter of a well-to-do brewer, a few
months before the birth of their son. Two girls followed, Charlotte
and Henriette (who died young), and a second son, Augustin, born
in July 1763, only eighteen months before the mother died giving
birth to a fifth child who barely survived her. The father, although
his practice prospered, had a restless and unstable character and made
off two years later, leaving his young family of four to be cared for
first by their maternal grandfather and later by aunts. So young
Maximilien was left a virtual orphan at the age of eight.

This inauspicious beginning to the revolutionary leader's career
has provided ample scope for the reflections and speculations of
biographers, novelists and specialists in "psycho-history". Among
these last, Max Gallo has suggested that his life henceforward became
dominated by a deep sense of his father's guilt.[1] How far this can
be verified is open to question; but it seems reasonable to suppose
that his father's desertion following so soon after his mother's death
left deep scars on his early childhood, forcing him to assume family
responsibilities unsuited to his years; and this may well account for
the precocious development of a deep seriousness and a passion for
solitude and silent study that never left him. What is even more
certain, and perhaps more significant for his future career, is that,
from an early age, he became acutely and personally aware – far
more than any of the other revolutionary leaders, with the possible
exception of Marat – of what it meant to be poor.

So it was as a poor scholar, supported by charitable foundations,
that he attended school first in his native Arras and later in Paris. The

collège at Arras was a former Jesuit institution, governed in Robespierre's day by a local committee appointed by the bishop. He stayed there for four years before moving on, with a scholarship from the Artesian Abbey of Saint-Vaast, to the far more illustrious College of Louis-le-Grand of the University of Paris. He was then eleven and he remained there until he was twenty-three. Here he studied Classics and Law under Oratorian teachers, began to read Rousseau, and became acquainted – though never on terms of intimacy – with two future political associates and eventual opponents, Camille Desmoulins and Louis-Marie Fréron. It is remarkable that neither they nor his teachers later retained any vivid impression of him; yet it may be accounted for by his lack of sociability and by the simple fact that he was poor. But, in other ways, he left his mark: he became the star classical scholar of his year and was chosen to deliver a Latin address of welcome to the young Louis XVI when the King and Queen passed through the capital on their return from the coronation ceremony at Rheims in 1775. It was intended by his teachers to be a signal mark of distinction; but for the young scholar it proved to be a humiliating rather than a rewarding experience, as the rain was falling in buckets and the royal couple, having heard the address drove on without even an approving nod or a word of reply. It has been suggested that the encounter left Robespierre with a deep resentment against royalty; it seems unlikely as he continued, for some years, to treat Louis with reverence and respect.[2] What is reasonably certain is that the impression of the event was eclipsed by the far more memorable one of a few years later when he caught a glimpse of Rousseau (or was it also an encounter?), then a recluse at Ermenonville in the Montmorency forest and near the end of his life.[3]

In 1780, young Robespierre was awarded a degree in law by the University of Paris; and, the year after, he was admitted as an advocate before the Paris Parlement; he rounded off his career at Louis-le-Grand with a prize of 600 *livres* and was allowed to pass on his scholarship to his younger brother, Augustin, then in his nineteenth year. He returned to Arras and began to practise law. It was not a particularly brilliant or eventful career and it was attended by few highlights. He lived modestly as a poor man's advocate, generally handling cases that allowed him to display his regard for virtue and respect for justice. He also, like so many other young lawyers of his day, assimilated the main ideas of the Enlightenment (of Montesquieu and Rousseau, in particular), wrote verse and joined the local debating society, the Rosati, where he met Lazare Carnot, a young mining engineer, who was one day to become his colleague on the Committee of Public Safety. He entered essays for literary competitions and won a 400-*livres* prize from the Academy of Metz, was elected to the Arras Academy and became its director in 1786. Certain writers of this time – Marat, with his *Chains of Slavery*, is an obvious example – were already exercising their talents and sharpening their knives in preparation for the revolution that lay ahead; Robespierre was not one of these. There are evident signs in these early writings and pleadings of a deep concern for greater justice and equity, of a man acutely sensitive to poverty and outraged by the abuses of power and one convinced that virtue alone was the basis of happiness; but there was no sign that he had any inclination to strike at the social order itself; in fact, he wrote as late as 1788 that "a general revolution" in France might be harmful as it would be unnecessary for dealing with her ills.[4] Yet the point must not be laboured too much, as though he had a sudden overnight conversion to overthrow this order in 1789; and it has been said of him with some justice that while he was not "a revolutionary before the Revolution", he already had potentiality for revolution that needed time to mature.[5] What is more than likely is that the Arras authorities sensed something of the kind. They did not take altogether kindly to the vigour with which he championed the poor and humble and denounced the rich and mighty; and it is perhaps significant, as one of his biographers has pointed out, that whereas he had been given thirteen causes to plead as a novice in 1782, the number had dropped to ten in 1788.[6]

Meanwhile, since early in the previous year, France had been convulsed by an "aristocratic revolt", which proved to be the curtain-raiser to the even more momentous events of 1789. Robespierre contributed to the spate of writing; it provoked his first published work of importance, the *Appel à la nation artésienne*. In it he called for a more just and more equal representation of the people; above all, he deplored that the parish clergy, whose interests bound them so closely to the *menu peuple*, should play so humble a role in the First Estate and that poverty should prevent the poor from winning the rights that were lawfully theirs. It was his first political manifesto and anticipated much of what he later said in the revolutionary Assemblies and Jacobin Club. So it was as a local notable of an already established reputation – as a politician, a lawyer and a man of letters – that he was elected as one of the eight deputies to represent the commons, or Third Estate, of Artois at the Estates General when it was summoned to meet at Versailles in May 1789.

1789

The Estates General met at Versailles on 5 May against a background of mounting crisis and popular unrest. In Paris the price of bread was at nearly twice its normal level, and there had been bloody riots in the *faubourg* Saint-Antoine and, in the provinces, a peasant revolt, which was to assume vast proportions, was already under way. As the great assembly opened, nothing was done to spare the commons' susceptibilities: they were ordered to wear the traditional black, to enter the meeting hall by a side door and, in every way, made to feel aware of their inferior status. The royal Council, though it had agreed to accord the commons double representation, refused to concede their further demand to deliberate in common. The estates were told to meet in separate assemblies and only to engage in joint discussion when invited to do so. The commons naturally protested as it was only by debates in common that they could hope to outvote the combined forces of the "privileged" orders, the nobility and clergy. So a long tussle ensued, which was only resolved when, on 17 June, the commons took the bull firmly by the horns and declared themselves to be the National Assembly and invited members of the other estates to join them. Three days later, when locked out of their usual meeting place, the deputies, by now joined by a number of parish priests, marched into a tennis court nearby and took a solemn oath not to disperse until they had given France a constitution. It was the first open act of defiance against monarchy and aristocracy and marked the opening round in the "bourgeois" revolution.

Robespierre had played a certain part in these events and had thus, like so many others of his colleagues in the *tiers*, been drawn into revolution by a combination of circumstance and personal choice. Soon after arriving at Versailles, he had joined the newly formed Breton Club, at first composed of the deputies of Brittany but soon developing into a national pressure group which included the most active elements in all the provincial delegations. Little known to the wider public at this time, he was first recorded in the journals as "Robes-pierre", "Robesse-Pierre", and even as "Roberts-piesse", or more simply as "Robert Pierre." But, after a hesitant start, he soon began to make his mark as a frequent contributor to debates: in fact, he spoke no fewer than 68 times in the year 1789 alone. He made his maiden speech barely ten days after the Estates General opened, on 16 May, when he proposed an alternative tactical device (which was not adopted) for bringing the clergy into closer association with the commons. His second intervention, on 6 June, was more characteristic and made a deeper impression. The Archbishop of Rheims had appeared before the commons to invite them to a joint discussion on how to alleviate the sufferings of the poor. In view of the existing relations between the estates, the commons sensed a trap; and Robespierre, while voicing their fears, chose the occasion to denounce the wasteful luxury of bishops. "All that is necessary," he declared, "is that the bishops and dignitaries of the church should renounce that luxury which is an offence to Christian humility; that they should give up their coaches, and give up their horses; if need be, that they should sell a quarter of the property of the church, and give to the poor." His words, we are told, were received in stunned, but approving, silence.[7] And, a couple of weeks later, we find him prominently displayed, and in characteristic pose (with hands clasped to his chest), in David's portrayal of the Tennis Court Oath.

The first act of revolution was quickly met by a counter-revolution inspired by a Court party centred on Marie-Antoinette and the King's younger brother, the Comte d'Artois. At first the King, having failed to persuade the self-styled National Assembly to disperse quietly, ordered the two other estates to join it. Then, prodded by the Queen and her advisers, he ordered troops to Versailles to intimidate the deputies and cut them off from Paris, dismissed Necker, his popular chief minister, and installed the Baron de

Breteuil, a nominee of the Queen, in his place. The news reached the capital on 12 July and touched off a popular insurrection in Paris which culminated in the assault and capture of the Bastille and the withdrawal of the army. Thus a popular revolution in Paris came to the rescue of the bourgeois revolutionaries at Versailles. The King had no option but to dismiss his new ministry, recall Necker from exile and recognize the National Assembly. Moreover, as a token of his acquiescence in the turn of events, he drove to Paris, donned the new tricolour cockade, and made his peace with the victors who had set up their local revolutionary government, or Commune, at the City Hall. He was accompanied by fifty deputies; and it is proof that Robespierre was already making some impression that he was elected to be one of them.

But the provinces had yet to have their say. As the news from Paris filtered through to the villages, provincial capitals and market towns, it touched off or intensified a chain-reaction of municipal upheavals and peasant revolts to which the Assembly – somewhat half-heartedly – had to give recognition by its August Decrees which took the first, but impressive, steps to dismantle the whole feudal and seigneurial régime. It also proceeded to deny the King any absolute right to annul or veto the laws enacted by the new Assembly and to issue a Declaration of the Rights of Man. These measures provoked a second attempt by the Court to undo what had already been done by carrying through a second *coup*. Troops were once more summoned to Versailles and there was more talk of dispersing the Assembly by force of arms. So Paris, in what have been called the October "days", intervened again. This time, it was the women of the markets who took the lead; followed by the armed battalions of the newly formed National Guard, they marched to Versailles, dispersed the royal guards defending the *château*, and brought the King and Queen as prisoners back to Paris. They were followed, ten days later, by the National Assembly which came to meet at the Archbishop's Palace before moving, soon after, to the old riding school, a stone's throw from the new royal residence in the Tuileries.

In these August and October "days" Robespierre played a very modest role. Yet he continued to build himself a reputation in the Assembly. He intervened several times in the debate on the Declaration of Rights; above all, in a speech on 24 August, he opposed all restrictions on the liberty of the press; for "freedom of the press goes hand in hand with freedom of speech". Two weeks later, he invoked Rousseau's law of the General Will to support his view that the King should have no right to oppose or delay the legislative measures proposed by the Assembly. He supported the majority in rejecting the absolute veto; but he also argued that even a "suspensive" veto (which the Assembly adopted) would leave "an open door for despotism and aristocracy".[8] On 5 October, when the women marchers noisily invaded the Assembly, he spoke to their leaders and helped to restore calm.

CONSTITUENT ASSEMBLY

Returning to Paris with the Assembly in mid-October, Robespierre went to live in the Rue Saintonge in the Marais quarter; he stayed there for nearly two years. It was a period of relative peace after the turbulence of the earlier months of 1789; and the National (or Constituent) Assembly now settled down to a prolonged spell of law-making that provided France with her first Revolutionary Constitution in September 1791. The Constituents, or Constitutional Monarchists, were essentially the bourgeois – the lawyers, merchants, former government officers and untitled landed proprietors – of the original Third Estate, shorn of a small number of *monarchiens* (such as Mounier and Malouet) and reinforced by the addition of some fifty "patriot" nobles, forty-four bishops and 200 parish clergy. Though they expressed themselves in the current language of "philosophy", they were men of property who knew which side of their bread was buttered. Owing to circumstances not entirely of their own volition and largely outside their control, the Old Régime of aristocratic privilege and royal absolutism had collapsed, and something had to be put in its place. They looked to new leaders – in the event, to the triumvirate of Barnave, Duport and Charles Lameth, the spokesmen for the Centre and moderate Left in the former Third Estate – and, under their direction, they enacted a long series of constitutional laws (ranging over government, suffrage, land, industry, war and peace, land, church and property rights) that,

for all the "philosophy" in which they were couched, were conceived in the image of a property-owning class whose common
interest it was to erect barriers against the triple danger of royal
despotism, aristocratic privilege and popular "anarchy".

Within this Assembly, Robespierre formed with Jérôme Pétion
and a small group of other more-or-less constant supporters (sometimes reinforced by the volatile Mirabeau) an extreme Left of liberal
democrats, who, while sharing the general "philosophical" principles of the majority, acted as consistent champions of democratic
and liberal ideas, as watchdogs against bureaucratic abuse and
government "tyranny", as vigorous critics of ministerial and royal
encroachments on the rights of the Assembly or on local initiative,
and as spokesmen for the rights of the people to express themselves
by all possible legal (or even "revolutionary") means. Robespierre
was an assiduous attender and sought every possible occasion to air
his views. This did not endear him to all and he was often abused or
shouted down; but he often succeeded in winning the Assembly's
attention, if not its approval, and made 125 recorded speeches in
1790 and 328 in the first nine months of 1791. With such a record he
could hardly have been seen as the sort of clownish performer that
both Michelet and Aulard made him out to be. He was taken
seriously enough, though the majority did their best to keep his
influence within reasonable bounds. He was, in fact, never admitted
to any of its committees; he served only once as secretary and, while
Pétion was on one occasion elected to the presidency, it was never
offered to Robespierre.

As a speaker, he lacked presence and colour and the conventional
graces and oratorical tricks: Carlyle saw him as an "anxious, slight,
ineffectual-looking man in spectacles, his eyes (were the glasses off)
troubled, careful; with upturned face, snuffing dimly the uncertain
future times". Yet he spoke with a quiet passion and intense conviction and expounded, and repeated, principles that remained
remarkably consistent and forced even his opponents to accord him
a grudging respect. Many of his critics conceded the point; and
Mirabeau, who was often among them, said of him: "That man will
go far; he believes all he says." An Englishman who closely watched
him in the Assembly in March 1791 wrote of him as "a stern man,
rigid in his principles, plain, unaffected in his manners, no foppery in

his dress, certainly above corruption, despising wealth, and with nothing of the volatility of a Frenchman in his character".[9]

It was in accordance with these convictions that, although he spoke so often and attempted to speak more, he always (apart from his impromptu interventions) chose the issues on which to speak with care. When the Assembly came to Paris, it took prompt steps to restrain the revolutionary ardour of the Parisian *menu peuple* by imposing martial law, the death penalty for rebellion and a censorship of radical journals like Marat's *L'Ami du peuple*; but not before Robespierre had spoken passionately against it. The next day, 22 October, he made his opening speech in a long verbal duel in support of a wider franchise. Prompted by the Abbé Sieyès, the Assembly proposed to distinguish between "active" citizens who should have the vote and "passive" citizens who should not and to limit "electors" in a two-stage electoral process to men of substance; while only those who paid a silver mark of 52 *livres* (or *marc d'argent*) in taxes should be qualified to serve as deputies. Robespierre countered by insisting that all adult Frenchmen should have the vote whether they paid taxes or not and that all property-qualifications of the kind should be withdrawn. He made further speeches on the *marc d'argent* in April 1791 and played a part in having these qualifications effectively annulled a few months later. On 23 December, in another famous intervention, he demanded civil rights for Jews, actors and Protestants; and, not having received full satisfaction, returned to the attack in July of the following year. He had played no significant part in the debate on feudal privilege and peasant rebellion in August 1789; but in February and March 1790 he opposed the repressive measures that were being taken to curb peasant riots and denounced the widespread enclosure of land. At the end of August, the Swiss guards stationed at Nancy rebelled against their officers for refusing to make up their arrears in pay and were shot down by their general, the Comte de Bouillé. While the Assembly sent the general a congratulatory message, Robespierre denounced his action in a vigorous speech in defence of the rebellious troops. In similar vein, in April 1791, he justified the people of Avignon for rioting against their Papal rulers and for demanding the right (which he had already supported) to become part of the French nation. In further speeches on the Constitution as it took shape during these years, he opposed the King's right to declare war without the express wish of the Assembly; supported clerical marriage; urged the creation of a Supreme Criminal Court; defended freedom of speech, press and assembly; opposed capital punishment, and demanded that all male citizens, irrespective of property, he admitted into the National Guard.

Mirabeau died in early April 1791 and was buried, with full civic honours, in the Pantheon; and, on the Left, there were many who saw Robespierre as his most worthy successor. Loustalot's *Révolutions de Paris* commented: "The Assembly has perhaps lost its foremost orator, but M. Mirabeau did not hold the same place among the small group of patriot deputies. The French people need not despair of the conduct of public affairs as long as they still have a representative of the calibre of M. Robespierre." Robespierre was, by this time, certainly gaining both new assurance and authority within the Assembly and Jacobin Club and among the wider public. In the Assembly, he won approval in May for a far-reaching proposal: that no member of the outgoing Constituent Assembly should be entitled to hold a seat in the Legislative Assembly that followed. This "self-denying ordinance" would, as we shall see, have a considerable effect on Robespierre's own fortunes in the year to come.

Soon after, the comparative calm that had prevailed since October 1789 was shattered and the Revolution entered a new stage of crisis. It was also the first great crisis in Robespierre's political career. The King, in spite of his promise to co-operate with the Assembly, attempted, in June, to flee the country and join an Austrian army that was waiting on France's eastern border. But he was recognized by a vigilant postmaster at Varennes, failed to link up with his Austrian allies and was brought back under a strong military escort to Paris. The city was in uproar; and, in the Jacobin Club (the name assumed by the former Breton Club when it moved to the Couvent des Jacobins in October 1789), Robespierre called for the King's deposition and demanded that the Executive be constituted "by other means". He also at first supported the preparations being made by the more plebeian Cordeliers Club (where Danton and Marat were the leading lights) for a petition and demonstration in the Champ de Mars. Meanwhile, the Assembly had, on hearing news of Louis' flight, suspended him from office pending an enquiry into the circumstances in which it had taken place. But, before the Cordeliers' demonstration could be held, the deputies had received their committee's report and decided to uphold the fiction that Louis had been the victim of an aristocratic *coup*, with the Comte de Bouillé as its main executor, and should be restored to office. At this point, Robespierre, either from deference to the Assembly once it had made its wishes known, or (which seems more likely) from fear of an intrigue to replace Louis by his cousin the Duc d'Orléans, persuaded the Jacobins to withdraw their support. So the Cordeliers Club went ahead on their own. Martial law was declared, the red banner of executive violence was unfurled, and General Lafayette's National Guard fired on an unarmed crowd of petitioners and demonstrators, leaving fifty dead and a dozen wounded on the Champ de Mars. Numerous arrests followed; other leading democrats, including Danton and Marat, went into hiding; while Robespierre's life was threatened and, after an emotional scene in the Jacobin Club, where hundreds rallied to his defence, he sought a temporary refuge in the carpenter Duplay's house at 366, Rue Saint-Honoré. Three weeks later, he moved from his Marais address and settled at Duplay's which was conveniently near to both the Assembly and the Jacobin Club. He remained there for the rest of his life, almost three years to the day.

After the June–July crisis the Assembly resumed its debates and the Constitution was ready for the King's signature on 18 September. Twelve days later, the Constituent Assembly wound up the last of its business and was dissolved. As Robespierre emerged from the final session onto the Terrasse des Feuillants, accompanied by his fellow "patriot" Pétion, they were seized by an enthusiastic crowd, garlanded with oak-leaves and carried through the streets of the city in triumph. He had already won the title of "Incorruptible": it was a tribute both to the "purity" of his principles and to his modest way of living and his refusal to accept financial rewards (he was living on an annual income of about 600 *livres* at the time). Since Mirabeau's death, in particular, he had won enormous popularity. His portraits hung in the Salon; Madame Roland, the future presiding hostess of the Girondin group, wrote him an enthusiastic letter; cities – Avignon, Toulon and Marseilles – showered honours on him; children were given his name in baptism; and even a bishop would have been proud to have been his brother.[10] He left Paris soon after to make what was to prove his final visit to Arras and, there too, was received with honours and illuminations.

JACOBIN CLUB

Robespierre had already been a frequent attender at the Jacobin Club during the days of the Constituent Assembly. His name first appears in the Club's records as president in April 1790; and between January and September 1791 he took the floor on thirty-five occasions. And when the moderate majority of deputies ceded from the Jacobins to found their own Club des Feuillants in the June crisis, and in the aftermath of the Champ de Mars "massacre" that followed, he performed a Herculean task in retaining the loyalty of the provincial societies to the parent-Club and persuading the waverers to return to its ranks. By the time the Legislative Assembly met in early October, the Jacobins' fortunes had been largely restored and it became the forum for all Robespierre's speeches until August of the next year. He barely missed a session and from early November, when he returned to Paris from his visit to Arras, he spoke there a hundred times or more.[11] So it was in the Jacobins that he levelled his main attacks against Lafayette in March–April 1792 and, between December and May, fought a long verbal duel with Brissot on the issue of war and peace, which threatened once more to tear the Club apart.

The possibility of war with Austria (and therefore with Prussia) had already existed in the summer of 1791. Even before this there had been tensions caused by the asylum offered to the Prince de Condé's army of *émigré* nobles by the Elector of Trèves, the Emperor's *protégé*, within his territory of Coblenz; and by the National Assembly's decision in August 1789 to abolish the feudal dues of the German princes in Alsace. Trèves would soon agree to disband Condé's army, and the princes' claims might also have been settled by negotiation if a new cause of friction had not arisen with Louis' flight to Varennes. The Emperor Leopold had shown no inclination to be provoked into war with France on behalf of his sister, Marie Antoinette; but when the King and Queen of France were brought back under military escort to Paris, he feared for their safety and issued the Padua Circular, threatening "vigorous measures"; and he followed this up, when Louis was reinstated in office and the danger appeared to be over, with the more innocuous Declaration of Pillnitz, which was more of a face-saver than a serious threat, but was a provocation nevertheless, that brought fresh grist to the mill of the strangely assorted war party that was developing in France. On the one hand, there was the party at Court, grouped around the Queen, which favoured war as it believed that military defeat would undo the work of the Revolution and restore the throne to its former authority. The Comte de Narbonne, the War Minister, also favoured war hoping that it would pave the way for a strong military government. But most effective of all in rousing the country to a state of warlike fervour was the new Left group in the Legislative Assembly, led by Jacques-Pierre Brissot, deputy for Eure-et-Loir, and composed of a score of deputies of whom several were from the south-western region of the Gironde, and supported outside the Chamber by a number of journalists like Carra and Gorsas and by Pétion, Robespierre's old comrade-in-arms, who was soon to be elected mayor of Paris. From October 1791 Brissot preached an armed crusade of the peoples against the crowned heads of Europe, in the course of which the peoples, liberated by their own endeavours or by the easy victory of the "armed missionaries" of France, would rally to the flag of revolution, while the King would be compelled to call on Brissot's supporters to take office. They also claimed that war would bring other and more tangible benefits as well. It would end the external danger to France; it would force Louis to behave as a strictly constitutional king; it would divert the *sans-culottes* from their present preoccupation with food prices and direct their energies into constructive channels; and (though this last point was not trumpeted quite so loudly abroad) victory in war would stabilize the currency and open up fresh markets for the commercial bourgeoisie.

The argument was an appealing one which at first won almost universal favour among the Paris militants and in the Cordeliers and Jacobin Clubs. Robespierre, too, was at first attracted by it and, in late November, made a speech in the Jacobins in which he threatened the Emperor with a "people's war" if he would not disperse Condé's *émigrés* from Trèves. But soon after, following Marat

and Billaud-Varenne, he changed his mind and became convinced
that war at this point would be a disaster and that to provoke it was
to fall into a trap baited by the enemies of the Revolution. He carried
the debate into the Jacobin Club where, between 9 December 1791
and 16 February 1792, he made half-a-dozen powerful speeches in
which he challenged Brissot's assumptions, sometimes in direct personal confrontation, one by one. War, he argued, would play into
the hands of the Court, expose France to a military dictatorship (he
was thinking of Lafayette rather than of Narbonne), divert attention
from the danger within, and thus severely prejudice the Revolution's
achievements before there had been time to complete them. Moreover, he insisted, to count on a friendly reception being given to
France's "armed missionaries" was to foster illusion and to court
disaster.

Such arguments were to prove, in the long run, to be soundly
based; and they are a reminder that Robespierre, in this instance as in
so many others, was concerned far less with abstract principles than
with their application to political realities.[12] But they had little effect
in stemming the tide that was flowing strongly in favour of war.
When negotiations broke down after the Emperor Leopold was
succeeded by the more bellicose Francis, Brissot won the day and
war was declared with Austria in April 1792. Long before this,
Robespierre's reputation had inevitably suffered from his staunch
opposition to a "revolutionary war" and he slipped into a period of
popular disfavour. He did little to redeem the situation, among
former middle-class admirers at least, when, in March, he told an
astonished and scandalized Jacobin audience of his belief in God and
the immortality of the soul.

FALL OF THE MONARCHY

The war started badly, as Robespierre had foretold; and the French
forces, far from acting as "armed missionaries", being quite un-
prepared for battle (let alone to carry the war into the enemy's
camp), fled in disorder before the Duke of Brunswick's armies, and
France lay open to the enemy. Even before the war began, armed

counter-revolution broke out in the south. The *assignat* (the revolutionary paper-money) had fallen to 63 per cent of its nominal value by January 1792 and grain riots followed in the provinces. In Paris, as the result of civil war in the West Indian colonies, the price of sugar had trebled and provision shops in the *faubourgs* were broken into by angry citizens, who compelled grocers to sell their wares at the former price. These developments led Robespierre – and for him it was a new experience – to take stock of the economic and social factors that lay at the base of the contests between political parties and groups. The case of Simoneau, mayor of Etampes, in the grain-growing belt to the south of Paris, seems to have brought the matter home to him. Simoneau, who was also a wealthy grain merchant, had been killed by local peasants and townspeople in a food riot in March 1792. When the Jacobins, and later the Legislative Assembly, proposed to honour his memory as a martyr for "property", Robespierre bitterly opposed it and denounced the speculator who had robbed the people of their bread in the same breath as the political groups that protected him. He did more: when Pierre Dolivier, the *curé* of Mauchamps, near Etampes, chose the occasion not only to blast hoarding and speculation but all the other evils he saw arising from private property in land, Robespierre published his text in full, with approving comments, in his journal, the *Défenseur de la Constitution*, which he had begun to publish in May of that year.

The war brought not only military defeat, speculation and rising prices, but treachery in high places as well; and it was widely believed (with ample justification, as it later turned out) that the Queen and her "Austrian Committee" were planning to restore the absolute monarchy with the aid of foreign arms. Brissot had boasted that such treasonable activities would serve his party's interests (*"il nous faut de grandes trahisons,"* he is reputed to have said), and he and his associates, several of whom now held ministerial posts, did not hesitate to inflame popular passions against the Court. So much so that the King felt obliged to dismiss the Brissotin ministers; while Pétion, by now a close ally of Brissot's, was suspended from his mayoral office. These actions provoked a popular demonstration in the city on 20 June, when the shopkeepers and craftsmen of the *faubourgs* Saint-Antoine and Saint-Marcel paraded in arms before the Assembly and broke into the Tuileries Palace, where they obliged the reluctant Louis to don the Cap of Liberty and drink to the health of the nation.

From this incident followed, by what appeared to be an almost inexorable chain of events, the far greater and more violent insurrection of 10 August that captured the Tuileries and toppled Louis from his throne. Yet the Brissotin party, though it had stoked up the flames and its ministers had been reinstated in office, derived no advantage from the result. For the Brissotins, alarmed by what they saw would be the eventual consequences of the storm they had unleashed, drew back in support of the King, whose removal they had been the first to call for, and surrendered the leadership of the popular movement to Robespierre and the majority that he had by now built up in the Jacobin Club. This Jacobin majority had had little to do with the June demonstration, as they suspected the motives behind it; and Robespierre himself, far from being a Republican before the event, had made it amply clear (he was writing in May) that he preferred a representative Assembly of "free citizens" under a king to an "enslaved people" governed by "an aristocratic senate and a dictator." And even after mid-July he argued that the future of the monarchy, as of the Constitution itself, must be decided by a popularly elected Convention rather than by a resort to arms. But events moved too quickly for such leisurely solutions. Lafayette had deserted the front to urge drastic measures against the Parisian democrats and the air was thick with rumours of counter-revolutionary plots and *coups*; and, before the end of the month, forty-seven of the forty-eight Paris sections had voted for the abdication of the King. Robespierre endorsed the demand in the Jacobins on the 29th; and the Jacobin leaders went ahead with plans for an armed insurrection that was given a greater urgency by the Duke of Brunswick's Manifesto of August, which threatened Parisians with summary vengeance should the invading Prussians find them arms in hand. So, partly as the outcome of a premeditated design and partly as a measure of self-defence, Jacobins, visiting contingents of militiamen from Marseilles and Brest and other cities and the Parisian sections and National Guard combined, under the direction of a newly formed "Revolutionary Commune", to capture the Tuileries by force of arms and drive the King to seek refuge in the Legislative Assembly.

Robespierre played no part in the military preparations or siege of the Tuileries; this was not a role that suited his talents. But the part he played in the Jacobin Club had been of prime importance; and on the afternoon of the 10th (a few hours after the fighting stopped) he attended his section – the Section des Piques, in the Place Vendôme – and was elected as its representative on the general council of the "Revolutionary Commune", which had been in session since the previous night. For the next three weeks, this council, acting as the embodiment of the sovereign people under arms, shared (and often usurped) the authority of the Legislative Assembly. It initiated measures of "public safety", closing the city's gates and collaborating with Danton, the new Minister of Justice, in rounding up suspects and carrying out thousands of house arrests; it insisted that a revolutionary tribunal should be set up and that the King and his family should be interned in the Temple prison, and it imposed on the Assembly Robespierre's demand that a National Convention should be elected by male adult suffrage to replace it and proceed to declare the Republic.

Meanwhile, the invading armies were advancing. On 16 August, the Austrians crossed the frontier to the north; in the east, the Prussians broke through into Lorraine on the 19th, captured Longwy on the 21st, and marched on the fortress of Verdun which fell a few days later. The road to Paris lay open, blocked only by the volunteers that Danton had hastily summoned to arms. Moreover, the Paris gaols were full (and believed to be fuller) of refractory priests, political enemies of the Revolution, and forgers whose faked *assignats* were held responsible for rising prices and inflation – all believed to be so many allies for the Duke of Brunswick and to be only waiting for the volunteers to leave in order to break out of prison and massacre the aged, women and children left behind. (The words of the *Marseillaise* were there to confirm it.) It was this atmosphere of exaltation, suspicion and panic that bred the gruesome episode known as the September Massacres, when the prisons of Paris were entered by armed bands, who set up hastily improvised "people's" tribunals and executed some 1,100 to 1,400 of their inmates – priests and political prisoners among them, but mainly common-law offenders: thieves, prostitutes, forgers and vagrants.[13]

What responsibility, if any, did Robespierre have for this affair?

Like others, he had warned that something of the kind might happen if the Legislative Assembly failed to take speedy and adequate measures to set up summary courts of justice of its own; and he was a member of the Commune whose "vigilance" committee had, in a memorable circular sent to the departments and believed to have been drafted by Marat, appeared to recommend the provincials to follow the Parisians' example: "... no doubt the whole nation ... will hasten to adopt this necessary means of public safety". (Yet it should be noted that similar summary acts of vengeance took place in the provinces before the news reached them from Paris.) Certainly, he did not condemn the massacres any more than Danton or Pétion or the "virtuous" Roland, or any other of the party leaders, at this time. But such responsibility as he had was not a direct one; and perhaps his feelings in the matter may best be gauged from the question he addressed to his Girondin opponents in the National Convention a couple of months later: "*Citoyens, vouliez-vous une révolution sans une révolution?*"

STRUGGLE FOR POWER

Before the Massacres ended, elections to the National Convention were already under way. On 5 September, Robespierre was returned at the head of the list of Jacobin deputies for Paris and was soon joined by Danton, Collot d'Herbois, Manuel (a leader of the 10 August uprising), Billaud-Varenne, Tallien, Camille Desmoulins, the painter Louis David and Robespierre's brother Augustin. These men who, with others like-minded, accounted for twenty-three of the twenty-four deputies returned by the capital, were joined soon after by two future Jacobin leaders from the provinces: Georges Couthon and Louis-Antoine de Saint-Just, one elected in Puy-de-Dôme and the second in Aisne. The whole group came to be known as the Mountain from the upper tiers they occupied in the Chamber. They acknowledged Robespierre as their leader; so from now on – for the next twenty months, at least – his story becomes inextricably bound up with theirs.

There were two other principal groups in the National Convention. Probably the largest was that formed by the "Marsh" or

"Plain",[14] who were not committed to any particular faction and whose support was therefore vital to one or other of the two parties struggling for control of the Assembly. Of these the larger, and certainly the more influential at the start, was that of the "Girondins" (as the former Brissotins now came to be called by their Jacobin opponents), who supplied most of the ministries. To this advantage they added their control of a large part of the Paris press and their solid support in the provinces, where the Paris Jacobins and clubs were viewed with considerable suspicion. The Mountain, on the other hand, while their followers in the provinces were thinly spread (and were probably not as prosperous as those of their opponents), had, as the acknowledged victors of August and founders of the Republic, the allegiance of the Paris clubs and *sans-culottes*. So the Mountain now emerged as the consistent champions of the capital; while the Girondins, partly from choice and partly from the nature of their following, appeared as spokesmen for provincial interests and even – and this became increasingly a bone of contention – for "federalism" against the Jacobin notion of "the Republic one and indivisible". Such tensions were compounded by others arising from sharply differing attitudes towards the control of food prices and the conduct of the war, in which not only principle but tactical considerations and the deep personal dislike of opposing leaders all played their part.

Such tensions inevitably came to the surface in each of the major debates that marked a bitter struggle for power which was only resolved by the expulsion of the leading spokesmen for the Gironde after another popular insurrection in June 1793. In the first round, the Gironde succeeded in persuading the Assembly to disband the "Revolutionary Commune", whose exercise of extra-legal authority naturally proved offensive to the nation's elected representatives once the crisis was over and the Republic proclaimed. So the Mountain did little to justify the Commune's continued existence and, after a few heated exchanges, gracefully consented to its liquidation. Far more stubborn and prolonged was the battle over the fate of Louis XVI, now a prisoner in the Temple. In early December, Robespierre proposed that he be brought before the Convention and sentenced to death as a traitor to the nation. There should be no formal trial, he urged in a famous speech, as the King had already been judged by the people: "The right of punishing the tyrant and the right of dethroning him are the same things; they do not take different forms." The people having passed judgment, the Convention had, therefore, merely to record a sentence of death. While accepting a part of this argument, the Assembly decided in favour of a trial, but in which it should be both prosecutor and judge. Several of the Girondin deputies wished to spare the King's life; but such was the weight of evidence against Louis (an iron chest containing his secret correspondence had recently been discovered in the Tuileries) that they chose to join in the unanimous verdict of guilty. Following this, they resorted to manoeuvre: having failed to obtain a stay of execution, they demanded a referendum; but again they were out-voted, and Louis was executed on 21 January 1793.

But as long as victories could be recorded for French arms the Girondins retained the balance of power within the Assembly. After their initial defeat, the troops of the Republic had routed the Prussians at Valmy and Jemappes in September–November and, in February, had annexed Belgium and stood ready to occupy Holland. In March, however, Dumouriez was driven back from the Netherlands and, failing to persuade his army to march on the Convention and proclaim Louis XVII as King, he deserted to the enemy. Mutual recriminations followed in the Convention. The Girondins, as close associates of the general, were the more exposed; but, to defend themselves, they turned the attack against Danton, who had been sent to parley with Dumouriez on the eve of his desertion. The attempt failed; but there emerged from it, partly on Robespierre's initiative – he had already on 10 March called for the formation of a strong central government – two of the most important institutions of the Revolution: the Revolutionary Tribunal and the Committee of Public Safety.

Meanwhile, the economic situation was also working to the advantage of the Mountain and to the detriment of their opponents. The *assignat* had fallen to only half of its nominal value in February, and the price of food, after remaining comparatively stable in the preceding summer and autumn, had taken another sharp upward turn in the spring. Once more, the prices of colonial products had risen out of all proportion; but, this time, the rise covered a far wider range of consumers' goods than in February 1792. The riots that followed were, consequently, more intense and widespread than those of the year before; and, on 25 and 26 February, grocers' shops in almost every section in Paris were invaded by *sans-culottes*, who refused to pay more than they had for such products in 1790, or even refused to pay anything at all. All parties joined in denouncing this infringement of the rights of property; and Robespierre deplored that "patriots" should be so misguided as to riot for what he termed *de chétives marchandises*. But though none of the Assembly's spokesmen was prepared to condone such activities, it was once more the Girondins, as the party most thoroughly committed to *laissez-faire* principles, that reaped all the disadvantages, while their opponents correspondingly benefited. In March, the Paris Commune, led by Jacobin supporters, decided to fix the price of bread at 3 *sous* a pound; and, two months later, the Assembly followed suit by passing its first "Maximum law", whereby local authorities all over the country were authorized to control the price and supply of bread and flour.

Long before this, a movement had begun in the Paris sections and streets, calling for a popular insurrection to purge the Assembly of the Girondin leaders. Such an uprising was, in fact, attempted on 10 March by the small group of extreme democrats known as the Enragés, whose leaders were Jacques Roux, the "red priest" of the Gravilliers section, Théophile Leclerc and Jean Varlet. But the Mountain and Jacobin leaders, while quite prepared to use the popular movement to promote their political ends, were in no immediate hurry. They had no intention of allowing the movement to fall into the wrong hands, either into those of the Enragés or of Hébert, the editor of the popular *Le Père Duchesne*, whose influence was steadily increasing in the Cordeliers Club and the Paris Commune. Besides, they feared that a premature rising would entail a too drastic purge of the Convention, whose Rump would be powerless to resist the economic demands of the *sans-culottes*; that it would be accompanied by a new outbreak of prison massacres and leave Paris isolated in the face of the combined hostility of the provinces. So they proceeded with caution; but by early April they were ready to formulate their programme, win the support of the sections and wrest the leadership from either group of "extremists". Accordingly, on 5 April, Augustin Robespierre publicly invited the sections to appear at the bar of the Convention and demand the expulsion and arrest of the "disloyal" deputies. On the 10th, Maximilien lent his official support; and, by mid-April, three in four of the sections had "named" twenty-two of the offending Girondins and declared themselves in favour of their removal. The Commune endorsed the demands; and, a month later, at the Commune's invitation, another central revolutionary committee, based on the sections, was formed to carry the operation through. Thousands of *sans-culottes* enrolled in the National Guard at a rate of two francs for each day spent under arms; and, in the bloodless uprising of 31 May to 2 June, twenty-nine deputies and two ministers of the discredited Gironde were handed over and placed under house arrest, leaving the Mountain as the dominant party in the Assembly.

Again, Robespierre took no direct part in the insurrection; yet his was the guiding voice and his the brain that inspired it. Long an ardent defender of freedom of speech and press and of the inviolability of the Assembly, he had been led by his experience of war and counter-revolution to shed his old liberal ideas. The Revolution could now, he believed, be saved, and its internal and external enemies be defeated, only if, with the aid of the armed *sans-culottes*, a strong central government were set up to restrain both the "selfish rich" and the remnants of aristocracy. The programme is nowhere precisely spelled out; but it may be deduced from his speeches at this time and the notes that were later found among his papers: "What we need [he wrote] is *a single will* . . . This rising must continue until the measures necessary for saving the Republic have been taken. The people must ally itself with the Convention, and the Convention must make use of the people." It was a programme that looked beyond the June "days" to the tasks facing the Committee of Public Safety in the autumn and winter of 1793.

But there was an even more immediate task: both as an act of good faith and to consolidate the Jacobins' victory over their opponents. Within three weeks of their victory, they passed through the Convention and primary assemblies the Constitution of June 1793 – a charter of the greatest historical significance in that, for the first time, a nation was provided – on paper at least – with a system of government both liberal and democratic, under which all male citizens had the vote and a considerable measure of control over their

representatives and governors. It certainly had its limitations: as
Jacques Roux pointed out to a resentful Assembly, it failed, for
example, to make adequate provision for the economic needs of the
poor. Meanwhile, however, there were other pressing matters to
attend to. Stirred by "federalist" agitation, the city of Lyons and
parts of the south and south-west had overthrown their Jacobin
authorities and risen in arms against the newly purged Convention;
Toulon was preparing to surrender to the English (at war with
France since early February); and the revolt of the Vendée peasants
in support of their landlords and priests had, since March, been
sapping the nation's military strength. Even in Paris, the moderates
were still in control of a dozen sections of the centre and west; and
Marat, the best loved of all the revolutionary leaders, was assassinated
in July. The economic situation continued to deteriorate; and the
assignat slumped to 22 per cent of its value in August. Food prices
rose again in the summer; and, in spite of controls on the price of
bread, there were shortages and queues at bakers' shops in June,
August and September. So it was impossible to continue to resist the
insistent popular demand for a general control of prices, and the
further demands for exceptional measures to restrain hoarders and
speculators and to ensure the supply of food to Paris and other cities.

These measures followed shortly after a new intervention by the
Parisian *sans-culottes*, who, after a massive demonstration on 4
September, persuaded Hébert and Chaumette, the leaders of the
Commune, to head a deputation to the Convention on the following
day. It resulted in decisions being taken to pay needy *sans-culottes* for
attending sectional meetings; to enact drastic laws against suspects
and hoarders; and to set on foot an *armée révolutionnaire*, recruited
from city *sans-culottes*, which, as an instrument of the Terror (now
put on the order of the day), was to ensure the adequate provision of
supplies to Paris from the neighbouring countryside. Three weeks
later, the Convention yielded to popular pressure and passed the law
of the *Maximum Général*, which pegged the price of not only bread
but of a large range of essential goods and services at levels prevailing
in June 1790 plus one-third, while wages were raised by one-half.
The law, government agents reported, was well received in the
streets of Paris.

Meanwhile, the peasants had also been given satisfaction. On

17 July, nearly four years after the August decrees, the peasants' outstanding debts to their landlords were finally wiped out, and the remaining feudal obligations were abolished without compensation. So the new Jacobin majority, with Robespierre at their head, entered upon a new phase of the Revolution with considerable peasant support and with the more solid support of the "small people" of the cities.

REVOLUTIONARY GOVERNMENT

Robespierre joined the Committee of Public Safety, the new governing committee of the Revolution, on 27 July 1793; he was to remain a member, and its outstanding spokesman, until his death a year later. Those composing the Committee for most of that year were the former *parlementaire* and nobleman, Hérault de Séchelles; two former members of the Plain, Bertrand Barère and Robert Lindet; four specialists in military and naval affairs: the two Prieurs, Jeanbon Saint-André and Lazare Carnot, whom Napoleon would call the "organizer of victories"; two men of the Left recruited from the Cordeliers Club after the September demonstrations: Collot d'Herbois and Billaud-Varenne; and, finally, three "ideologues" who now became closely associated: Couthon, Saint-Just and Robespierre himself. Though the divisions among these twelve proved fatal in the long run, for close on a year they made a remarkable team: "a stranger set of Cloud-Compellers", Carlyle wrote of them, "the Earth never saw".

To these men fell the task of organizing the nation's defence and of solving the economic problems that continued to be pressing; though they already formed the nucleus of what Robespierre had meant by a government of "a single will", it was only in the course of these new trials and experiences that a "revolutionary government" took shape. First they took the west-country rebellion in the Vendée firmly in hand and achieved early success. Then the insurgent cities – Caen, Bordeaux, Nantes, Lyons and Marseilles – were restored to revolutionary authority; and the siege of Toulon by an English fleet was raised, largely through the skill and initiative of Napoleon Bonaparte, then a young artillery officer. In August, the Convention accepted the principle (though Robespierre had at first opposed it) of a *levée en masse* for mobilizing the whole nation for war. State workshops were set up to manufacture arms; armies were recruited, trained and equipped by the organizing genius of Carnot; while representatives were sent on continuous missions to the front to strengthen the troops' morale, keep a watchful eye on the generals and ensure supplies. Thus the Republic, with close on a million men under arms by the following summer, began to clear its soil of the invaders: Jourdan defeated Coburg at Wattignies in October; Hoche pursued the enemy across the Vosges; Kellermann freed Savoy; the Spaniards were driven back across the Pyrenees; and, finally, in June 1794, Jourdan's victory over Coburg at Fleurus drove the last Coalition soldier across the frontier. It was a fateful moment in the Revolution's, and Robespierre's, history, as we shall see later.

Meanwhile, through "economic terror", the Committee had at last brought currency speculation and inflation under control; and the *assignat*, having fallen to 22 per cent of its value in August, rose to 33 per cent in November and to 48 per cent in December. During these months too, in spite of war, the supply of food to the population of the cities was probably more regularly assured than at any time since the autumn of 1791. Nor were other, more far-reaching, social measures neglected. In addition to writing off the peasant debt, some provision was made to enable small peasants to combine and purchase the lands of *émigrés*, now put up for auction in smaller lots. Possibly more radical in intention, though they came to nothing, were the Convention's later decrees, inspired by Robespierre and Saint-Just, to divide and distribute the confiscated properties of "suspects" among poor and needy "patriots" (laws of Ventôse, February–March 1794). The Committee also looked to the future by laying before the Assembly a succession of drafts relating to education, industry, the civil code and public assistance. While some of these did not survive the fall of their promoters, others became part of the legacy that the Revolution left to its successors.

But to prosecute the war both within and without, and to realize these further aims, the new rulers of France were compelled to abandon the haphazard methods of government accepted by their predecessors. So it was through the logic and pressure of events, far

more than through obedience to "philosophical" precepts, that
Robespierre's conception of a government of "a single will" began
to take shape in the autumn. Its basis had, as we noted, been laid by
the exceptional measures adopted in the crisis of March 1793; and
others had followed in August and September. But to call the nation
to arms and institute the Terror against hoarders and speculators was
one thing; to see that such measures were carried out was quite
another. In fact, during the autumn, something like anarchy prevailed in a number of departments, in which contingents of the
armée révolutionnaire were almost running wild and "pro-consuls"
like Fouché, Tallien and Carrier were applying the law pretty well
as they pleased. So the needs of war, of civil peace and public order –
quite apart from any personal considerations – combined to persuade
Robespierre and his colleagues to take further steps to tighten their
control in Paris. This inevitably meant putting aside the democratic-
liberal provisions of the Constitution of 1793, for the time being at
least. Robespierre urged it in a speech on 8 October; and, on the
10th, Saint-Just persuaded the Convention to declare that "the
provisional government of France is revolutionary until the peace".
So the Constitution, so recently adopted, was to be put into cold
storage "for the duration" and a new, more authoritarian, system of
government put in its place.

Of course, this was not at all what the *philosophes* had ordered.
Robespierre admitted as much when he explained the purpose and
significance of the new system in a great speech to the Convention
on 25 December. "The theory of revolutionary government," he
declared, "is as new as the Revolution that created it. It is as pointless
to seek its origins in the books of the political theorists, who failed to
foresee this Revolution, as in the laws of the tyrants ... The object of
revolutionary government is to preserve the Republic; the object of
constitutional government is to establish it." So, as neither Rousseau
nor Montesquieu, in whom the revolutionary constitution-makers
had sought their models hitherto, could have foreseen the situation of
France in the autumn of 1793, it is not surprising that they should
have provided no recipe for the system of government that emerged
with the law of 14th Frimaire (4 December 1793) – a system, it
should be noted, that, under the circumstances, was as readily
accepted by the Plain as by the Mountain. By the new law, the two

Committees of General Security and Public Safety, while deriving their authority from the Convention, were vested with full executive powers. The first was made responsible for police and internal security, including the operation of the Revolutionary Tribunal. The second had far more extensive powers: to control ministers, appoint generals, conduct foreign policy, and to purge and direct local government. In fact, the restrictions on local authorities were far more stringent than those placed on the Convention: departments were left with purely routine functions, districts were made respons- ible for executing "revolutionary" decrees, and the old *procureurs* of departments and communes were replaced by "national agents" answerable to the central government. Even Paris had its independ- ence severely curbed: the Commune lost its right to send commis- sioners to the provinces and its control over the National Guard, and the local "revolutionary" committees – another product of the crisis legislation of March 1793 – were placed firmly under the direction of the Committee of General Security. The Terror remained and resumed its work, but it was institutionalized and directed from the centre. It was the end of anarchy and of prison massacres, but it was the beginning of the end of popular initiative as well.

Thus, strong government had finally emerged and it is doubtful if the Republic's achievements could have been realized without it. Yet, for many, it was a heavy price to pay and the government was soon to encounter a chorus of protests from former supporters and injured parties. The opposition arose, in the first place, from within the Jacobins' own ranks and from their allies of the Cordeliers Club; but the opponents soon divided into mutually hostile factions. The opposition of the Right gathered round Danton and the so-called party of the Indulgents; and that of the Left round Hébert and the leaders of the Paris Commune and Cordeliers Club. Danton, who had retired from political activity after being removed from the first Committee of Public Safety in July, was persuaded by friends to return to the capital in November and began to lead what was alternately a pressure-group and an organized opposition within the Assembly. Insofar as the Dantonists had any settled political pro- gramme, it was to break up the Revolutionary Government, restore the freedom of action of local authorities, dismantle the machinery of the Terror, liberate the national economy from controls, and to negotiate a peace, in the first place by detaching England from the European coalition. They divided their activities: Danton himself was their spokesman for matters of higher policy; Desmoulins founded a new journal, *Le vieux Cordelier*, which preached "clemency" and the release of "suspects"; while others – Fabre d'Eglantine and Philippeaux among them – dabbled in shares and in shady business ventures.

Unlike the Dantonists, the Left opposition had little following in the Convention: their main hunting-grounds were the Cordeliers Club, the Paris Commune and the clubs and sections, among whose militants they continued to enjoy considerable support. In his popular organ, *Le Père Duchesne*, Hébert called day in and day out for a more vigorous prosecution of the war and more vigorous measures of "public security" to be taken against hoarders, speculators and merchants. He also, with Chaumette and Fouché, played a leading part in stoking up a campaign of "de-christianization," in the course of which churches were closed wholesale, priests and bishops were compelled to give up their functions, and the Goddess of Reason was solemnly enthroned, to civic incantations, in the Cathedral of Notre-Dame. It is probable that the earlier agitation of the Hébertists was intended to spur the Jacobins and Mountain to greater energy rather than to usurp their authority; but the law of 4 December, by extending the power of the Committees at the expense of the Commune and sections, the denunciations of the Dantonists and the growing hostility of Robespierre, who viewed their "de-christianizing" activities with the greatest alarm, gradually drove them into more open opposition.

The *sans-culottes*, too, had their reasons for alarm. They had become a force to be reckoned with by those in authority, dominating the Paris sections, and even the Commune, as they did by the end of 1793. Thus there arose a problem of divided counsels, as it was not surprising that the political ideas and social aspirations of small shopkeepers and craftsmen should differ in important respects from those of the lawyers, tradesmen and civil servants who sat in the National Convention and in the Jacobin Club and its provincial affiliates. While both Plain and Mountain now favoured strong government to destroy the Revolution's enemies and win the war, the *sans-culottes* clung to the discarded Constitution of 1793; they passionately believed that popular sovereignty was essentially vested in the primary assemblies, and therefore in the Paris sections; and they demanded the frequent recall and constant accountability of deputies to their constituents. Such being their views, they could hardly fail to challenge the Jacobins' claim that, "for the duration", the Convention and the Committees should be the sole custodians of the General Will. Again, while the Jacobins and the Convention – even the Robespierrists among them – were prepared to tolerate controls and State-direction of the nation's economy merely as exceptional and temporary measures, to the *sans-culottes* they appeared to ensure a more permanent degree of security and social justice. And while the Jacobins, both as employers and as politicians, were concerned to check the upward movement of wages, the wage-earners among the *sans-culottes* (particularly numerous in Paris) had every motive and, owing to the shortage of labour in time of war, every opportunity for pushing up earnings as high as employers would be willing to pay. So, for all these reasons, the alliance between Jacobins and people was already beginning to wear thin.[15]

At first, it was the Hébertist challenge that faced Robespierre and his fellow-rulers with the greatest danger. The activities of the "de-christianizers", both in Paris and the provinces, filled them – and Robespierre most of all – with particular concern. They had enough difficulty already in checking the spread of the peasant rebellion in the west without gratuitously throwing into the arms of counter-revolution great numbers of Frenchmen whose religious beliefs persisted, and who could not fail to be outraged by violent attacks on priests and the closure of churches. So when, in November, the Commune closed down every place of worship in Paris, Robespierre riposted by denouncing Fouché, Chaumette and their associates as atheists and diversionists and even as agents of a "foreign plot" – and called for a return to the Convention's agreed policy of allowing worship in churches prescribed by law. Danton, seeing an opportunity for driving a wedge between Robespierre and his one-time Hébertist colleagues (he had Collot and Billaud in mind), joined in the fray. So a complicated three-cornered fight ensued, variously fought out in the Jacobin Club, the Convention, the two Committees and the press, in the course of which the government's spokesmen, led by Robespierre, alternately sought allies in one faction or the other, but more frequently leaned towards Danton and the Indulgents in order to weaken and destroy the Left. Thus encouraged, the Indulgents stepped up their own campaign; and the growing violence of their denunciations, particularly those of Desmoulins in *Le vieux Cordelier*, compelled Robespierre to break with the Dantonists and engage both factions at once; all the more so as Fabre d'Eglantine, a lieutenant of Danton's, had been guilty of falsifying a decree relating to the Indian Company and as Danton's own efforts to end the war were endangering the government's military operations. So the outcome was the almost simultaneous destruction of both groups, with the Hébertists preceding the Dantonists to the guillotine by a matter of days, in late March and early April. In all these proceedings, though he had been temporarily deterred by his affection for Desmoulins, Robespierre had played the principal role.[16]

Danton's fate, though distasteful to former associates and used by them later to settle accounts with Robespierre himself, caused not a ripple of excitement or protest in the sections or among the *sans-culottes*. Hébert's fall was another matter. Though not loved, like Marat, he had had an uncanny knack of echoing the feelings of the *menu peuple* in his *Père Duchesne*; and his departure left a political void and an ominous silence. Besides, his fall had been followed by an attack on those popular institutions in which his influence had been strongest: the Parisian *armée révolutionnaire* was disbanded and those local "popular" societies which had been set up to evade the censorious scrutiny of the Jacobin Club were dissolved. And as the "revolutionary committees" had already had their wings clipped by becoming firmly tied to the Committee of General Security, the sections themselves soon ceased to reflect the independent views and activities of the *sans-culottes* and tended to become mere rubber-stamps for Jacobin directives and government decrees. Saint-Just noted the change and summed it up in a sentence: *"La Révolution est glacée."* The high water-mark of revolution had already been passed.

The months from Germinal (April) to Thermidor (late July) have often been presented as an inexorable sequence of events, leading to the final act of a tragedy before the curtain is rung down. Such a view is plausible enough; besides, it appeals to "Dantonist" historians (historians are rarely "Hébertists"), because it places high on the list of explanations for Robespierre's own fall and execution the punishment he meted out to the "factions" in the spring of 1794. This is presumably how it appeared to the unnamed deputy who hurled at Robespierre, when he appeared for the last time in the Assembly and was refused a hearing, "the blood of Danton chokes you"; and Georg Buechner, the young German author of *Danton's Death*, must have had something similar in mind.

Yet it is hardly realistic, as such an explanation lays too much weight on the elimination of the "factions" and, accordingly, too little on the further succession of crises, some closely related and others not, that intervened between Germinal and Thermidor; not to mention any weaknesses in Robespierre's character that may have helped to precipitate his fall. To return, in the first place, to the relations between the Jacobin rulers and their *sans-culotte* allies. We have seen already that the latter were silenced *politically* by Hébert's removal and the subsequent restrictions on popular means of expression. But this was not all: they were further estranged by the government's economic measures, directed against wage-earners and small consumers. The Maximum laws, after rousing early enthusiasm, had proved a disappointment. For a while, prices remained stable; but the laws could only be enforced in a country of predominantly small producers and distributors by further measures of coercion and repression; and these the government, anxious to retain the support of peasants, merchants and manufacturers in order to win the war, was quite unwilling to take. So producers, large and small, began to resort to wholesale evasions of the law; and shopkeepers, in turn, passed on the higher prices that followed to their customers. The *sans-culottes*, as small consumers, reacted violently, demonstrated against butchers and grocers, and demanded more vigorous measures of control. By January, the authorities had already been faced with the choice of either intensifying the Terror against law-breaking merchants and producers or of officially relaxing the regulations at the expense of the protesting consumers. They hesitated but, urged by Barère, whose feelings for the *sans-culottes* were never more than lukewarm, they decided on the second course: in late March, an amended Maximum was published providing for higher prices and profit margins; currency speculators were allowed to show their faces again; and the *assignat*, having risen to 48 per cent in December, had, by July, slipped back to 36 per cent of its nominal value. Consequently, the agitation in the markets revived and the Jacobin leaders had their share of the epithets hurled at merchants, speculators and shopkeepers. And more was to come. The Maximum law of September 1793 provided, as we saw, for the control of wages as well as prices; under existing circumstances, this meant that local authorities were required to *reduce* wages to a level 50 per cent above that of 1790. This had been done in many districts where employers dominated the local committees; but not in Paris, where wages had risen two or three times above their pre-revolutionary level and where the Commune, as long as the Hébertists were in charge, had had little intention of enforcing this part of the law. The government itself, however, was responsible for wages in its own workshops and had introduced new scales for its arms-workers and others. Meanwhile, to prevent wages in private industry from getting out of hand, it had on more than one occasion invoked the Le Chapelier law against workers' "combinations" and had even sent strikers before the Revolutionary Tribunal. Yet the greater problem remained and, even after the fall of Hébert, the now-Robespierrist Commune hesitated for many weeks before taking so dangerous a step as to reduce the current earnings of a large part of the Parisian population by one-half, or even more. When they took the plunge and published the new scales on 23 July, it was at an unfortunate time; and the hostility of the wage-earners no doubt played a part in Robespierre's fall from power a few days later.

Yet this abandonment of their *sans-culotte* partners might, under other circumstances, have served to strengthen, rather than weaken, the hold of the Jacobin leaders on the National Convention. There were plenty of men, in both the Mountain and the Plain, to whom the *sans-culotte* alliance appeared, at best, an unwelcome necessity and whom such experiments as the laws of Ventôse – whatever their real intention – filled with evident alarm. Yet the opposite happened and, far from increasing their hold on the Convention and its Committees, the estrangement of the *sans-culottes* was accompanied by the estrangement of a large part of their middle-class partners as well. On 22 and 23 May, attempts were made to assassinate Robespierre and Collot under circumstances that suggested a royalist plot. An atmosphere of panic and uncertainty followed: there were further rumours of prison conspiracies and of projected retributive action by the *sans-culottes*; and, three weeks later, Couthon presented to the Convention the text of a Draconian law – the law of 22nd Prairial (10 June 1794), which was rushed through the Assembly with maximum speed. The law, drafted by Robespierre and Couthon, accelerated the process of justice within the Revolutionary Tribunal and deprived the prisoner of the aid of defending counsel; but it also appeared to many deputies to threaten their parliamentary immunity. Was the law intended, in fact, to be used to weed out a number of "corrupt" men at whose presence in the Assembly Robespierre and Couthon were already beginning to hint without giving them names? Was its purpose to "liquidate" the suspects held in prison in order to operate more quickly the laws of Ventôse (as claimed by Albert Mathiez)? Or was it, rather, imposed (as argued by Georges Lefebvre) to forestall another prison massacre that appeared imminent following the attempted assassination of Robespierre and Collot? Whatever the truth of it, the law proved a disaster to its authors and a godsend to their political opponents. In the first place, it thoroughly alarmed a great many *Conventionnels* who, though they had accepted without much demur the successive purges of Girondins and Dantonists, now felt a grave uncertainty as to what the future might have in store. In the second place, it provided a handy weapon for Robespierre's and Couthon's – and Saint-Just's – critics on the rival Committee of General Security to use against them. Inevitably, the new law led, as was presumably foreseen or intended, to an intensification of the Terror; and the "Great Terror" that followed accounted for 1,350 victims of the guillotine in June and July where there had been only 1,250 in the nine months before. These were months when Saint-Just, on mission

47

to the front, was away from Paris; and when Robespierre and Couthon were also, though for other reasons, rarely present at the Committee's meetings. Moreover, Robespierre, from 9 July onwards, made speeches criticizing the excesses to which the new law had given rein. But he and Couthon and Saint-Just were recognized as the nation's outstanding leaders and as the architects of the Prairial law; so it is hardly surprising that it was on their heads, and not on those of the men who had ordered the executions, that the resultant revulsion – or *nausée de l'échafaud* – should eventually rebound.

Some weeks before the law of Prairial, Robespierre had persuaded the Assembly to accept another of the Committee's proposals: to introduce a new civic religion, the Cult of the Supreme Being. It was based on Rousseau's teaching and a cult that, while providing little comfort for either "atheists" or "fanatics", was calculated to appeal to the bulk of religious-minded revolutionaries, whether professedly Christian or not. Thus "virtue" should serve not only as an end in itself but as a moral shield for "terror"; and, to mark the occasion, Robespierre himself, as current President of the National Convention, marched, a few days later, at the head of a great procession to attend a colourful pageant designed by the painter David, in the Champ de Mars. It was another innovation that rebounded on the head of its promoter. To "de-christianizers" and Voltairian deists it appeared a deliberate attempt to revive Catholic "fanaticism", and Robespierre was suspected of aspiring to become the "pontiff" of a new religion. Amar and Vadier, in particular, members of the Committee of General Security, saw it in this light; and when Catherine Théot, an old fanatic and self-styled "Mother of God" who claimed to have had visions of Maximilien, was brought before the Revolutionary Tribunal and released on Robespierre's intervention, they made the most of the embarrassment and excited whispers that the whole incident provoked.[17]

The very day that Robespierre pleaded for Catherine Théot's release (26 June), there took place an event of far more momentous importance that was in no way related to it and one which, in other circumstances, would have assured the government of almost universal acclaim. This was the victory won by French arms over the Prussians at Fleurus, which cleared the Republic of foreign troops and once more opened the road to Belgium. Moreover, Saint-Just, the man most closely associated with Robespierre at this time, had made a notable contribution to the victory by the vigorous role he had played as representative on mission to the northern front. Yet, paradoxically, the event, far from strengthening the Robespierrists' hold on the Assembly, weakened it further. For, it began to be asked, particularly among those who had long sat silent on the benches of the Plain, why continue to support a policy of Terror and tightened belts, reluctantly accepted at a moment of danger, when that danger no longer existed?

So internal crisis and dissension and a release from tension from outside combined to raise doubts as to the desirability of retaining Robespierre and his group in power. And, to make matters worse, there had developed other divisions in the two governing Committees, both within the Committee of Public Safety and in the relations between the two. Since the law of December 1793 that prescribed their respective duties, there had always been a certain overlap in function: the Committee of General Security was nominally responsible for all matters relating to police and security, but the other Committee, as the senior partner, had its own right of access to the Revolutionary Tribunal. Recently, the overlap had become more serious when the Committee of Public Safety, in April, created its own police department for bringing erring and dishonest public officials to justice; and this inevitably drew the anger of the rival Committee's members onto the heads of Robespierre and Saint-Just, who had made the new department their special concern.[18] Tension became the greater when Robespierre and Couthon, having drafted the law of 22nd Prairial, pushed it through the National Convention without consulting those who considered themselves most directly concerned with its operation. We have seen how the Security Committee reacted both by stacking the tumbrils in the months that followed and by wringing the maximum possible political advantage from the Catherine Théot affair.

Within the major Committee, too, a conflict of principles and personalities had been waged since May. Bitter disputes had broken out between Carnot and Saint-Just on the conduct of military operations: Carnot accused Saint-Just, who had been a successful emissary to the armies in Alsace and the north, of meddling with matters beyond his competence. The "practical" men, Carnot and

Lindet, who tended to be moderates, clashed increasingly with the "ideologues", Robespierre, Couthon and Saint-Just, whom they accused of being over-indulgent towards the *sans-culottes*: Lindet, for one, objected on this score to the laws of Ventôse. Robespierre in turn, found himself increasingly at variance with the views of the "terrorists", Billaud and Collot, who continued to parade Hébertist sympathies. Collot had been Fouché's partner in the savage pacification of Lyons and was closely associated with another group of "terrorists" who had been similarly employed – Barras and Fréron at Toulon, Tallien at Bordeaux, and Carrier at Nantes. As the crisis within the Committees developed, such men, fearing the hostility of Robespierre, who had several of them recalled by the Assembly to account for their excesses, tended to rally round Billaud and Collot and stand together in common defence against their accuser.

By the end of June, the atmosphere within the Committee of Public Safety had become so charged with suspicion and mutual recrimination that Robespierre withdrew in disgust from its meetings and confined his activities to his private office in the Rue Saint-Honoré and the forum of the Jacobin Club. The gesture could not fail to rouse further suspicion against him, and rumours became rife of conclaves held behind closed doors between the "tyrant" and his closest lieutenants. To make matters worse, Robespierre chose to nail his critics as "intriguers" in a number of speeches to his loyal supporters in the Jacobins. He made them worse still when, refusing Barère's offer of mediation and apparently ignorant of his dwindling support in the Plain, he decided to appeal to the Convention itself against his dissident colleagues. So, in a long speech on 8th Thermidor (26 July), he passionately defended his conduct against his critics and pleaded that the Revolution could once more be saved and the reign of "virtue" finally triumph if only one last surgical operation were performed – the removal of a small group of "corrupt" men, at whose identity he continued to hint but whom he obstinately refused to name. It was a fatal gesture or miscalculation – of which Saint-Just, who was aiming at a compromise, appears to have heartily disapproved. What prompted him to do it? Historians, both defenders and detractors, have argued about the matter ever since. Jean Massin, a staunch supporter, believes it was due to excessive exhaustion, which had become evident since the attempts made on his life in May. Some (and they include Georges Lefebvre) have suggested that he may have deliberately courted martyrdom when he saw no other clear solution in sight. Gérard Walter inclines towards a similar view: that he felt that his destiny as a champion of "virtue" against "vice" had by now been fulfilled; while Max Gallo, for his part, believes it was a personal choice which put an end to the "too long unbearable waiting for martyrdom and rest".[19] (The advantage of this "death-wish" argument is, of course, that it cannot be proved or disproved; so it is a simple case of heads I win, tails you lose!)

Whatever the true explanation, Robespierre had evidently lost his grip. He was heard in silence and the Convention declined to allow him the usual courtesy of sending his speech to be printed; while Barère, ever susceptible to changing winds, threw in his lot with Robespierre's enemies. The same evening, the identical speech was enthusiastically applauded in the Jacobin Club. But the alliance of moderate Jacobins, Plain and "terrorists", temporarily united by a common fear, proved to be the stronger. During the night, the confederates concerted their plan of action for the Convention's session on the morrow. Saint-Just, who had sat up all night preparing a speech for the occasion, rose to defend his colleague but was shouted down; Robespierre was greeted with shouts of "Down with the tyrant!" and refused a hearing. Saint-Just, the two Robespierres, and their brother-in-law Lebas were placed under arrest, and sent under close escort to the Committee of General Security.

Yet, even now, the day might not have been wholly lost (or perhaps its outcome might have been postponed) if the Paris sections had rallied in support of the Jacobin leaders, as in August 1792 and June 1793. Not only the Jacobin Club but the Commune continued to voice support for the arrested men; Hanriot, Robespierrist chief of the National Guard, escaped from the squad sent to arrest him; and the turnkey of the prison to which Robespierre and his group were directed refused to acknowledge their escort's mandate, so that they were free to seek refuge among their friends at the City Hall. Moreover, the conspirators acted with caution, being still uncertain which way the wind would finally blow. But, though urged by his companions to issue a call for insurrection, Robespierre hesitated too long – either through legalistic scruple or because he lacked the will to act. More important, perhaps, was the simple fact that, when it came to the point, the *sans-culottes*, estranged by his recent policies, showed little inclination to take up arms for a cause they no longer believed in. It was certainly not for lack of time or opportunity to make up their minds. All through the afternoon and evening, the two contending parties, based respectively on the Commune and the Convention, sent mutually conflicting orders, threats, pleas and declarations to the sections and battalions of the National Guard, appealing to their loyalties. At one time, in response to the Commune's summons, 3,000 armed men, supported by thirty-two pieces of artillery, were drawn up outside the City Hall. But they lacked both leadership and purpose and, as the tide of debate in the sectional assemblies and "revolutionary" committees turned against the Robespierrists, the whole of this force gradually melted away.

Meanwhile, the Convention had screwed up its courage and declared the "conspirators" to be outlaws; and Barras, armed with the Convention's mandate, appeared at the City Hall with 6,000 men in the early hours of 10th Thermidor (28 July). He encountered no resistance and found Robespierre with his jaw shattered by a bullet (either from his own pistol or from that of a trigger-happy soldier). Barras carried off his prisoners for final identification by the Revolutionary Tribunal; and, a few hours later, they were hustled to the Place de la Révolution (the present Place de la Concorde) for execution. Among twenty-two victims, Robespierre was the last but one to mount the scaffold. It was typical of his austere probity that, after a year in high office, he should have left little more than £100. The next day, 71 councillors of the Commune, also implicated in the "Robespierrist conspiracy", followed him to the guillotine. With them perished not only a man or a group but a system. The democratic Republic of the Year II, created with the aid of the *sans-culottes*, gave way to the property-owners' Republic of Thermidor and the Directory, when gentlemen and *honnêtes gens* once more came into their own. The "single will" was put into cold storage and remained in abeyance until Bonaparte, five years later, restored it on the new foundation of a military dictatorship.

PART II

The Changing Image

It is inevitable that any public figure of eminence – and particularly one who divided opinion so sharply in his day and played so dramatic a part in such remarkable events – should have had his reputation continually reassessed by subsequent generations of writers and critics. And none more than Robespierre: it is now more than 180 years since he mounted the scaffold and the volume of literature that has been written about him and around his name would fill a well-stocked library.[1] In the course of this reassessment the questions have been asked again and again: was he a statesman or a mere small-town lawyer turned politician? was he a democrat who loved the people or a tyrant and despot who used them to further his own ends? was he a revolutionary who knew what he was about or was he a hypocrite, a pedant or a sophist besotted with theories and words? or such more impersonal questions as: what did he achieve? what role did he play? what social forces, or classes, did he represent or seek to advance?

In the shaping, or re-shaping, of any historical judgment there are – quite apart from the historian's own personal idiosyncrasies – at least four main factors at work. One is the country to which he belongs. It is obvious that, in a case of this kind, Frenchmen will feel far more involved than others. The French Revolution was *their* revolution before it was anyone else's and it has played so important a part in their subsequent history that they are inclined, even today, to debate anything that touches on it, whether they reject or accept it, with a remarkable degree of commitment. Citizens of other countries, too, that have been through revolutions in the last century and a half may also be inclined to see revolutions and revolutionaries in a more personal and less abstract way than (say) those of a country like England that has been singularly free of revolutionary movements and has not had a revolution for over 300 years. This may help to explain some of the differences we shall note between English and French attitudes towards Robespierre. Of perhaps equal importance is the generation, or epoch, to which the writer belongs. He may be writing in an age of revolution – like that of the 1830s and 1840s or 1870 or 1945 – or in a period of tension and conflict like that of the two world wars; and such experiences are far more likely to sharpen insights into what happened in an earlier period of stress than one of gradual development, affluence or consolidation, such as the 1850s and 1860s in France and England or the middle years or *"la belle époque"* of the French Third Republic. A third factor, and one of considerable importance in a case of this kind, is the social prejudice or political bias that the writer brings to his task. No one, not even an Englishman or an American, is likely to be politically neutral about a historical character like Robespierre. To make a broad generalization, he is not likely to elicit much sympathy among conservatives or Whigs; while radicals and socialists are liable to feel a certain regard for him. But by no means all: anarchists and socialists of the "left", like Blanquists and Trotskyists, are likely to reject him, and many student "revolutionaries"of the 1960s had no more use for him than they had for Stalin. And, finally, a fourth factor is perhaps as important as any. It is the documentary evidence that the historian has at his command to enable him to arrive at a reasonably balanced judgment. If this has been substantially preserved and is freely available, the subject has a chance of being fairly judged by posterity; if not, the dice may be heavily loaded against him. And here Robespierre was, for long, singularly ill served. Not only were the mass of his personal papers destroyed, but those that survived were carefully combed and selected by his "Thermidorian" enemies and successors. In consequence, the first generation of post-Revolution historians were presented with a motley collection of memoirs and reminiscences that were either counter-revolutionary and royalist or, if Republican, were uniformly hostile to Robespierre and his group. The first important breach in this web of conspiracy came in 1828 when the rest of Robespierre's surviving speeches and the memoirs of a sympathizer, Levasseur de la Sarthe, were published in Paris. Even more important for Robespierrist scholarship was the publication, in the 1830s, of the 40-volume *Histoire parlementaire de la Révolution française* by Buchez and Roux and of Laponneraye's 5-volume edition of the *Oeuvres de Robespierre*; and the reprinting of *Le Moniteur*, the official record of Revolutionary debates, was completed in 1845. It was at about this time, too, that John Wilson Croker, a conservative Englishman and

Macaulay's *bête noire*, deposited his collection of 48,000 pamphlets on the Revolution with the British Museum. So, by the mid-century, it was possible for historians at last to shake off their dependence on memoirs and recollections that were, to say the least, highly coloured and often highly unreliable, if not spurious, as well.

Since then, after a lull during the Second Empire and the aftermath of the Paris Commune, a rich flow of new documentation has followed: starting with Aulard's 6-volume edition of the proceedings of the *Société des Jacobins* (1889–97) and his *Recueil des actes du Comité de Salut public* published in 12 volumes between 1889 and 1899 (later in 23), which were in turn succeeded by the great volume of economic literature sponsored by Jaurès on the eve of the First World War and by the recent edition of Robespierre's complete speeches and writings by the Société des Etudes Robespierristes in Paris.[2] So the historian or biographer of today, whatever his loyalties or affiliations, has a far greater chance of doing justice to his subject than his predecessor of a couple of generations ago, let alone the historian or chronicler of a hundred years before.

AFTER THERMIDOR

With these points in mind, let us now follow Robespierre's "changing image" through its successive stages. To start with the Thermidorian and Napoleonic period, when he was almost universally portrayed as a mean and cowardly monster and a blood-thirsty tyrant aspiring to dictatorship and made the scapegoat for all the excesses of the Terror; and these were among the more restrained of the epithets voiced in the flood of literary tracts and libels that greeted his downfall. Two years after Thermidor, there appeared in Paris a *Secret History of the French Revolution* by F. X. Pagès, a former admirer, who now attributed to the fallen leader a "base envy, engendered by the consciousness of his inferior abilities" and "a desire of reigning solitary sovereign over ruins and carcases";[3] while Des Essarts' *Les crimes de Robespierre et de ses principaux complices*, published in Paris a year later, described him as "the greatest rogue that human nature has produced" and as "the most hypocritical, cowardly and ferocious monster that has appeared on the world's stage to the misfortune of humanity".[4] Some of these extravaganzas went further still. Who would now, for instance, believe it possible, as Galart de Montjoye did in a widely read piece called the *Histoire de la conjuration de Maximilien Robespierre* (1796), that the Incorruptible took part in orgies with prostitutes; or, with the Abbé Proyart (alias Le Blond de Neuvéglise), that he drank the blood of his victims, ate the roasted flesh of priests and sent their skins to the tanneries to make shoes for the *sans-culottes*?[5] Not to be outdone, a London pamphlet, entitled *The History of Robespierre Political and Personal* (1794), told its readers that Robespierre was a nephew of Damiens, Louis XV's would-be assassin, and had worked in a shop in Dublin before coming to Paris to become a lawyer and a favourite and "prime minister" of the Duc d'Orléans; and it pinned on him the responsibility not only for the Terror but for all the blood-letting in France from the fall of the Bastille on.[6] More sedately, Helen Maria Williams, a lady of Girondist sympathies and the author of *Memories of the Reign of Robespierre* (1795), confined herself to attaching to him such commonplace labels as "tyrant", "malevolent genius" and "great conspirator against the liberty of France".[7] And it was with literature to draw upon that England's earliest historian of the Revolution, John Adolphus, published his *Biographical Memoirs of the French Revolution* in 1799. The *Memoirs* included a long chapter on Robespierre, who appears as a "bloodthirsty tyrant" and an "execrable monster" who "no longer knew any bounds to his desire for blood"; and the whole account is liberally seasoned with such epithets as "ungrateful", "jealous", "envious", "cowardly", "vain", "treacherous", "perjured" and "depraved".[8]

There were, however, a few exceptions to this almost unrelieved presentation of Robespierre as a classical stage-villain of Grand Guignol proportions. Some came from unexpected quarters. Louis XVIII, for example, both when in exile and after his return to France, thought the Jacobin leader had been seriously maligned, that he possessed statesmanlike qualities and might reasonably be compared with Sully, or even with Richelieu.[9] Napoleon, too, had grave doubts about the authenticity of the Thermidorians' picture. While Consul and Emperor he had excellent political reasons for refusing to see any virtue in either Robespierre or any of his leading Jacobin colleagues. But once in exile in St Helena such inhibitions disappeared and, prompted by Cambacérès, one-time member of the Convention and now a loyal servant of the Emperor, he more than once expressed interest in the "mystery" attending Robespierre's fall. He fell from power, he told the small circle of his intimates, not because he wanted to extend the Terror but to end it. "The people of Paris [he told them] thought that in removing Robespierre they were destroying tyranny, whereas the purpose of his removal was to make it flourish more luxuriantly than ever. But once Robespierre had fallen, the explosion was such that, in spite of all their efforts, the Terrorists were never able to gain the upper hand again."[10]

THE RESTORATION

With the fall of Napoleon's Empire and with the Restoration in France, there came a change in opinion both in regard to the Revolution itself and to Robespierre's role within it. Whereas, in the earlier period, critics of the Revolution had been disposed, as Edmund Burke had been, to condemn it as a whole, it now became a subject of debate between conservatives, who continued to see it as an unmitigated evil, and liberals who saw great virtue in its earlier stages. While conservatives thus remained entrenched within prepared positions, liberals, as champions of Louis XVIII's Charter, were anxious to prove that the Charter set the stamp of official approval on the work of the "men of 1789" and that the Revolution, far from being a disastrous aberration, had its roots in France's national past.[11] Among them, Germaine de Staël, Necker's daughter, considered the Revolution "one of the grand eras of social order; the same movement in the minds of men which brought about the revolution in England was the cause of that in France in 1789"; and François Mignet wrote that, for the abuses of the past, "the Revolution substituted a system more conformable with justice and better suited to our times".[12] But, being monarchists as well as liberals, such writers could hardly condone the removal and execution of Louis XVI; and so, with them the Revolution tended to fall into two parts: the years 1789 to 1791, which they generally approved of, and the years 1792 to 1794 (or 1799 or 1804), which they generally condemned. They made some exceptions to this rule: they commended the exploits of the French armies during the Terror and they had a certain sneaking admiration for Danton. "Danton's mind", wrote Adolphe Thiers in his *History of the French Revolution*, "was uncultivated, but it was noble, contemplative and, above all, possessed simplicity and firmness"; and Mignet wrote of the death of Danton and Desmoulins: "Thus perished the last defenders of humanity and moderation, the last who sought to promote peace among the conquerors of the Revolution and pity for the conquered." [13] Robespierre, however, still remained beyond the pale and, while the grosser epithets were spared him, continued to be written off as a mean-spirited fanatic and hypocrite or petty tyrant. Madame de Staël, it is true, believed that some of his colleagues on the Committees – Collot and Billaud, for example – were no less detestable than he was and overthrew him in Thermidor for no nobler purpose than to save their skins; and Thiers allowed him the saving grace of possessing "strong conviction and acknowledged incorruptibility". Yet, for all this, Thiers described him as being "of the worst species of men"; as "a devotee without passion, without the vices to which passions are exposed, but yet without the courage, the greatness, and the sensibility which ordinarily accompany them; a devotee living for nothing else than to satisfy his pride and his creed, hiding himself in the hour of danger, coming forth to attract adoration after the victory had been gained by others".[14]

Yet, once more, a few voices were raised to question the validity of this totally unflattering portrait; and, once more, as with Cambacérès, they were raised by men who had been members of the National Convention. The first to do so was Paganel, whose *Essai historique et critique sur la Révolution française* was seized by the Imperial police when it appeared in 1810 but was reissued under the Restoration in 1815. Paganel had felt no regrets at Robespierre's fall, but he now paid tribute to his high ideals, acknowledged his great influence and popularity, and believed that the memory of his achievements would endure together with those of the Republic he had helped to found.[15] Other apologists were Guillaume Laurent, author of an 18-volume collection of Revolutionary speeches and reports, published between 1818 and 1821, and Laurent de l'Ardèche, who, in 1827, wrote an account of the French Revolution in reply to a "liberal" history of France by the Abbé de Montgaillard. In both praise was tempered with criticism; but both claimed that Robespierre possessed qualities of eloquence, leadership and moderation that his liberal critics had unfairly denied him.[16] A more incisive admirer was Levasseur de la Sarthe who, as mentioned before, published his *Memoirs* in 1828. Levasseur vindicated the conduct of Robespierre and Saint-Just in the course of the Terror. The execution of the Girondin leaders and of Danton and Hébert he justified as "acts of legal vengeance that must not be confused with the bloody holocaust that horrified all France". And for this later, excessive violence he believed that neither Robespierre nor his closest associates had any responsibility at all. For, if they had, he asks, "how comes it then that they broke with the vile and stupid demagogues of the Paris Commune . . . how comes it that the enemies who overthrew them had at their head Collot d'Herbois, Billaud-Varenne, Carrier and all the murderers and human tigers of that tragic and glorious period?"[17] It was much the same question as the one Napoleon had asked at St Helena a dozen years before.

1830-1848: A NEW AGE OF REVOLUTION

So, by 1830, the first steps towards a rehabilitation of Robespierre had been taken: the process would be carried considerably further during the next round of revolutions, both in France and in other parts of Europe, in the 1830s and 1840s. For one thing, as monarchy once more came under attack, more survivors from the 1790s came forward to sing the praises of the First Republic and its Jacobin leaders. Among them were some of Robespierre's enemies and critics of Thermidor who had been chastened by exile and were now willing to see qualities in him that they had previously denied. The most distinguished of these repentant Thermidorians was Bertrand Barère, former member of the great Committee of Public Safety, who, when interviewed in old age in 1832, described Robespierre as "a man without personal ambition, a Republican to the fingertips"; and added: "Would to heaven there were in the Chamber of Deputies today someone to point to those who conspire against our freedom! We were then in the middle of a war, and we did not understand the man. He was a nervous, choleric individual, whose mouth twitched when he spoke. His was the temperament of many great men, and posterity will not refuse him the title."[18] And Filippo Buonarroti, Babeuf's young lieutenant of the "Conspiracy of the Equals" of 1796, who had with Babeuf joined in the hue-and-cry against "the tyrant" in Thermidor, acclaimed him in his *Observations sur Maximilien Robespierre* (1837) as "the victim of immorality"; and "the people [he added] never had a more sincere and a more devoted friend. Great efforts have been made to sully his memory: now he is accused of aiming at dictatorship, and now he alone is held accountable for every necessary measure of severity taken by the revolutionary government. But happy, we say, would France and humanity have been if Robespierre had been dictator and had been allowed to carry out his great reforms!"[19]

New voices were also heard to praise the Incorruptible, some of them inspired by the new socialist ideas being promoted by Buonarroti and others. Among them was a young teacher and militant Republican, Albert Laponneraye, who spent a great part of his early manhood in gaol. While in the prison of la Force in Paris in 1831, he prepared a course of lectures for worker-students. One of them was devoted to Robespierre whom he described as a "great citizen . . . whose memory the people should bless, because he was the people's friend, who loved them as a mother loves her children and never ceased to make war on the hungry wolves that batten on their substance". The lectures were closed down by the police; but, during a further spell of gaol, he began to prepare for publication the first edited edition of Robespierre's works; and, later, having met Maximilien's sister Charlotte, he inherited her *Mémoires*, and the *Mémoires* and the second part of the *Oeuvres* were published together in 3 volumes in 1840–2.[20] The work was to give a great stimulus to Robespierrist studies in France; yet it was eclipsed in importance by the almost simultaneous publication of Buchez and Roux' *Histoire parlementaire de la Révolution française*, which appeared in 40 volumes between 1834 and 1838. This, too, served as a monumental vindication of Robespierre's role in the Revolution; for Buchez, a Christian Socialist, believed that the Revolution marked the climax of Christian civilization and that Jacobinism was its gospel and Maximilien its apostle.[21] These works between them touched off a spate of histories by socialist writers that generally presented Robespierre in a new and favourable light. Among them was Tissot's edited *Histoire de Robespierre* (1844), Cabet's *Histoire populaire de la Révolution* (1845) and Esquiros' *Histoire des Montagnards* (1848); and, by far the most influential and the most richly documented of them all, Louis Blanc's 12-volume *Histoire de la Révolution* (1847–62). Blanc sat down to write his *History* before the beginning of the Revolution of 1848, in which he played an outstanding role; but it was the defeat of that revolution and the weaknesses that its leaders had shown which prompted him, when in exile in London, to offer his readers the record of the *Montagnards* of 1793–4 as an example that should have been followed. So Robespierre, quite naturally, became the central figure and the one to be most admired. From the start he is cast for a hero's and statesman's role; and even in that opening ceremony at Versailles, when the deputies to the Estates walked in procession to meet the King, he is shown to be the only one among them who, "strong in his convictions, had the vision to foresee the ultimate consequences" that would flow from the event. Above all, he is praised for his draft of the Constitution of 1793; this, Blanc believed, laid the foundations of a new social order in France. And, like others before him, Blanc was inclined to play down Robespierre's part in the Terror, and he thought that his reputation as High Priest of the Cult of the Supreme Being had been grossly and mischievously overplayed.[22]

It was during this period, too, that admiration for Robespierre began to be expressed in other countries: among them, England, Germany, Russia and the Austrian Empire. In Russia, in April 1842, Vissarion Bielinski wrote to a friend of the great regard he had formed for Robespierre and Saint-Just; and Alexander Herzen wrote in the same year: "Maximilien is the only truly great man of the Revolution; all the others are only brilliant and necessary manifestations of it, nothing more."[23] In Hungary, meanwhile, the poet Sandor Petöfi was hanging the walls of his rooms with portraits of Robespierre, Marat and Saint-Just; and, in the spring of 1848, there appeared in Budapest a Hungarian translation of a speech Robespierre made to the Convention on 10 May 1793.[24] In England, James Bronterre O'Brien, the Chartist, translated Buonarroti's *Conspiracy of the Equals* in 1836; and, a year later, he wrote a *Life and Character of*

Maximilien Robespierre, which was followed, after an interval of twenty years, by a *Dissertation and Elegy on the Life and Death of Maximilien Robespierre*. Neither work is distinguished by original or critical scholarship. They are essentially political tracts cast in the spirit of the times and reflecting both O'Brien's conversion to *babouviste* ideas and the social and political tensions that attended the birth of industrial society in England. But they are remarkable for the reverence that the writer expresses for the memory of a man whom he considered to be "the greatest reformer and legislator that the world has yet known" and one whose "birth was the greatest honour ever conferred upon France"; and for his conviction that "the more magnanimous, the more god-like I prove Robespierre's conduct to have been, the greater will be the horror in which his memory will be held by the upper and middle classes". They are remarkable, too, in that O'Brien condemned the Terror – and not only its "excesses" – and believed that his hero had no part in it whatever.[25]

In Germany, Robespierre found a more critical and cautious admirer in the young Karl Marx. Marx was at this time editing the *Rheinische Zeitung* at Cologne and, in contests with the Young Hegelians, was developing his own theories on the struggle of classes, the role of ideas and the nature of the State. He chose the French Revolution as a testing-ground for his new ideas and saw it, at this time, as a mainly *political* revolution in which the rising class, the bourgeoisie, while welcoming the "plebeians", or *sans-culottes*, as their allies, turned their energies to their own exclusive advantage and to further the growth of a bourgeois State. In this operation, Marx recognized that Robespierre and the Jacobins had a particular and necessary part to play in that they used the Terror to harness the nation to the needs of a revolutionary war; but once the danger from invasion was over they were inevitably cast aside, as they held the illusory and anachronistic belief that the new State could be built on a model drawn from the Classical past instead of coming to terms with a "bourgeois" model better suited to the times. In this picture, Robespierre was presented neither as villain nor hero, but as a Utopian who had played a necessary, though limited, historical role.[26] We shall see that Marxists were by no means to remain tied to this interpretation in the century that followed.

It was inevitable that some writers, whose interest in the French Revolution had been awakened by the events of their day, should be attracted not so much to the Incorruptible as to his opponents – to the Gironde or Danton rather than to Robespierre himself. This was the case, among others, with a number of the Romantics. In England, Sir Walter Scott, a Tory Romantic who had a certain regard for Danton, wrote in his *Life of Napoleon* (9 volumes, 1827): "Marat was a madman, raised into consequence only by circumstances; Robespierre, a cold, creeping, calculating hypocrite, whose malignity resembled that of a paltry and second-rate fiend – but Danton was a character for Shakespeare or Schiller to have drawn in all its broad lights and shades."[27] In Hesse, in Germany, Georg Buechner, a young Romantic of a more radical stamp than Scott who had been exiled for playing a part in the political underground of the early 1830s, also turned to the French Revolution and, having read Mignet and Thiers, chose Danton as hero and Robespierre as villain. In his play, *Danton's Death*, Danton is represented as a red-blooded man of vigorous good sense who chooses to enjoy the fruits of a revolution that he believes to be completed; while Robespierre, a self-righteous and narrow-minded bigot, persuades himself – but fails to persuade Danton – that the revolution must go on. In the last encounter between the two, in March 1794, Robespierre is made to say, "The social revolution is not yet complete. If you leave a Revolution half finished, you dig your own grave . . . Vice must be punished. Virtue must rule through Terror"; and Danton counters: "The guillotine is your private washtub – you wash your dirty linen in other people's blood."[28]

In England, Thomas Carlyle, another Romantic, but one who had read *Le Moniteur* and the *Histoire parlementaire* and had also a certain pitying indulgence for the Parisian *sans-culottes* ("poor lackeys, all besoiled, encrusted with dim effacement"), wrote *The French Revolution* in 1837. As an admirer of the Great Man in history, cast in the mould of a Cromwell or Frederick the Great, Carlyle was naturally more attracted to earthy characters like Mirabeau and Danton than he was to an intellectual like Robespierre. Mirabeau he describes as "royal Mirabeau . . . a man, a reality"; and Danton: "with all dross, he was a Man, fiery-real from the great firebosom of Nature herself". In contrast to these two, Robespierre cuts a very sorry figure indeed: "a sea-green Incorruptible", a "Jesuit doctor", "Mahomet-Robespierre", the "Dalai-Lama of patriot men"; and, for good measure, "arid, implacable-impotent, dull-drawling, barren as the Harmatten wind". And, like Buechner, Carlyle stages a final, dramatic encounter between the two protagonists: "One conceives easily the deep mutual incompatibility that divided these two; with that terror of feminine hatred the poor sea-green Formula looked at the monstrous colossal Reality, and grew greener to behold him . . . Two such chief products are too much for one Revolution."[29]

Ten years later, the French Romantic poet and politician, Alphonse de Lamartine, who was to play a leading part in the events of 1848, published a long history of the Revolution under the title of *L'Histoire des Girondins*. Some clue as to its nature is afforded by the note that Alexandre Dumas, the great novelist, sent the author, congratulating him on having lifted history to the level of romance: at least, so Acton tells us. And it accorded well with Lamartine's own political inclinations and his romantic view of history that he should have cast the Girondins, the great failures of 1793, as the heroes of his piece. By contrast, Robespierre emerges as a Utopian idealist who, much in the style of Buechner's presentation, allows himself to become a tyrant and terrorist, a Marius where he might have been a Cato, and therefore unsuited to be a model for the "liberal" revolution of 1848. Yet Lamartine's revulsion is tempered with a certain admiration; for, in the course of writing, he had been persuaded (partly through a meeting with Souberbielle, Robespierre's doctor, and with one of Duplay's daughters) that the Incorruptible had had "a thirst for truth and just laws" and that it was his "great tragedy" that he had sought to achieve admirable ends by criminal means. In consequence, some of Lamartine's readers became confused and alarmed: his wife wrote that she regretted Alphonse's growing respect for such a man; and the author himself felt obliged to issue a later disclaimer, in which he said that "the accusation of having flattered Robespierre is the calumny that has saddened me more than any other".[30]

Another champion of Danton and critic of Robespierre was Jules Michelet, who was probably, for all his romantic fantasies, the greatest Revolutionary historian of the century. To Michelet, however, the real hero of the Revolution was neither of these leaders but "the people": "*l'acteur principal* [he wrote in the preface to the first volume of his *History of the French Revolution*, published in 1847] *est le peuple*". It was to "the people" that the Bastille surrendered in July 1789 "because its conscience troubled it", and the Revolutionary wars were fought with mystical fervour by the whole nation under arms. Like the liberals of the 1820s, Michelet saw the need to divide the Revolution into two; but, being a Republican democrat and not a constitutional monarchist, he drew his dividing-line not at 1791 but at 1792–3; and he saw a sharp distinction between the "glories" of 1789 to 1792 – "*l'époque sainte*" – when the nation was united, and the "heroic" but "sombre" days of 1793–4 – "*l'époque des violences, l'époque des actes sanguinaires*" – to which the Republic had been driven by dangers, both real and imaginary, from within and without. In consequence, Danton, the man of August–September 1792, is portrayed throughout as a heroic figure, while Robespierre, who destroyed Danton and lived to preside over the "sombre" days of '93 and '94, is an ambivalent figure, a mixture of good and bad. Michelet esteemed him as "a man of great will and as hard-working and poor as myself"; but, having been reared in "the sombre and austere city" of Arras and "within the great sombre walls of Louis-le-Grand, blackened by the shadows of the Jesuits", he had emerged as a solemn, solitary, brooding figure, devoted to the cause of justice, yet lacking in political audacity and "lacking, above all, in the knowledge of men and affairs". He had, moreover, read more deeply than was good for him of Rousseau and Mably and slid all too easily into his self-destructive role as priest of the new Cult (for Michelet the greatest sin of all) and patron of the Terror.[31]

ENGLISH TORIES AND WHIGS

So, in France and other countries involved in the Revolutions of 1830 and 1848, the French Revolution and Robespierre's role in it tended to be discussed as part of a great political debate which related almost as much to the present as to the past: in fact, Blanc, Lamartine and Marx all played significant roles in the Revolution of 1848, and even Buechner (as we saw) played some part in that of 1830. But in England the case was a somewhat different one. Here, too, in addition to the Romantics and the Chartist O'Brien, there were historians of the 1830s and 1840s, both Tories and Whigs, who debated the rights and wrongs of the Revolution and its leaders. In so doing, they, too, did not fail to betray their political sympathies; but for them it was more of an intellectual exercise than a demonstration of loyalty to party or cause, and they naturally lacked the sense of immediacy and direct involvement of the Germans and French.[32] Whigs as well as Tories were, perhaps not surprisingly, inclined to be hostile or lukewarm towards the Revolution; and hostility to Robespierre was as likely to be found in the one party as in the other. The first of these historians to write at this time was a Tory, Sir Archibald Alison, whose *History of Europe during the French Revolution* was published in 1833. It is a dreary and pedantic piece, adorned with copious marginal references; but it was not over-critical in its use of sources, drawing heavily on royalist memoirs (on Chateaubriand and Lacretelle) and on the spurious *Mémoires révolutionnaires*, which purported to relay the more bloodthirsty declarations of the Jacobin leaders: Robespierre, for example, is credited with the phrase: "A nation can only be regenerated by mountains of corpses"; and Collot and Saint-Just are made to say much the same. "Such", observes the author, "were the principles daily carried into practice for months together in every town in France." And what, he asks, would have been the consequence if the Revolutionary Government's policy had been fully carried out? "To sink the whole human race to the level of the lowest classes, and destroy everything which dignifies or adorns human nature."[33] It is, in fact, old-fashioned Grand Guignol, harking back to the tracts of the late 1790s. So it is all the more remarkable to contrast Alison's *History* with the scholarly writing of a fellow-Tory, John Wilson Croker, which began to appear at about the same time. Croker's *Essays on the Early Period of the French Revolution* were not published until 1857; but they had already appeared as separate pieces in the conservative *Quarterly Review* in the 1830s: among them a 130-page essay on Robespierre in 1835. Croker was both a scholar and a collector (we have mentioned the Collection he left with the British Museum) and had, unlike Alison, read just about everything that had been made available on the French Revolution up to his day. However, his Tory sympathies drew him towards Burke rather more than to any other previous writer or observer, and he shared Burke's view that the Revolution was the outcome of a conspiracy and was an almost unmitigated disaster from start to finish. In consequence, he was highly critical of the liberal histories of Mignet and Thiers; he detested Danton and Desmoulins, whom he represented as agents of the Duc d'Orléans; he thought the Girondins to be beneath contempt; and he denounced Robespierre's Thermidorian opponents as terrorists without principle, whose only motives for overthrowing him were fear and hatred compounded with ambition. In fact, the only leader for whom Croker has a kind word to say is Robespierre himself; and, if we except O'Brien, he was the first English historian to do so. Moreover, he traces Robespierre's career from 1789, when he already casts him for the future leader of the Mountain, through to Thermidor; and all with the most scrupulous care and attention to detail. He blames the Gironde for the divisions that split the Convention after September 1792; he analyses minutely the meaning of Robespierre's note of June 1793 on the need for "a single will" (*la volonté une*); he carefully examines the problems and choices facing the Jacobin Government in 1793–4; and he adopts Napoleon's "scapegoat" theory to explain the events of Thermidor and concludes: "Obscure and unaccountable as Robespierre's later conduct was, we repeat our inclination to believe that the chief cause of his fall was his being suspected of an intention of returning to some system of decency, mercy and religion".[34]

Compared with Croker, the Whig historians were more charitably disposed towards the Revolution itself but far less so towards its leader. Like Croker's own work, the definitive edition of William Smyth's *Lectures on the History of the French Revolution* did not appear until the 1850s (a first, incomplete edition was published in 1840), though they were delivered, in their original form, at Cambridge, where Smyth held the Chair of Modern History, in the 1820s and 1830s. Six of them, including a pen-portrait of Robespierre, were presented under the title of "The Reign of Terror". The portrait is almost unrelievedly unflattering. Epithets abound: "this dreadful Robespierre", "the Moloch of the French nation", "the most perfect poltroon", "a tyrant so mean and unworthy to command", and so on; and, surprising in one who had dipped so widely into every available source, he tells us that "wine and liquors, which he used to drink immoderately, must have made him commit some indiscretion, for latterly he drank but water". Yet Smyth allows him one virtue at least: a love of austerity and contempt for luxury, "a virtue always intelligible to the populace". This does little, however, to offset the severity of the final verdict: "It is a mortifying passage in the history of mankind that a man like this should obtain domination, and such a domination, over one of the first Kingdoms of Europe."[35]

Among English Whigs who wrote occasional pieces on the Revolution were Henry Brougham and Lord Macaulay. Brougham's *Historical Sketches* (1843) include chapters on both Robespierre and Danton. His first reaction to Danton was an unfavourable one; but he later toned it down and allowed him a grudging admiration. Robespierre, however, was given no such charitable dispensation and emerges as an arch-enemy of liberty whose virtues are hard to find. Macaulay, too, was concerned with "liberty" and believed that revolutions were salutary if they promoted or achieved it; and he applied a similar test to the leaders and parties. So, among the French revolutionaries, he thought that the Girondins, for all their obvious lapses from virtue, were the only group that commanded respect. The Jacobins hardly fitted the bill at all: Danton, though he died "the martyr of mercy and order", was the author of the Terror and "the captain of the ruffians of September"; and Barère he wrote off as the most depraved and consummate villain of them all. Robespierre, on the other hand (and here Macaulay may, surprisingly, have been influenced by Croker), was disinterested and zealous for principle and was made the scapegoat for the crimes of others; and it was Macaulay's judgment that he and his fellow-"triumvirs" were better men than the conspirators who overthrew them.[36]

George Henry Lewes, a man of many talents and the last of the Whig historians to write on the Revolution in the 1840s, has the distinction of being the author of the first full-length biography of Robespierre in English. He was also the only English historian who, in writing of these events, was acutely conscious of the impact of the Revolution of 1848. The experience was not an altogether agreeable one, and he wrote in the preface to his *Life of Maximilien Robespierre* (1849) that what happened in that year had brought "Robespierre's name and doctrine into alarming prominence". Lewes had read widely but with little discrimination, and his book is a curious hotch-potch of the views of Lamartine, Michelet, Alison, Croker and Louis Blanc, giving the impression that he was trying desperately hard to be fair to his subject. But it was evidently Lamartine that influenced him most and his total picture is that of a remarkably unattractive fanatic. Robespierre, he concludes, was "honest, sincere, self-denying and consistent; but he was cowardly, relentless, pedantic, unloving, intensely vain and morbidly envious"; more-over, "he has not left the legacy to mankind of one grand thought, nor the example of one generous or exalted action".[37]

HISTORIANS OF THE SECOND EMPIRE

By 1850 or 1851, the second phase of the "age of revolution" was over. Chartism was dead or moribund in England; and in France, as in other European countries that had had revolutions in 1848, a conservative government now sat firmly in the saddle. So, for the next twenty years and more – years of conservatism and "consolida-tion" – there was little public debate on revolution, whether that of 1789 or any other. Besides, such new work as appeared lacked originality and inspiration. (There was, of course, one notable exception: Tocqueville's *Ancien Régime and the French Revolution*, published in 1856; but this made no mention of Robespierre and made little impression in its day.) In France, Imperial historians, in writing of the great events of the 1790s, only showed sympathy insofar as they could be seen to have contributed to the rise and glory of the first Napoleon. On the other hand, there were those, among the Empire's critics, who championed the Jacobins' cause and looked back to Robespierre with reverence as their outstanding leader. Among these were two popular novelists, George Sand and Eugène Sue. To George Sand (she was writing in 1856) Robespierre was "the greatest man of the revolution and one of the greatest men in history".[38] Sue returned to the debate of the "mystery" and "para-dox" of Thermidor and, having considered the virtues and vices of the two main parties to the dispute, asked the rhetorical question: "Does not this prove that the *journée* of the 9th Thermidor marked *the triumph of the scoundrels* over *the men of honour and integrity*?"[39] To this period, too, belongs a long, rambling, uncritical eulogy of

71

Robespierre, 2,200 pages long. This was Ernest Hamel's *Histoire de Robespierre*, published in Paris in 1865. Hamel, a democrat of 1848 whose grandfather had been a friend of Saint-Just, reacted violently to the criticisms of Michelet and other historians and set himself the task of correcting the score. To do so, he thought it best to arrive at total truth by tracing Robespierre's career "day by day" and "hour by hour" and, where there were gaps in the evidence, he padded his account with a recital of every single event in the long history of the Revolution. The result was a long-winded piece of hagiography that, far from winning converts to the Robespierrist cause, lent grist to the mill of his detractors.[40]

As an antidote to Hamel – though it was not so intended at the time – came Edgar Quinet's *La Révolution*, which was published in the same year. It is the work of a liberal conservative, hostile to the Second Empire, to popular democracy and (his mother was a Protestant) to the Roman Catholic Church. Like Brougham and Macaulay in England, he praises the Revolution as a struggle for "liberty"; but he condemns it where it makes concessions to Catholicism, as when it recognizes a "constitutional" (Catholic) clergy and, even more, when, in the course of the Terror, it promotes a new (disguised Catholic) cult. So Robespierre comes in for an assault on two fronts: as a terrorist who suppresses "liberty" and as the "pontiff" of a new under-cover form of the Catholic faith. Indeed, Quinet, unlike most of the historians of his day, is inclined to lend some credibility to the Thermidorians' case: "Contemporaries", he writes, "never believed that Robespierre was a stranger to the Terror; it is only a number of historians that have denied it."[41]

TAINE AND THE PARIS COMMUNE

Quinet had condemned the Terror, not only for the havoc he believed it to have caused in France but because its "savage grandeur must still terrify posterity". So, with him as with so many other French historians, concern for the present served as a stimulus to re-write the history of the past. But in no case was that preoccupation as intense as with the next Revolutionary historian to appear on the scene, Hippolyte Taine. Taine had, like Michelet, been a liberal democrat in 1848 and had, at that time, been enthusiastic for the popular cause. But the Paris Commune of 1871 had soured and disillusioned him, for this was indeed the Terror writ large; and, five years later, he published the most eloquent, bitter and scathing indictment of the Revolution that has ever been penned. But whereas earlier conservative writers had presented the Revolution as an unfortunate accident or the result of a conspiracy, Taine saw it as the logical sequel of the dissolution of government and of the old social order (which, incidentally, he condemned); thus "spontaneous anarchy" was let loose and "the mob" took over. And to Taine "the mob" was by no means "the people" as seen by Michelet, but "bandits and vagabonds", "*la lie de la société*", "*la dernière plèbe*", in short "*la canaille*" or the lowest riff-raff of the streets. And from this compost-heap of revolution, as Taine viewed it, there emerged the sort of leaders – unstable characters, social failures and misfits, riddled with dogma and self-importance – that were best qualified to fill the role. "*Ce sont là nos Jacobins; ils naissent dans la décomposition sociale, ainsi que des champignons dans un terreau qui fermente.*" And as the Revolution was a disaster from start to finish, he was no more inclined to spare one ·group of leaders the shafts of his savage wit than any other. Thus Marat is a madman, Danton a barbarian, and Robespierre, the best suited of all to preside over this monstrous saturnalia, an empty babbler, a hypocrite and self-infatuated pedant – that is to say, "a mind both vapid and inflated which, because it feeds on words, believes itself to be rich in ideas, toys with phrases and deludes itself the better to lord it over others".[42]

THE THIRD REPUBLIC AND DANTON

While Taine's study, bitter and pathological as it so evidently was, came to be largely discounted as a work of serious history, it has had a profound influence on conservatives and counter-revolutionaries ever since. In its own day, it found a number of imitators – among them P. Lanfrey, author of an *Essai sur la Révolution française* (1879), for whom Robespierre was a hypocrite and a besotted follower of Rousseau: "*C'est le* Contrat social *fait homme.*" [43] But though Taine had his admirers, his heated denunciation of the Revolution as a whole did not appeal to the academic and intellectual climate of the Third Republic which, after a shaky start in the seventies, now began to settle down. This new climate of opinion was anti-clerical, bourgeois, anti-Terrorist and anti-socialist; but it was also Republican and formally democratic. To men who embraced such views the Republic of 1793 could not be summarily dismissed or laughed out of court as it had been by Taine; moreover, memories of the Prussian War, which had stripped France of a part of her eastern provinces, and the stirring speeches of Gambetta were still fresh enough to give added lustre to the tradition of national revolutionary defence that sprang from those times. It is, therefore, not surprising that Danton, the hero of September '92, should now become restored to favour and be given a street and a monument in the heart of Paris in the centenary celebrations of 1889. Moreover, a historian was found to put the seal of academic approval on the event and become one of the most vocal and respected of Danton's admirers. Alphonse Aulard, a typical Radical of the Third Republic, was appointed to the new Chair of the French Revolution at the Sorbonne in 1886 and wrote a *Political History* of the Revolution that appeared at the close of the century. Like the work of so many other historians, the book was both a work of scholarship and a tract for the times. In his preface, the author wrote that he wished "to write the political history of the Revolution from the point of view of the origin and development of Democracy and Republicanism"; and Danton fell naturally into place as the hero of the book. Not only was he suited for the role by his solid Republican virtues, but he was also a convinced anti-clerical, a fighter and a man of action, a worthy forerunner of Gambetta, the hero of 1871; and, besides, although he lacked a system and a programme and was careless of his reputation and personal safety, he was a stranger to hatred and vengeance and undeserving of the charges of cruelty and venality that both contemporaries and posterity had heaped upon him. Robespierre, on the other hand, for all his integrity and the undoubted services he rendered, is presented as a meaner type of mortal altogether: as a man who attuned his policies to win popular applause, who destroyed the Girondins to avenge a personal affront and who killed Danton who looked to the future while he looked to the past: in short, a reactionary as well as the "pontiff" of a new religion and a Republican after the event. "It is for these reasons [Aulard concludes] that he seems to us today a hypocritical demagogue, and also because he points out the desirable but not the possible; he says what ought to be done but never tells us how to do it." [44]

In England as in France, the study of the Revolution had fallen into the doldrums by the early 1850s; but, in England, this "fallow" period lasted longer and the revival of interest came later. In 1876 (the year of Taine's *Les Origines*), the Radical John Morley had contributed an article on Robespierre to the *Fortnightly*, in which he broke fresh ground by shifting attention from his subject's personality to the role he had played in an important historical event.[45] But this was a brief interlude; and it was only under the impact of the centenary year in France and the scholarly publications it unleashed (Aulard's *Political History* and his edited volumes on the Jacobin Club and the Committee of Public Safety were prominent among them) that English historians began, as the French had done in the 1870s, to look at the Revolution afresh. Among the fruits of this revival were Hilaire Belloc's *Robespierre* (1901) and *French Revolution* (1911) and the lectures that Lord Acton gave on the Revolution at Cambridge between 1895 and 1899 and published in a single volume in 1910. Acton and Belloc were both Roman Catholics, who considered the conflict between Church and State to have been of paramount importance and who saw the events of those years as a battle of ideas and a battle for men's souls. But Belloc, unlike Acton, shared Michelet's view of the Revolution as a great regenerative episode in the history of the people of France to which Danton and Robespierre had, each in his own way, made a distinctive contribution. Danton is his particular hero and is commended for his intelligence, courage, patriotism, eloquence and powers of leadership. Yet Belloc was anxious to dispel the "legend" that Robespierre was a man of blood: "He has left no monument; but for the intensity of his faith and for his practice of it, his name, though it will hardly increase, will certainly endure." [46] Acton saw the Jacobin leaders in quite different terms. As an aristocratic Whig enamoured of personal "liberty", he was more indebted to Tocqueville – and even to Smyth, his predecessor at Cambridge of half a century before – than he was to Michelet; and though he had an almost exaggerated

regard for Aulard's scholarship, he had little else in common with
a Frenchman of the Third Republic. Being a Whig, he detested the
Terror and the Revolutionary Government; and, like Tocqueville,
he recoiled before the social and political consequences of equality
and democracy. To him Robespierre was the embodiment of Terror
and popular democracy combined. So he wrote him off – or
appeared to do so – in terms almost as violent as Thiers' and Taine's
as "the most hateful character in the forefront of history since
Machiavelli reduced to a code the wickedness of public men". But,
as a moralist (and here he differed sharply from Tocqueville), he
applied other standards of conduct as well; and this had the effect of
toning down the sweeping severity of the judgment just quoted. For,
as it turns out, it is of Danton rather than of Robespierre that he has
the lowest opinion of all; and he has no use whatsoever for the
"opportunism" that Aulard saw as one of Danton's principal virtues.
"With Danton and his following", he writes, "we reach the lowest
stage of what can still be called the conflict of opinion, and come to
bare cupidity and vengeance, to brutal instinct and hideous passion";
whereas Robespierre, for all his crimes, acted "in the service of some
form of democratic system". And once more, like Croker, he
returns to the "mystery" surrounding Robespierre's fall and quotes
Cambacérès' remark to Napoleon that his case had been "judged but
never pleaded".[47]

REHABILITATION

We have now seen that, by the eve of the First World War, Robespierre's reputation had had its ups and downs, but that the typical
view of him, among writers and historians, was still of a pedant or
sophist and, if no longer of a "tyrant" or man of blood, of an
unpractical dreamer and demagogue with little capacity for action.
His personal integrity, or "incorruptibility", was seldom called in
doubt; though many, preferring the very human frailties of Danton,
rated it low in the list of virtues, or even as a form of hypocrisy;
while to a few it was a mask for something else and therefore a
downright fraud. Moreover, in France at least, Danton's rehabilitation, a product of the 1880s, far from proving to Robespierre's

advantage, tended to down-grade him further. Yet, in the twenty years that followed, the roles would be reversed and now Robespierre would emerge as the Revolution's hero and Danton as its villain.

This reversal of opinion may be attributed to four main causes: to the experiences of the First World War, the growth of Marxism from the 1880s on, the outbreak of the Russian Revolution and the work of Albert Mathiez. But rather than consider each of these four factors in turn, it may be best to see how the first three of them, at least, were reflected in the work of a number of historians. And here the point of departure must be Jean Jaurès, the author of the *Histoire socialiste* (1901–4), who, though not an unqualified admirer of the Incorruptible, made a significant contribution to the new image of him that was only to reach its full maturity in the 1920s and 1930s. In spite of its tendentious title, Jaurès' work was by no means a narrow party piece: he accepted Michelet's and Aulard's thesis that the Revolution was a struggle for the democratic Republic, and he claimed to owe his inspiration in more-or-less equal proportions to the narrative vigour of Plutarch, the mystical-nationalist fervour of Michelet and the materialism of Marx. But he was a socialist deputy and Labour leader as much as he was an academic historian, and as such Marx's influence was very strong indeed and, in some respects though by no means always, it surpassed the other two. In fact, he wrote, a few years before he published his book, that "the Revolution is a great drama whose chief actors are the social classes";[48] and, in the preface to his *History*, he took Aulard to task for not "conceiving of the social and political upheavals [of the Revolution] as intimately linked."[49] So now, for the first time, in a full-length history of the Revolution, the struggle of classes became not just an occasional interlude but a central and systematically presented theme. And for Jaurès the inter-play of classes was not confined to that between nobles and commoners and peasants (which would, in itself have been nothing new), but it was extended to include the "small people" of the towns – the small masters, shopkeepers and workers, or *sans-culottes* – to whom he gave a greater importance than historians had done before. In consequence, the role and actions of the leaders had to be tested not only as orators and Parliamentarians, as members of the Jacobin Club or the Committee of Public

77

Safety, for their conduct of public affairs or in their relations with the "bourgeois" political groups, but in their relations with the common people and their spokesmen as well. So naturally Robespierre who, far more than Danton, appeared as the foremost leader of popular democracy, was lifted into greater prominence and won Jaurès' praise as a champion of the aspirations of the lower classes. In addition, Jaurès, as a pacifist (he was assassinated as a war-resister in 1914), approved strongly of Robespierre's opposition to war in 1791–2 and his later condemnation of territorial conquest. Yet his praise is tempered with caution: like Michelet and Aulard, he deplores certain qualities of meanness and envy that he noted in Robespierre's dealings with the Gironde; he observes his hesitations and shortcomings at certain moments of crisis (as in the summer of 1792); and, in general, he is not more inclined to see virtue in Robespierre than he sees in Danton, or even in Mirabeau and Barnave, until the decisive turning-point of June 1793, when he emerges as the foremost and undisputed leader of the Revolution in its most critical year. Thus, in the interests of Revolutionary defence, of national unity and of France's future (and of social democracy, as Jaurès sees it), he applauds Robespierre's condemnation of "atheism" and his use of the Terror to eliminate the factions; yet he stops short of expressing either praise or blame for his conduct in the last dramatic months that led to Thermidor. So, in Jaurès' picture, the positive aspects of the leader far outweigh the negative; and, in his view, the Incorruptible was no unpractical dreamer, but a political realist who constantly kept his ear to the ground: "In fact, he kept himself abreast of every detail of revolutionary activity both in the armies and through the length and breadth of the land; and, with an incredible agility of mind and an extact concern for realities, he attempted to assess the qualities of the men whom the Revolution summoned to serve it." [50]

So a long step had already been taken towards Robespierre's rehabilitation; it was left to Mathiez and some of his supporters to complete it. Mathiez began his academic career as a student of Aulard and it was under Aulard's direction that he wrote the first of his books (in 1904) on the Revolution's religious cults. This and his reading of Jaurès awakened his interest in Robespierre; and, from 1907 on, he began to make him the centre of all his research. He broke with his old master and the prevailing orthodoxy of the Sorbonne and founded, with Charles Vellay, the Society for Robespierrist Studies, whose proclaimed object was to render to Robespierre "the justice that is his due"; and, in the following year, the society began to issue the *Annales révolutionnaires* (later the *Annales historiques de la Révolution française*) which, from then on, became France's leading organ for the promotion of Robespierrist scholarship. One of Mathiez' own early contributions (in 1910) was a study of Robespierre and religion. He opened it with the challenge: "The figure of Robespierre has been so much misrepresented during the past twenty years, even by republican historians, that to talk of the Incorruptible's religious ideas nowadays may seem a rash undertaking"; and he rounded it off by commenting on Robespierre's report to the Convention that inaugurated the Cult of the Supreme Being in tones of filial devotion: "His speech was listened to amid a truly religious silence, only interrupted from time to time by frenzied applause. This speech has all the force of a testament: not the testament of one man, but that of a whole generation, the generation which created the first Republic and believed that by the Republic they were regenerating the world." [51]

We have seen that earlier historians, when anxious to elevate Danton, had generally found it necessary to deflate or denigrate Robespierre: thus a kind of logical antithesis had been established between the two. Mathiez had a similar problem, though, in his case, the roles were reversed; and the long series of books and papers he now devoted to the Incorruptible, both in the *Annales* and elsewhere, were systematically studded with attacks on Danton, who now became a total villain, not only in the crisis of the winter and spring of 1794, which led to the execution of the Indulgents, but throughout his career from the summer of 1789 onwards. For, in Mathiez' view, Danton was a rogue from beginning to end; and he based this opinion not only on a careful study of the memoirs and documents of the Revolutionary period, but on the new insights given him by his experience of the shortcomings of the Radical politicians of his day. As a Jaurèsian socialist, Mathiez did not take much persuading that the series of financial scandals of 1902 and 1906, involving a number of these politicians, was an additional pointer to the character of Danton whom these same politicians so much admired. So, by association, Danton became a typical Radical, or Radical-socialist, of the Third Republic, opportunistic and venal; while Robespierre, in contrast, was a model of revolutionary high-mindedness, exemplary virtue and incorruptibility. Mathiez' experience of the First World War completed the picture: added to his other vices Danton now appeared as a "defeatist" moving in a circle of shady "foreigners". And the Russian Revolution, which Mathiez enthusiastically welcomed, justified *post facto* the earlier revolutionary dictatorship in which Danton had shown such obvious failings and Robespierre had been such a pillar of strength.

Mathiez died in 1932, at fifty-eight, and he had no time to write that definitive biography of Robespierre which he must have had in mind; and the nearest approach to a synthesis of his Robespierrist studies must be sought in the history of the Revolution that he wrote in the early 1920s. In it, he presents the Incorruptible as a man dedicated to social justice who, through the laws of Ventôse (March–April 1794), attempts to redistribute wealth by dividing the properties confiscated from arrested "suspects" among the poor. Like Jaurès, he commends Robespierre's efforts to stop the war in 1791–2; but he also exculpates him from any direct responsibility for the Great Terror of 1794 and attaches the blame for the misuse of the law of 22nd Prairial on his enemies in the Committee of General Security; and finally (like Croker and others), he explains the events of Thermidor in terms of a conspiracy hatched, in the main, by a clique of corrupt and bloodthirsty "pro-consuls" around Fouché and Carrier, whom Robespierre had recalled to Paris to account for their crimes.[52]

Such heights of reverence for Robespierre were never to be reached again, in works of scholarship at least. But Mathiez was a persuasive lecturer, writer and polemicist and, though he died young, he lived long enough and wrote well enough to topple the established orthodoxy of the Aulard school and to put another in its place. This new orthodoxy, while not uncritical of Robespierre, has generally continued to assign him to the role for which both Jaurès and Mathiez cast him and, accordingly, reduced the stature of Danton who has never recovered the clean bill of health that Aulard had given him.

Among historians who came under Mathiez' direct influence

were Gérard Walter, Georges Michon and Jacques Godechot in France; Crane Brinton, Louis Gottschalk and Ralph Korngold in America; and J. M. Thompson in England. Some of them wrote excellent biographies as well: perhaps none better than Gérard Walter, whose 2-volume *Robespierre* was published in Paris in 1936. In his preface, Walter admonished his readers: "Whatever your attitude may be to the French Revolution, do not forget that the name of Robespierre counts among the four or five that represent France in the Pantheon of all humanity. You therefore have no right to retain a false or superficial image of him." And, in preparing his second edition for the press a quarter of a century later, he stated that he "had nothing to withdraw and nothing to add" to what he had said before.[53] A similar, underlying sympathy pervades Ralph Korngold's *Robespierre and the Fourth Estate* (New York, 1941), which is the only biography of the Incorruptible of any distinction to have appeared in the United States. Curiously, Korngold first became interested in Robespierre through reading Thiers; yet he owed a great deal more to Mathiez; and it may be, as Crane Brinton suggests in an Introduction, that the collapse of the Third Republic in 1940 gave him a greater awareness of the problems that had faced the First. Thus Korngold tries to put himself in Robespierre's shoes as he grapples with the tasks of war, national unity and social regeneration. For, as with Mathiez, the social problem plays an important part in the book; and the struggle of parties and factions was (in the author's words) "at bottom not a struggle between groups of ambitious individuals and their followers, but the effort of society to find its political equilibrium after the shifting of great economic forces". In this context, Robespierre, as "the leader of the Fourth Estate – the proletariat", had a particular role to play; and, following Mathiez again, he believes that, through the laws of Ventôse, he made a determined attempt to redress the economic situation in favour of the "working classes" and the fact that the attempt was made was a major factor in his overthrow and execution.[54]

But the best biography of Robespierre in English – and perhaps, with Walter's, the best in any language – was that written by J. M. Thompson at Oxford in 1935. As a liberal-radical brought up in the British parliamentary tradition, Thompson, though profoundly influenced by Mathiez, owes perhaps as much to Croker and Acton in the picture he paints of the Jacobin leader. Unlike earlier British historians, Thompson saw Robespierre as playing a role of the greatest importance through the Revolution as a whole: as the undisputed leader of the Left following Mirabeau's death in April 1791 and, at this and every other stage, as the principal spokesman for political and social democracy. His greatness, Thompson believed, lay in "the thoroughness with which he embodied the main ideas and experience of the Revolution, from the enthusiastic liberalism of 1789, through the democratic aspirations of 1792, to the disciplined disillusionment of 1794". But he also believed that he was "too visionary, too narrow-minded, and a man of too little worldly experience or tact to be a statesman"; and, unlike Jaurès and Mathiez, he made no secret of the fact that he far preferred the earlier Robespierre to the later. In fact, he makes a sharp distinction between the liberal of 1789 to June 1793 and the spokesman for the Jacobin Dictatorship of 1793–4. To explain this transformation from liberal to authoritarian, Thompson was inclined to look for answers in personal failings, such as a deterioration in character or a lack of statesmanship, rather than in the changing conditions of war and counter-revolution that may have faced leaders with choices and solutions that were not necessarily to their personal taste. Nevertheless, he closes his biography on an almost Mathiezian note: "So long as the French Revolution is regarded, not as the 'suicide of the eighteenth century', but as the birth of ideas that enlightened the nineteenth, and of hopes that still inspire our own age; and so long as its leaders are sanely judged, with due allowance for the terrible difficulties of their task; so long will Robespierre, who lived and died for the Revolution, remain one of the great figures of history." [55]

SINCE 1945

So, by the outbreak of the Second World War, Robespierre's reputation among writers and scholars stood very high indeed. He had become a household word, and not only with the Left. Romain Rolland, the great French novelist, might justly complain (as he did in 1939) that Paris had not thought fit to erect a monument to "the greatest man of the Revolution";[56] but, at least, some other cities had done so: streets had been named after him at Arras and Rheims and at Arras, his birth-place, he had a public monument as well. But the image of Robespierre has changed again; and, in some respects, it is a more diffused and uncertain image than it was in the years following Mathiez' death.

With France's defeat in 1940, Revolutionary studies ground virtually to a halt and Georges Lefebvre's *1789* was burned by order of the authorities. But the Liberation brought a fresh and intensive revival of interest in the Revolution and its leaders. A year later, a Gallup poll was held to see what Frenchmen thought of Robespierre after four years of military occupation and oppression. Of the 69 per cent who knew who he was, 34 per cent approved of him, 37 per cent disapproved and 29 per cent had no opinion to offer; and among the one-third who approved, the main reasons for approval were that he had saved the Republic, that he had no fear of the Right, that he was not in the pay of the foreigner, and that "a man like him is what we need today".[57] As such discussions are generally conducted within the sanctum of universities and not in the forum of public debate, the outcome is not as negative as it may seem; and one wonders what it would have been if a similar enquiry had been held half a century before. So, ambivalent as the results may appear, they suggest that Robespierre at this time had a fairly large and appreciative circle of admirers. And the trend that Jaurès started and Mathiez continued of deepening and extending the study of Robespierre has certainly gone on apace; and, sometimes, as in a number of recent biographies, admiration for the role he played is accompanied by expressions of deep personal regard. Jean Massin, for example, whose biography is perhaps the best that has appeared since the war, writes in his preface: "I do not try to hide the affection I have for him or that his existence is bound up with my pride in being a Frenchman." [58]

But work on Robespierre has, far more frequently, strayed from the path of single-minded devotion that Mathiez traced a half-century ago. At one extreme, there have been those, as in every generation, to whom revolutions – even comparatively remote ones – are far less of a blessing than a curse. Such "counter-revolutionary" observers and historians of the events of 1789 have appeared in the

wake of nearly every fresh revolution or convulsion that has happened since.* Among them we have noted Burke and the pamphleteers and writers of the mid- and late 1790s; and we have seen
how Taine reacted to the Paris Commune. The Russian Revolution
of 1917 also touched off a spate of angry comment on the earlier
revolution in France. There was Nesta Webster, an Englishwoman
who, writing in 1919, followed the Abbé Barruel (a French *émigré* of
1797) in denouncing the Revolution as an "illuminist" plot and
repeated the old legend that Robespierre and his associates had
promoted the Terror for the express purpose of decimating France's
population.[59] In France in the 1920s Pierre Gaxotte also followed
Burke and Barruel – and Augustin Cochin, a later writer – in
tracing the origins of the Revolution to a conspiracy. Moreover,
with his eyes on the revolution in Russia, which horrified him as
much as the Commune had horrified Taine, he believed that the
Mountain had stood for communism and that Robespierre's overthrow marked the end of a communist Terror; and such being his
beliefs, he engaged in a polemic against the Revolution, the Jacobin
leaders and the *sans-culottes* whose virulence and colourful epithets
would have done credit to Taine himself.[60]

Compared with these counter-revolutionaries of the previous
post-war era, those writing after the Second World War and the
spread of People's Democracy and communism in Eastern Europe
have been more sophisticated, scholarly and restrained. Among them
one writer of distinction, J. L. Talmon, the Israeli political scientist
and historian, has had something new to say about Robespierre.
Talmon's *The Origins of Totalitarian Democracy* (1952) was the first
part of a trilogy whose aim it was to trace the concept of "political
Messianism" or "totalitarian democracy" from its genesis in the
ideas of Rousseau, Mably and Morelly via the Revolutions of 1789
and 1848 to the Communist governments and People's Democracies
of the twentieth century. So *The Origins* is a political-philosophical
treatise whose starting-point lies in the ideological battles of the
present and in which the French Revolution serves as an illustration
to a theme. The Revolution as a whole is condemned, because it is
seen not as a criminal act or the conspiracy of a few (and Gaxotte
saw it as both), but as the first episode in a long chain of events,

*The Revolution of 1848 appears to have been an exception.

launched by a group of eighteenth-century thinkers, which has tended to deny man his most cherished possession, political freedom. The main carriers and executors of these "totalitarian-democratic" ideas in the first revolution, Talmon argues, were Robespierre, Saint-Just and Babeuf; and the lesson he draws from the whole experience is "the incompatibility of the idea of an all-embracing and all-solving creed with liberty . . . To attempt to satisfy both at the same time is bound to result, if not in unmitigated tyranny and serfdom, at least in the monumental hypocrisy and self-deception which are the concomitants of totalitarian democracy".[61]

Another hostile view of Robespierre, which reflects the tensions caused in France by the Occupation and Liberation, is that voiced by Jean Anouilh in his play, *Pauvre Bitos* (1956). Robespierre had been the frequent subject of literature, or of literary opinion, before: we have seen the different views of him held by Scott, Buechner, George Sand and Eugène Sue in the previous century; and, in 1912, Anatole France wrote of him with mixed feelings of admiration and revulsion in his novel *Les Dieux ont soif.* (Elsewhere, France described him as "the greatest statesman to appear on the scene between 1789 and 1794"; though he believed the Terror to have been an avoidable and regrettable mistake.)[62] Anouilh divides his play into two parts, of which the first is set in a French country town immediately after the Liberation and the second in Paris during the Terror. Robespierre is made to play two roles, the first being a thinly disguised version of the second. First, we see him as Bitos, a prissy, self-important official of the Public Prosecutor's Department, descending like an avenging angel from the coach at Clermont-Ferrand, "in grey woollen gloves and carrying a *curé*'s briefcase stuffed with principles", and all set to send collaborators before the firing squad. Later, he reappears as the Incorruptible himself, a fastidious, twitchy, envious and vindictive hysteric, who plans with a coldly bloodthirsty and cynical Saint-Just to use religion and terror to teach the people "respect" and to settle old scores.[63] So, with Anouilh, we are back once more with Adolphus and Taine.

Another trend has been to treat Robespierre as a psychological case. The intention may be a friendly or a hostile one, but the result has generally been to show him up as being slightly deranged. An early study of this kind was Reginald Somerset Ward's *Maximilien Robespierre: A Study in Deterioration*, published in 1934: the very title betrays the evident bias of a writer who had learnt his history from Taine. Ward sets himself the task of "examining the mysterious process of spiritual deterioration by the analysis of the life of a notable historical character". In this case, the "deterioration" set in early, as we find Robespierre, from 1789 onwards, "turning his back on that reverence for the idea of law which is the uplifting and spiritual part of a lawyer's profession" by encouraging the lawlessness of the riotous "mob". And, in 1793, he rises to power by trampling on "the ideals of Freedom and Justice"; so, Ward concludes, "in obtaining what he desired he had grievously injured his soul".[64] A far more sympathetic treatment is Max Gallo's in his recent "psycho-biography", which was first published in Paris in 1968 under the title of *Maximilien Robespierre: Histoire d'une solitude*, and was renamed *Robespierre the Incorruptible* in its later English translation. Gallo's theme derives from Freud: that the clue to a man's political career and the decisions he takes must be sought not so much in the impact of events or of the actions of other parties and groups as in his own "deepest personal impulses" and "those secret phantasms" that are born in his childhood. In Robespierre's case, according to Gallo, the key to an understanding of "why Robespierre became Robespierre" is provided, in essence, by the fact that he was abandoned by his father at an early age. This gave him a profound sense of failure and guilt and isolation and a devouring need to prove himself worthy of public applause; and from this follows, almost inexorably, the long road from election as deputy for Arras, through his rise to power, to his final overthrow and execution. And, within this chain of ascension and decline, Thermidor becomes a form of self-sacrifice, a personal choice rather than the outcome of a clash between opposing groups – a choice "forced upon him by his own psychic necessities: his obligation to speak, to justify himself, to offer himself up in order to bring an end to the too long, unbearable waiting for martyrdom and rest".[65]

Robespierre has also found critics on the Left. This, again, is nothing new. In the early 1850s, he was condemned by Blanqui, the revolutionary activist, and Proudhon, the anarchist, in turn: both dismissed him as being a dangerous liability to the revolutionary cause.[66] Later, there was Prince Kropotkin, an anarchist like Proudhon, who, in his *Great French Revolution* (1911), described him as a fanatic who, "to establish his authority over men's minds, was ready, if necessary, to pass over the dead body of his opponents".[67] A more recent critic from the Left has been Daniel Guérin, whose 2-volume work, *La lutte de classes sous la Ière République: bourgeois et "bras-nus"* (*1793–1797*), appeared in 1946. At that time Guérin (who later became an anarchist) held Trotskyist views and he was strongly influenced by Trotsky's theory of "permanent revolution". He challenged the interpretation of most earlier writers – both opponents and supporters of the Revolution, Radicals as well as socialists and more orthodox Marxists. Radicals and Marxists have certainly differed as to the degree of importance to attach to the divisions that arose within the Third Estate and between the *sans-culottes* and the Jacobin leaders; but they have generally agreed that, despite these divisions, such groups had the common objective of seeking to destroy the foreign enemy without and the remnants of feudalism and aristocracy within. For them, therefore, the predominant social conflict has not been at any stage one of bourgeoisie against *sans-culottes*, still less of Capital versus Labour. To Guérin, however, the *sans-culottes*, or *"bras-nus"* (a term borrowed from Michelet), constituted a pre-proletarian vanguard and the Revolution, from 1793 onwards, takes on the form of a proletarian revolution in embryo. In this context, Robespierre, as the leading spokesman of Jacobinism, becomes a reactionary who deliberately stems the revolutionary tide in the autumn of 1793; and Thermidor becomes a continuation rather than a break – the continuation, by other means, of a bourgeois dictatorship that had already been established to defeat the challenge of the resurgent *"bras-nus"*.[68]

In Guérin's work there remains a residue of the personal polemics that characterized Mathiez and many of the historians of the nineteenth century. But, more particularly, it belongs to a new type of social and political history that has come into greater evidence since the last war and has had an important effect on the direction of Robespierrist studies. This history has tended, far more than that of the past, to play down personal virtues and vices and to direct greater attention to the historical role and the social forces that leaders like Robespierre represented or unleashed than to what they were in themselves – or to such questions as Gallo's, "Why did Robespierre become Robespierre?" And even biography, that last redoubt of the cult of personality, has not entirely escaped the contagion. (The present volume may be considered a case in point.) This trend may be attributed, in part, to a growing interest in the methods and outlook of social science; but, in this instance, perhaps even more to a development of Marxist writing on the Revolution and to attempts made by historians, in the last decades, to treat history "from below".

We have already noted the impression Robespierre made on Marx in the 1840s. He saw him as playing a necessary, but purely temporary, role in using the Terror to promote the needs of a "bourgeois" revolution in one of its stages; but once military victory was assured by the Prussian defeat in the summer of 1794, he became expendable and was overthrown; and Engels, with some embellishments, repeated the same argument to Victor Adler over forty years later.[69] So there was no attempt as yet to present Jacobinism as a worthy forerunner of socialism or to harness it to the proletarian cause; in fact, rather the reverse. But Lenin, writing under the very different historical conditions of 1917, did precisely this; for he saw the "revolutionary democratic dictatorship" of the Year II as a precursor and model for the one he was preparing to establish himself. "The bourgeois historians", he wrote, "see in Jacobinism a *downfall*. The proletarian historians regard Jacobinism as the greatest expression of an oppressed class in its struggle for liberation. The Jacobins gave France the best models of a democratic revolution; they repelled in exemplary fashion the coalition of monarchs formed against the republic . . . It is natural for the bourgeoisie to hate Jacobinism. It is natural for the petty bourgeoisie to fear it. The class-conscious workers and toilers have faith in the transfer of power to the revolutionary oppressed class, for *that* is the essence of Jacobinism . . ."[70]

So Jacobinism became the ally of Bolshevism in its struggle for power; and, after October, and to mark the occasion, Robespierre was given a monument under the walls of the Kremlin and, later, a quay was named after him along the Neva in Lenin's new capital city. This interest in Robespierre in the young Soviet Republic was further marked by the publication of two biographies: the first by

N. M. Lukin in 1919 and the second by J. M. Zakher in 1925. Both authors, like Marx and Lenin, were little concerned with Robespierre's personal vices or virtues and far more with the part he played in the Revolution; but they gave it a new slant: rather than stressing his leadership of an "oppressed class in its struggle for liberation", they reverted to Marx's more guarded interpretation and pointed to his limitations and to the contradictions to which he was driven by being a spokesman for the petty bourgeoisie.[71] There followed a thirty-year lull in which studies of Robespierre and Jacobinism were generally discounted; and it was not until the bicentenary year of 1958 that a further biography, A. Manfred's *Maximilien Robespierre*, was published in Moscow. Manfred has followed this up with several important books and articles, of which the latest, "La Nature du pouvoir jacobin", appeared in the French rationalist journal, *La Pensée*, in April 1970. His interpretation is far closer to Lenin's than it is to that of the historians of the 1920s. He does not see Robespierre or the Jacobins as belonging to, or representing, any particular social class, let alone a mere "petit-bourgeoisie". In his view, they represented a *bloc* of social groups ranging over a middle and lesser bourgeoisie, the peasantry and the urban "plebs" (or *sans-culottes*); and it was with the aid of these groups that they came to power and in their interests (which was, broadly, a *national* interest) that they set up their Revolutionary Government, fought a revolutionary war and carried through a sweeping programme of reforms in 1793 and 1794. And far from that Revolutionary Government (or "democratic dictatorship") being slavishly modelled on a Rousseauesque blue-print – as so many historians have argued – it was a brand-new Jacobin invention, engendered by political need and the necessities of war both within and without. For, Manfred argues, "the historical greatness of Robespierre, Saint-Just and the other Jacobin leaders lay in the fact that . . . they behaved not as doctrinaires and pedants, who followed the letter of the law, but as revolutionaries", who embarked on a new and uncharted course. Why, then, did their government collapse and why was Robespierre sent to the guillotine? It was, he writes, because the former allies fell apart; because, at a certain stage of the war, the bourgeois and peasant proprietors had had enough of Terror and tightened belts and sought other solutions. This, then, as Manfred sees it, was the essence of Thermidor rather than a conspiracy of "pro-consuls" or a rift between the *sans-culottes* and the Jacobin leaders – still less, of course, the expression of a "death-wish" on the part of Robespierre.[72]

Broadly, Manfred's view is shared by his fellow-Marxists in Eastern Europe.[73] But these historians, though committed to the study of revolutions, have shown a greater interest in the conflicts of parties and groups and in the emergence of radical, socialist and communist ideas than they have in the popular movements of peasants and *sans-culottes*. Thus, among Soviet historians, J. M. Zakher went on to study the Enragés and V. N. Dalin is an authority on Babeuf; and, in the German Democratic Republic, Walter Markov, besides editing a bicentenary volume on Robespierre, has done extensive research on Jacques Roux, the "red priest", and his followers. The study "from below" of popular movements and classes, though influenced by Marxism, has been rather the work of a group of historians in the West. This again, like the rehabilitation of Robespierre, may be traced back to Jaurès. Jaurès, as we saw, criticized Aulard for neglecting the Revolution's social and economic factors and advanced the frontiers of knowledge by extending his canvas to the provinces and paying more attention to the needs and aspirations of the poor. Later, after the publication of his *Socialist History*, he went on to found, with government support, a *Commission de recherche*, whose purpose it was to collect and publish the most important economic documents relating to the French Revolution. It was a resounding success and 57 volumes of documents had appeared by the time of his death in 1914, with several more to come later; and it had a great influence on the work of economic historians and others in the half-century that followed. Among those influenced by Jaurès was C.-E. Labrousse, whose studies in the movements of wages and prices in the last century of the Ancien Régime have thrown a new light on the crisis out of which the Revolution emerged. Mathiez was more of a political historian; but he followed up Jaurès' earlier work on the urban lower classes with a study of his own, *La Vie chère et le mouvement social sous la Terreur* (1927), which was the first serious attempt to show how the Revolutionary Government grew out of the social conflicts and economic pressures of 1793. Meanwhile, Georges Lefebvre, a greater scholar than Mathiez, had written his masterly account, *Les Paysans du Nord* (1924), and went on to open up new fields of research with his studies of the psychology of crowds and the "Great Fear" of 1789.[74] Lefebvre was, in fact, the real progenitor of the attempt to focus on the Revolution "from below". What Lefebvre had done for the peasants, Albert Soboul, one of his students, did, thirty-five years later, for the *sans-culottes*. His main work (published in 1958) for the first time gave them a clear-cut identity where they had previously lingered, somewhat uncertainly, on the fringe of events; and, by subjecting their activities, institutions, composition, ideas and aspirations to a microscopic enquiry, he integrated them within the revolutionary mainstream and, in so doing, enriched the political history of the Revolution and its leaders as well.[75] A few years later, Richard Cobb, an Englishman, in a massive study of the *sans-culotte*-based "revolutionary armies" of 1793, extended this vista beyond Paris to France as a whole; his work threw a new light on the "de-christianizing" of the countryside and provincial towns, on the problems of requisitioning and of feeding the cities during the Terror, and on the "anarchy" of local government before Robespierre and the two governing Committees took matters firmly in hand in the winter of 1793.[76]

So this group of historians may justly claim to have opened up new perspectives and to have shifted the focus to the social and economic aspects of the Revolution and to the hitherto largely "submerged" classes of the towns and countryside. But, in so doing – and this is where the "changing image" of Robespierre comes in – they have also served to draw attention away from the centre of government and debate in Paris, from the Revolutionary Assemblies, the Jacobin Club and the Jacobin leaders; and this has naturally tended to reduce their relative importance as heroic or tyrannical figures towering over the mass. So Robespierre, Danton, Marat, Mirabeau and the rest are no longer the subject of such intense preoccupation as they were with the historians of the past. Another consequence has been that the steam has tended to go out of the debate on the relative merits or vices of this leader or that; and in order to justify Robespierre it has not been found necessary to denigrate Danton as Mathiez did a generation before. In fact, Lefebvre, who had a portrait of Robespierre on his desk until the day he died, did not fail to give Danton his due.[77] Not only this; but Robespierre, though kept at the top of the pyramid of Revolutionary leaders, finds critics even among those who rate him most highly. His shortcomings in dealing with economic affairs and his failure to understand the basic needs of the poor have, in particular, come under attack: Soboul's great study has as a major theme the inevitability of the clash between the Jacobins and their *sans-culotte* allies, which he sees (and here he differs from Manfred) as a primary cause of the catastrophe of Thermidor; and several articles in the *Annales historiques*, which Soboul edits with Godechot and Labrousse, have underscored this and similar points. But Cobb goes a great deal further than this, and he is the only one of these historians who has returned to the epithets and vendettas of the past. For, while he holds no brief for Danton, he has a personal dislike for Robespierre and seldom misses an opportunity to make snide digs at "Saint-Maximilien's" expense.[78]

But, whether recent historians have been personally attracted to Robespierre or not, they are almost unanimous in accepting Mathiez' verdict that he was the outstanding figure of the French Revolution. And Danton has, accordingly, been toppled from the pedestal to which Michelet and Aulard had raised him; and there are no signs that even the most bitter of Robespierre's critics have any inclination to put him back. So, to this extent at least, Robespierre's image, though still subject to change, has been radically, perhaps permanently, transformed from that of the vindictive and bloodthirsty tyrant of Thermidorian and Napoleonic times and of the second-rate sophist and pedant as seen by Taine and the early historians of the Third Republic. But he has, in the process, become tarred with a communist brush and political prejudice dies hard; moreover, Parisians have been slow to keep up with the times. So Danton still dominates the Carrefour de l'Odéon and Robespierre was once more refused a statue in his bicentenary year.[79]

PART III

The Ideologue

Chapter 1

THE POLITICAL DEMOCRAT

A common observation about Robespierre – and it has been made by both admirers and detractors – is that he was a man of unshakable principles. Again and again, throughout his writings and his speeches, there occur certain familiar refrains as he returns to the restatement of a number of fundamental truths to which he remained unswervingly attached. These truths, he believed, were both eternal and universal, unalterable and imprescriptible, they belonged to no particular time or place and were as readily applicable to one country as to any other.[1] What were these truths? Briefly, that the end of politics must be the embodiment of morality in government; that morality, or goodness or "virtue", emanates from the people and from the people alone; and, therefore, it is the people's will, and not that of their fallible and corruptible rulers, that must be sovereign and prevail.

But what is "virtue"; what is "sovereignty"; and who indeed are "the people"? To Robespierre virtue is essentially that which contributes to the public good: love of country and the subjection of the private to the public interest. "Virtue", the young Artesian lawyer had written in 1784, "produces happiness as the sun produces light"; and, ten years later, in one of his greatest speeches to the National Convention, he declared that "immorality is the basis of despotism as virtue is the essence of the Republic".[2] And to promote that happiness and public good sovereignty must be undivided and exercised by the people as a whole. Yet some people, he believed, were more trustworthy as depositories of virtue and therefore more fit to exercise sovereignty than others. These were the small, independent producers – craftsmen, shopkeepers, peasant proprietors and manufacturers – those who were "honourably" poor and not corrupted by the extremes of either wealth or destitution. And the main purpose of the Revolution, as Robespierre conceived it, must be to create a republic of such socially independent citizens, exercising a common sovereignty and restored by good government to

---

their natural and inalienable rights of personal freedom, political equality and the pursuit of happiness.

Such truths were, of course, by no means peculiar to Robespierre even if he voiced them with greater conviction and tenacity than the great majority of his contemporaries: they formed part of a common stock of ideas which he shared with many Englishmen, Americans and Frenchmen of his time, and more particularly with his fellow-revolutionaries of 1789. As with others, they derived both from his reading and his personal experience. At Paris and Arras, his Oratorian teachers had given him a solid grounding in the Classics: he was well acquainted with the history of Athens and Sparta and the Roman Republic, and his imagination had, from an early age, been fired by the republican virtues of Brutus and the Gracchi. Yet, like other Frenchmen of his day, he owed remarkably little to the earlier, English, revolution: the Levellers were unknown to him and Cromwell was a "tyrant" and "dictator", like Charles I or George III, and nothing more. Even Geneva, the stronghold of democracy for many of his contemporaries, he hardly referred to except as the birthplace of Rousseau. Far greater, of course, was his debt to the *philosophes*, whose ideas were widely disseminated in French schools, colleges and seminaries in the half-century before the Revolution; and, as a young advocate, we find him quoting freely from Montesquieu, Condillac, Mably, Turgot and Voltaire, and even from Bacon and Leibniz. For several of the Encyclopedists, it is true, he always felt a certain aversion, which increased with time: he was repelled, for example, by the "materialism" of Holbach, Diderot and Helvétius and by their known antipathy to Rousseau. Montesquieu, on the other hand, made an early and lasting impression and, although he rarely invoked his name, his conception of republican virtue probably owes even more to him than to his study of the Classics. But the greatest debt of all he owed to Rousseau. It was a debt he shared with many others and it is remarkable how frequently the revolutionaries of 1789, irrespective of party and whether they were intimately acquainted with Jean-Jacques' political writings or not, bandied his name about and appealed to his authority in all the great political debates. Among Girondins, Madame Roland and Louvet were among the most fervent of his admirers; Babeuf gave his son the name of "Emile"; and even the

Abbé Maury, who sat on the extreme Right in the Constituent Assembly, cited Rousseau's authority to support his views.[3]

In Robespierre's case, attachment to Rousseau took the form of a deep and personal involvement. How deeply and continuously he studied Rousseau after his college days is a matter of dispute. It may be that Rousseau's works found no place in his private library;[4] it may be, too, that the encounter with Rousseau at Ermenonville during his school-days was more fictitious than real;[5] and it is more than likely that the copy of *The Social Contract* that is said to have lain by his bedside at Duplay's was the only one of Rousseau's political works that he ever read. Yet his close acquaintance with *that* work, at least, is clearly established: so much appears both from the frequent invocation of his name during his speeches and the evident Rousseauist inspiration of many of his own basic political ideas. Among these we may cite his constant relating of political to ethical ends; his definition of utility in terms of morality; his faith in the natural goodness of the people; his belief in the social utility of a civil religion stripped of revelation and superstition; his distrust of representation; his emphasis on equality; his assertion of the sovereignty of the people and of the expression of the General Will; and his social ideal of a republic of small and "middling" property-owners and craftsmen uncorrupted by extreme poverty or wealth. Even more: as has been noted, there was a Rousseauist quality in his choice of imagery and turn of phrase, in his manner of thinking and way of life; and no other revolutionary leader identified so closely with Rousseau as he did in both word and deed.[6]

It would, however, be a great mistake to imagine that Robespierre formulated his opinions and was drawn to Rousseau and to Rousseauist ideas purely through his reading and the instruction he had received from his Oratorian teachers. They derive equally from his own background, his character and the circumstances under which he grew up. We have seen that he was poor, suffered deprivation and had, as the result of his mother's early death and his father's desertion, to take on family responsibilities well beyond his years. So, quite apart from his studies at Louis-le-Grand, it was natural that, as a young lawyer, he should be inclined to identify closely with the poorer and middling citizens rather than with the wealthy and privileged and to champion their interests and aspirations against those of the arirstocacy or rich. And so to him – and this is a matter of some importance in understanding the development of Robespierre's ideas – poverty was not a social disgrace provided a man had the will and the means to rise above destitution, to make his living by his own hands and to enjoy a measure of social independence. Moreover, he grew up at a time when France was still at its "pre-industrial" stage of development, when it did not appear inevitable that the small producer would become absorbed or squeezed out by the rise of large-scale industry and it still seemed possible that a hard-working craftsman or small manufacturer might, while remaining poor, achieve a fair degree of independence and gain or recover such "natural" rights as a reformed political system would allow him. Such men tended to be frugal and modest in their way of life and social ambitions, looking on luxury as a curse and wasteful spending as a vice. It was an attitude that Robespierre reflected admirably in his own comportment and style of living: in his neat and fastidious dress, which remained that of a "petit-bourgeois" of the Old Régime (he abhorred ostentation and later refused to don the revolutionary *bonnet rouge*) and in the frugal habits he brought with him to the Duplay household and of which ample evidence survives. It was, in fact, no mere oratorical flourish when he told the Jacobins, "*Je suis peuple mon-même, je n'ai jamais été que cela*". So it is not surprising that, such being his character, his temperament and upbringing, he should have taken to Rousseau as a duck takes to water and made Rousseau's political and social ideas his own.

Yet though devoted to Rousseau and the most constant of his political disciples, Robespierre was by no means so slavishly attached to the letter of his master's teachings as has sometimes been made out.[7] Like others placed as he was, he adapted them to suit the occasion; and it must not be forgotten that Rousseau himself departed significantly from the letter – and even the spirit – of his *Social Contract* when he came to write constitutions for Corsica and Poland. Robespierre was also to face problems for whose solution the undiluted message of Rousseau provided no answers. For example, he virtually abandoned the mythical notion of the social contract which Rousseau had taken over, and adopted, from Locke: there are few passages in his speeches where any reference is made to it at all. Again, it is well known that Rousseau, as a true countryman of

Calvin, would allow for no religious toleration in his ideal republic and prescribed banishment, or in extreme cases death, for incorrigible dissenters from his civil religion. Robespierre would have none of this; and, in a great speech to the Jacobins on 21 November 1793, when he denounced the "de-christianizing" activities of Hébert, he stated bluntly that "whoever would make a crime [of atheism] is a madman".[8]

A knottier problem still was how to put to practical use Rousseau's ideas on sovereignty and representation. In *The Social Contract* – the only one of Rousseau's political works with which, as we have seen, Robespierre was familiar – he had claimed that sovereignty could, by its very nature, not be represented; and he went so far as to state that "the instant a people gives itself representatives, it is no longer free: it no longer exists". Rousseau realized that to apply such a principle literally in a country as large as France would be quite unpractical and, to get over his difficulty, he wrote that, in such cases, deputies chosen by the people must act not as representatives but as agents (*commissaires*), without power to make decisions unless instructed by the *mandat impératif* of their constituents. Robespierre, for his part, ignored the *mandat impératif* when that mandate would have tied him to a line of conduct at variance with his political aims, and he showed a consistent hostility to the closely related device of the plebiscite. Again, like other Revolutionary politicians, he made a distinction between the sovereignty and sovereign rights of the people. The former, it was firmly held, was vested in the people alone and was the ultimate source of all political power; but the latter could be, and indeed must be in the case of a country like France, delegated to the people's elected representatives. So while the people were the source of all sovereignty, once their chosen deputies had formed themselves into a National Assembly, they and they alone were deemed to be capable of expressing and interpreting the General Will; and, in fact, the title of Representative of the People came to be the proudest title that a revolutionary could hold.[9] This soon became the prevailing view which Robespierre, generally, shared with others. Yet, on this point, there was a great deal of ambivalence in his attitude, depending on the political situation at hand. In the early days of the Constituent Assembly he was inclined to go along with the majority view that the people, having exercised their sovereign right of election, must leave the power of legislation to the nation's representatives, while at the same time constantly invoking Rousseau's theory of sovereignty to restrain the authority of the King and his ministers But, as he became more convinced that the majority of deputies themselves were almost incurably "corrupt", he began to move more closely to the letter of Rousseau's teaching and, on one occasion at least, reminded the deputies that a nation that delegated its authority to an Assembly was no longer free. As we have seen, Robespierre was not a member of the Legislative Assembly that followed, but he stood for election to the National Convention in September 1792. Election was still held in two stages; and, before it was known that the Jacobins held a majority in Paris, he insisted that the electors – at the secondary stage – should cast their votes aloud and "in the presence of the people"; and, moreover, that the deputies returned should, before their election was considered valid, be subject to the revision and scrutiny (*scrutin épuratoire*) of the primary assemblies to ensure that they were worthy of the people's confidence. But once it became apparent that the electors had returned a majority of good Montagnards, these procedures were allowed to lapse.[10] Similarly, he rejected the Girondin proposal of an appeal to the people in the course of the King's trial; and we shall see later how Robespierre and his colleagues of the Committee of Public Safety departed even more dramatically – and not only as a short-term tactical device – from Rousseau's teachings in creating their Revolutionary Government in the winter of 1793–4.

So it may be argued, and with ample justification, that Robespierre, far from literally or slavishly following Rousseau's teachings, only did so when they accorded with the interests of the Revolution as he understood them. But, whether this entitles him to be called a consistent Rousseauist or not, he was, far more certainly, a consistent champion of popular democracy; and from the first day he set foot in the National Assembly he insisted that sovereignty belonged to the people as a whole and that all their "natural" rights must be restored to them. The first of these rights, in Robespierre's view, was the right to vote. It was a principle that appeared to be solemnly enshrined in the Declaration of the Rights of Man of August 1789; but, two months later, the Assembly, following the advice of the Abbé Sieyès, decided to restrict the vote even at the primary stage to "active", or property-owning, citizens while imposing higher qualifications for electors and deputies. Robespierre assailed this law, in a number of speeches, as a serious breach of a principle that had already been accepted. In one of these (printed in April 1791, though not reported in the official *Le Moniteur*), he asked, "Can the law be termed an expression of the general will when the greater number of those for whom it is made can have no hand in its making?" And he went on to declare: "All men *born* and *domiciled* in France are members of the body politic termed the French nation; that is to say, they are French citizens. They are so by the nature of things and by the first principle of the law of nations. The rights attaching to this title do not depend on the fortune that each man possesses, nor on the amount of tax for which he is assessed, because it is not taxes that make us citizens: citizenship merely obliges a man to contribute to public expenditure in proportion to his means. You may give the citizens new laws, but you may not deprive them of their citizenship." [11]

It was in accordance with the same principle of equal rights as citizens that Robespierre demanded that membership of the National Guard should be open to all Frenchmen of fixed abode: "To be armed for self-defence," he told the Assembly that same month, "is the right of all men without distinction; to be armed for the defence of the fatherland is the right of every citizen." [12] Some months before, he had insisted that all discriminatory laws previously restricting the rights of Protestants, Jews and actors should be repealed and that their right to vote and to hold public office should be the same as for any other Frenchman. Referring to the Jews, he asked, "How can you blame the Jews for the persecutions they have suffered in certain countries? These are, on the contrary, national crimes that we must expiate by restoring to them the imprescriptible rights of man of which no human authority can deprive them . . . Let us give them back their happiness, their country and their virtue by restoring their dignity as men and citizens." [13] Nor, he argued on another occasion, could such rights be denied to French citizens overseas, such as the free men of colour (though not the slaves) in the West Indian colonies. The occasion was the debate that followed a report of one of the Assembly's committees which recommended that the question of the eligibility to vote in these territories should be left to the decision of a colonial assembly. Such a proposal, Robespierre insisted, would leave the men of colour to the mercies of the white settlers controlling the assembly who, in refusing the right to vote, would virtually deny them rights of citizenship which they previously possessed.[14]

But formal rights of citizenship, Robespierre realized, would not ensure that they would be exercised in practice. As he had noted back in his Arras days, to lay legitimate claim to a "natural" right was one thing but to have the means to enjoy it was something else. It was, in fact, cold comfort for a poor man to be offered the vote, access to public office or membership of a jury or the National Assembly without some financial inducement to compensate him for time lost from work. To quote his own words: "What purpose does it serve for the law to pay hypocritical homage to equality of rights if necessity, the most imperious of laws, forces the most sane and most numerous section of the people to renounce them?"[15] So it logically followed that the demand for equality of civil rights must be accompanied by a demand for payment for public service. Robespierre had already begun to voice this view before the Estates General met at Versailles; and when the *cahiers* of the Third Estate had been drawn up at Arras he had proposed, though with little success, that the craftsmen attending the meetings should be paid for the four days they had taken off from their work;[16] and he went on, during the next couple of years, to press for payment for service on juries and in the National Guard. He met with no success at the time; but the principle was accepted when the Paris Commune agreed to pay "indigent" citizens for taking part in the armed insurrection of June 1793 and the Convention decided to subsidize attendance at meetings of the Paris sections in the following September.

Yet to Robespierre there were other ways as well in which the people might legitimately exercise their sovereign rights. In addition to electing their representatives, they had the right – if not the sacred obligation – to ensure that the deputies did the job for which they had been chosen. One way to ensure this was to make the galleries of the assembly hall as spacious and as accessible to the public as possible: thus the direct impact of popular sovereignty could bring neglectful or "corrupted" deputies to heel. It was common, once the Assembly moved to Paris, for several hundred citizens to crowd into the galleries and to make their feelings known in no unmistakable manner, often to the profound discomfiture and irritation of deputies of the Centre and Right and others whose views were not to the public's taste. Robespierre, however, was not satisfied and, in the early days of the Convention, he proposed that the legislators should meet in the presence of ten thousand spectators, a figure that he later raised to twelve.[17] Similar considerations led him to justify, or at least to condone, public demonstrations, or even riots and rebellions, provided they were directed against "tyranny" or an abuse of executive power. Thus, in a letter to a friend ten days after the fall of the Bastille, he refused to condemn the lynching of Foullon on the ground that "the people had sentenced him".[18] And, in the Constituent Assembly – we have noted some of these occasions before – we find him justifying the actions of peasants rioting against enclosure, of Savoyards and Avignonnais who rebelled against their own governing authorities and vociferously demanded a closer union with France, and of the soldiers of Châteauvieux who mutinied against their officers over pay.[19] Equally, the nation as a whole – and not only a small part of it – might justifiably rise in rebellion against their rulers if denied justice by other means (or if the occasion so demanded): we have already seen how Robespierre prepared and reacted to the events of August–September 1792 and May–June 1793; and the "sacred right of insurrection" was to be written into the Jacobin Constitution of 1793.

As Robespierre was a consistent champion of the rights of the "sovereign people", he was equally – for the duration of the Constituent and Legislative Assemblies at least – a consistent champion of the legislature against the executive. Here he by no means stood alone and his frequent attempts to build safeguards against royal or ministerial "despotism" were, on the whole, far better received by his fellow-legislators than his interventions in support of the "licentiousness" of the people. In fact, the Constitution of 1791, which emerged from the long debates of the first two revolutionary years, reflected the common interests of the majority of deputies that the executive power must be subordinated to the legislature and held severely in check. Under its terms, the King – by now become the

"King of the French" – would hold hereditary office, be granted a civil list as the first servant of the State, and have the right to appoint his own ministers (from outside the Assembly), his ambassadors and military commanders. He would also, by the so-called "suspensive veto", have the power to suspend or delay all laws, other than financial, initiated and adopted by the Assembly for a period of up to four years, or the duration of two consecutive parliaments. But, in other respects, his powers were definitely circumscribed: he could not dissolve the Assembly; his ministers would virtually be answerable not to himself but to the Assembly and its numerous committees; the armed forces (army, navy and National Guard) had been largely removed from his control; and, while he might take the first steps in declaring war or making peace, such measures would be subject to the approval of parliament. This was a far cry indeed from the plan advocated by Mirabeau with its strong executive, centred on a monarch with an absolute power of veto, with an army at his command and served by ministers drawn from the Assembly itself.

These constitutional provisions were generally acceptable to Robespierre before the summer of 1792; and until then, for reasons to be considered in a later chapter, he was no more inclined than the majority to look to alternative, republican solutions; and he preferred to keep the King in office even after his attempted escape to Varennes. Moreover, like most of his colleagues in the Assembly, he insisted on a strict separation of powers. But he drew sharper distinctions between their respective spheres of authority and would have reduced the King to a mere agent (or *commis*) whose sole function was to carry out the will of the nation as interpreted by its elected representatives, and he accused the Assembly's majority of having left him with too much power. To give him even a "suspensive" veto was, he argued, to allow him to obstruct the legislative process and thus to usurp a part of the sovereignty which belonged to the people and the Assembly alone. "Everything tells me," he concluded, "that there is no power in the State which is not eclipsed by his own; and everything proves that we have spared no effort to make the Constitution agreeable in his eyes." [20] It was on the same principle of maintaining a clear separation between the legislature and the executive that he warned the deputies against allowing themselves to be involved in a detailed discussion of the ministers' functions. When the question arose on a committee report in April 1791, he argued against its adoption on the grounds that it was the King's and not the Assembly's responsibility to allot the ministers their tasks and that by separating the ministerial from the royal authority it threatened to open the door to an extension of ministerial power.[21] It was one aspect of a theme to which he continually returned: that neither the King nor his ministers, nor the administrators that staffed the departments of government, formed any part of the "national representation" or had any share in the general will. They were agents or *commis* of the people and Assembly and nothing more; and, as such, they needed to be continually reminded of their proper functions and to be kept in their places by the supervision and vigilance of the people and its elected representatives. But vigilance was not enough: constitutional safeguards also had to be found to avert the constant danger of the abuse of authority by ministers and public servants. In a speech of 10 May 1793, made shortly before the expulsion of the Girondin leaders, he suggested a number of remedies: to make frequent changes in executive appointments; to forbid the plurality of offices; to distribute authority among many hands (it was better to multiply the number of public servants than to leave excessive power to a few); to maintain a strict separation between legislature and executive; to refuse entry of public officials to popular assemblies; and to remove the public purse from ministerial control.[22] In addition, the Assembly must assume the responsibility of checking administrative abuses by stripping "corrupt" officials of their duties and sending them before specially created tribunals. It was a problem that became all the greater with the creation of the Revolutionary Government in December 1793. Two months later, Robespierre warned the Convention in one of the most notable of his speeches: "In order for government to keep in the closest harmony with the law it is over its own head that it must wield the heaviest stick. Once the people has set up its representative body and invested it with full authority, it is for that body to watch, punish and control all public servants." [23] And it was to meet this need that, in the following April, the Committee of Public Safety set up its own police department to ensure that erring officials should not go unpunished.

The case of deputies, as the nation's representatives, was something different. They must be able to speak freely against executive abuse and to call ministers and public servants to account; so they must enjoy the privilege of parliamentary inviolability. But they also had the duty to be "virtuous" and "incorruptible" and, through frequent report-back meetings and elections, be continually accountable to the people they represented. Moreover, their immunity from prosecution must not extend beyond the Assembly: erring deputies, like erring officials, should be subject to the justice of the courts as all other citizens.[24] It was a principle that was to be applied to the Girondins in the spring and autumn of 1793 and to Danton a few months later.

As a champion of political democracy, Robespierre also played an important part in the debates held in the Constituent Assembly on the rights and liberties of the individual, particularly when these were designed to protect the individual citizen against executive encroachment or abuse. These debates mainly took place in the spring and summer of 1791, shortly before the Constitution was finally adopted; and Robespierre intervened on such matters as freedom of petition and speech and freedom from arbitrary arrest. On the right of petition, he argued, in a speech on 9 May, that it was "the imprescriptible right of every man in society". The Assembly wished to restrict the operation of the law to "active" citizens; but, characteristically, Robespierre opposed this on the grounds that "passive" citizens were in greater need of protection; for "the weaker and the more unfortunate a man is, and the greater his wants, the greater is his need to have an answer to his prayers." [25] Two days later, he argued in the Jacobin Club for a "complete and unrestricted" freedom of the press; and when the matter was further debated in the Assembly in August, he proposed that every citizen should have the unhampered right to express his opinions in writing, provided he did not formally incite to a breach of the law, and that public officials should be denied the right to prosecute in cases of libel.[26] And in his last speech as a member of the Constituent Assembly, before going out to receive the acclamations of the crowd, he protested against any police supervision of public meetings and demanded the right of popular societies to publicly criticize government servants.[27]

So far, we have followed the expression of Robespierre's political ideas in a somewhat piecemeal fashion, as he voiced them over a period of three years and in the heat of verbal exchanges that were largely conducted in an Assembly that was more often hostile than sympathetic to his views. For something of a more formal and concise political testament and one that probably sums up his political philosophy better than it is summed up anywhere else – we must look to his contribution to the discussions that prepared and accompanied the adoption of the Constitution and Declaration of Rights of 1793.

The discussions began in December 1792, when a committee of nine, composed of the Abbé Sieyès, six Girondins and two Jacobins, was appointed to prepare a plan of work. A week later, Barère, in presenting a first report, invited the deputies to send in proposals. They came in a flood and it was not until 15 February that Barère and Condorcet submitted a first draft, which was debated at length. Other, more urgent, matters now intervened and debate was adjourned until 15 April. Then Buzot, a Girondin, proposed that, in view of the prevailing emergency, discussion should leave aside such "metaphysical abstractions" as a new Declaration of Rights and centre on the terms of the new Constitution itself. Robespierre objected strongly; for "to propose to begin with government is to propose nothing at all, or it is to put the consequence before the principle"; and he reminded the Convention of the excellent precedent set by the Constituent Assembly when it drew up the first Declaration of the Rights of Man as a firm basis for the Constitution that followed: the Convention, he insisted, should do the same. His advice was accepted and the Assembly spent the next five days deliberating on a new Declaration of Rights. During this period, Robespierre intervened on two notable occasions: once to show that he no longer believed in the unrestricted freedom of the press; for "the interest of the Revolution [now that France had become a Republic] may impose certain measures to suppress a conspiracy founded on the liberty of the press": thus a particular liberty might have to be sacrificed to safeguard the greater liberty of all. On the second occasion, he presented the outline of an entirely different declaration of his own which he repeated, in greater detail, in a long speech on 24 April after the thirty articles of the official (Girondin-inspired) declaration had already been adopted. In his own draft, he pointed to certain important omissions of which the Assembly had been guilty. First, in defining property, they had failed to take account of the limitations that must be opposed to its free exercise by the rights of others; and among four clauses devoted to this question (to which we shall return in a later chapter) he specified that "the right of property is limited, as are all other rights, by the obligation to respect the rights of others". A second omission was that the Assembly had failed completely "to record the obligations of brotherhood that bind together the men of all nations, and their right to mutual assistance". (He had already stated, ten days before, that the new Constitution might serve not only for France but for all other nations as well.) Here he proposed four clauses which are so unique to the speaker himself that they are worthy of being quoted in full:

"1. The men of all countries are brothers, and the different peoples must help one another according to their ability, as though they were citizens of a single state.

2. Whoever oppresses a single nation declares himself the enemy of all.

3. Whoever makes war on a people to arrest the progress of liberty and to destroy the rights of man must be prosecuted by all, not as ordinary enemies but as rebels, brigands and assassins.

4. Kings, aristocrats and tyrants, whoever they be, are slaves in rebellion against the sovereign of the earth, which is the human race, and against the legislator of the universe which is nature."

During the next five weeks, when the Convention was torn apart by the struggle for survival of Gironde and Mountain, only one long session (that of 10 May) was devoted to a discussion of the Constitution itself. So it was not until after the expulsion of the Gironde in early June, which left the Mountain in control of the Assembly, that the debate could be resumed. It began on 11 June and was completed on the 24th. The new Declaration departed significantly from the Gironde-inspired text adopted two months before. In fact, it came far closer to Robespierre's version and eighteen of its clauses appear to have been modelled on his own. Yet it is equally significant that fourteen of his clauses find no reflection at all in the draft finally accepted by an Assembly that now acknowledged Robespierre as its outstanding spokesman and guide. For a detailed examination of these differences the reader is referred to the patient analysis of Gérard Walter.[28] Here it will suffice to note a few of the most important. Once more, he failed to carry his point that the rights of property should be circumscribed and that only that part of it that was "guaranteed by law" should be at the citizen's free disposal. Again, where he had wished to make the right to work or assistance open to all, it was decided to confine this right to *"les citoyens malheureux"*, thus reducing a brand-new social principle to a restatement of the need for public charity. (The matter was to arise again, in a different form, when the Convention decided, in September, to pay "poor citizens" 40 *sous* a day for attendance at sectional meetings.) And, finally, the Montagnard majority were no more eager to include Robespierre's clauses on international brotherhood in their Declaration than the Girondins had been before them.[29]

But, even so, with all its shortcomings (and Jacques Roux, the "red priest", was able to point out more), the Declaration and Constitution of 1793 marked the highpoint in the "liberal" phase of the Revolution. Here for the first time in history a nation was provided (on paper at least) with a system of government both republican and democratic, under which all male citizens had the right to vote and a considerable measure of control over its representatives and rulers. Yet, as is well known and to many a melancholy fact, within a few months it had been put into cold storage "for the duration", elections were suspended, and a highly centralized and authoritarian government came into being through the law of 14th Frimaire (4 December 1793). Commenting on this transformation, which so intimately concerns the history of Robespierre and the evolution of his political ideas, historians have naturally drawn widely different conclusions. Ernest Hamel, an uncritical apologist, sees virtually no change in Robespierre's political thinking or behaviour between 1791 and 1793–4: *"Tel nous le voyons à l'Assemblée constituante, tel nous le retrouverons à la Convention nationale."* [30] Others, while accepting that the change was real enough, have thought that it shows that the Jacobin Constitution was a fraud, a political manoeuvre or a piece of window-dressing to outbid their Girondin rivals; or, again, that the new system of government, even if new enough in itself, reflected "fixed attitudes of mind" that its promoters had held all along.[31] Others, again, while regretting the change,

109

have, more charitably, thought of it as marking no change of principle or ultimate intent on Robespierre's part, but rather as a temporary withdrawal from a liberal course undertaken "for strategical purposes".[32] And there have been plenty of other interpretations besides.

It is obviously a complex question that allows of no ready-made answers; but we may perhaps arrive at something reasonably near the truth if we consider how and why the Revolutionary Government came about, what part Robespierre played in its development, and what effects it had on his political thinking and behaviour in the months that followed its creation.

It may be best to begin by attempting to clear up two common misunderstandings. First, it needs to be emphasized that Robespierre was never at any time a "liberal" in the British-traditional sense of the term as used by J. M. Thompson: such a label ill accords with his views on popular sovereignty and the role of the individual within the State as we have already seen them expressed in the Constituent Assembly. Secondly, it is evident that his conversion to the need for a "revolutionary" government, or something akin to it, did not happen overnight. The conception is already there, in germ, in the measures of "public safety" that he and his colleagues on the Paris Revolutionary Commune took to meet the crisis of August–September 1792 during the six weeks of its existence at a time when that body challenged, and often superseded, the authority of the Legislative Assembly itself: we noted in an earlier chapter its domiciliary visits, its promotion of a "revolutionary" tribunal and its toleration, if not its actual incitement, of the prison massacres; while known monarchist supporters were removed from the electoral roll. At that stage, such measures were piecemeal and largely limited to Paris, Orléans and other cities and formed no part of a national plan. But, later, during the crisis created by General Dumouriez' defection in March–April 1793, the National Convention was persuaded to carry the process far further by setting up a Revolutionary Tribunal and "revolutionary" or vigilance committees in the sections and began to send out its own members, armed with extraordinary powers, on mission to the provinces where they imposed the Assembly's instructions on departments and communes. These were followed, in turn, in the next crisis of

August–September, by the decree of the *levée en masse*, the Law of Suspects, the control of food prices and the establishment of the *armées révolutionnaires* as a punitive, perambulating force empowered to raise supplies and to apply "revolutionary" justice to the country-side and provincial towns.

Such measures were clearly both extraordinary and exceptional and were devised in order to deal with critical situations as they arose; but their control remained strictly within the hands of the Assembly itself and did not, in themselves, entail any strengthening of the executive at the expense of the legislature; in short, they were perfectly compatible with the provision of the Constitution proclaimed by the new Jacobin majority in June. But it was hardly likely, as inflation ran riot and the crisis deepened, that they could remain so for long; moreover, it became amply evident, as the *représentants en mission* imposed their own solutions on the local authorities in the summer and autumn, that constitutional niceties were being brushed aside.[33] Yet it was still a long step to take to arm the government itself – and not simply the Assembly and its emis-saries – with exceptional powers; for any strengthening of govern-ment and consequent weakening of the direct authority of the Assembly would run counter to the basic constitutional principles to which all parties – including both Gironde and Mountain – sub-scribed. Once more, as so often in such matters, it was Robespierre who set the pace: in a speech made to the Convention, as the Dumouriez crisis developed, on 10 March 1793. In it he argued that in order to secure unity of action it was necessary to form an emergency government, composed of a committee of proved patriots of all parties and armed with powers to deal with the national crisis: this was, of course, a direct challenge to the long cherished view, which he held with others, that there must be a strict separation of functions between the legislative and executive powers. The next day, he followed up this declaration in more specific terms, when he gave tentative support to a daring proposal by Danton that ministers should be chosen from members of the National Convention.[34] Thus the ground had already been prepared for the Committee of Public Safety, which, armed with far greater powers than was at present envisaged, emerged from this initial exchange of views.

The Ideologue

The matter rested there until the expulsion of the Gironde and the proclamation of the Jacobin Constitution. But we know, from two long notes that were later found among Robespierre's papers and were probably written in late June or early July, that he was already thinking further along the lines he had already outlined in March. In the first note, he asks the question, "What is our aim?" and he answers, "To carry out the Constitution in favour of the people". But serious obstacles (he notes further) stand in the way: one is the egoism of "the rich" who, to realize their ambitions, hire mercenary scribblers to mislead the people; and another is the ignorance of the people, whose poverty (and here he returns to his theme of the Artesian days) makes it an easy target for the impostures and deceptions of "the rich". To overcome these obstacles (he continues), the people must be educated and given bread and the scribblers must be silenced or brought to justice. To these general aims the second note gives greater precision and outlines a whole programme of revolutionary action. "What we need," he writes, "is *a single will*." It must be either republican or royalist; and, for it to be republican, "we need republican ministers, republican journals, republican deputies and a republican government. The foreign war is a mortal disease as long as the body politic suffers from internal upheavals and . . . divided counsels. The internal danger comes from the *bourgeois*; to defeat the *bourgeois*, we must rally the people [or else suffer the fate of Marseilles, Bordeaux and Lyons, a fate we have only escaped in Paris through the June insurrection]. The present insurrection must continue until the measures necessary for saving the Republic have been taken. The people must ally itself with the Convention and the Convention make use of the people." [35] So two new principles were being advanced: the need for a strong and republican government of "a single will" to replace the weak and reactionary governments of 1791 and 1793; and the need to base such a government on a firm alliance between the Jacobin majority and the *sans-culottes*.

The first of these new principles was, of course, far more contentious than the second. (Danton's earlier proposal to draw ministers from the Assembly had, in spite of Robespierre's hesitant support, been dismissed almost out of hand.) So Robespierre and his intimates proceeded warily, and the late summer and early autumn went by without any further constitutional innovations being advanced. Meanwhile, however, inflation ran further riot; the demands of war and civil war became more pressing; the Parisian *sans-culottes*, encouraged by their earlier successes, were voicing new and highly embarrassing demands; and the *armées révolutionnaires* and their leaders were running amok in the provinces and imposing policies which were often at variance with instructions received from Paris. So, to meet the needs of war and the growing administrative "anarchy" (the term is Richard Cobb's), the Jacobin leaders decided to give formal substance to earlier piecemeal measures and to Robespierre's private thoughts by establishing a new, more centralized and authoritarian, or "revolutionary", form of government. They proceeded in two stages. First, on 10 October the Convention was invited to endorse Saint-Just's declaration, made on behalf of the Committee of Public Safety, that "the provisional government of France is revolutionary until the peace"; and this was followed, eight weeks later, by the enactment of the law of 14th Frimaire (4 December), which introduced a brand-new system of government and yet one which, under the circumstances, was as readily accepted by the Plain as by the Mountain.

Yet it has been suggested that the Jacobins, as good Rousseauists, were merely carrying out, under conditions that suited them best, a system which they had long prepared and for which they could as easily find the recipe in *The Social Contract* as for the earlier system based on the separation of powers.[36] Robespierre and the Committee – and, one suspects, the majority of the Assembly's members – knew otherwise. We certainly know what Robespierre thought; for he told the Convention in his speech on "the principles of revolutionary government" on 25 December: "The theory of revolutionary government is as new as the Revolution that created it. It is as pointless to seek its origins in the books of the political theorists, who failed to foresee this revolution, as in the laws of the tyrants, who are happy enough to abuse their exercise of authority without seeking out its legal justification." But he admitted that the term "revolutionary", used in this way, might be for many "an enigma" and that it would therefore be desirable "to explain it to all in order that we may rally good citizens, at least, in support of the principles governing the public interest". So he went on to explain that such a form of government was not a permanent feature or a desirable end in itself, but corresponded to new needs and to circumstances of emergency that neither he nor any other of the revolutionaries who had subscribed to the earlier "principles of 1789" could possibly have foreseen. Its aims, functions and methods were, therefore, not the same as those of the constitutional governments which the Revolution could afford in more settled times. "The object of constitutional government [he explained] is to preserve the Republic; the object of revolutionary government is to establish it. Revolution is the war waged by liberty against its enemies; a constitution is that which crowns the edifice of freedom once victory has been won and the nation is at peace." And he added: "The revolutionary government has to summon extraordinary activity to its aid precisely because it is at war. It is subjected to less binding and less uniform regulations, because the circumstances in which it finds itself are tempestuous and shifting, above all because it is compelled to deploy, swiftly and incessantly, new resources to meet new and pressing dangers." Moreover: "The principal concern of constitutional government is civil liberty; that of revolutionary government public liberty. Under a constitutional government little more is required than to protect the individual against abuses by the state, whereas revolutionary government is obliged to defend the state itself against the factions that assail it from every quarter." And he asks: "Is a revolutionary government the less just and the less legitimate because it must be more vigorous in its actions and freer in its movements than an ordinary government? No! for it rests on the most sacred of all laws, the safety of the people, and on necessity, which is the most indisputable of all rights. It also has its rules, all based on justice and on public order . . . It has nothing in common with arbitrary rule; it is public interest that governs it and not the whims of private individuals." [37] In short, the "revolutionary" government was an innovation promoted by the revolutionaries themselves; it was armed with exceptional powers to meet an exceptional situation; and once the war was over and the crisis that engendered it had passed, there would be a return to the "normality" of the Constitution that had recently been adopted.

Two questions immediately arise: first, was Robespierre sincere in claiming that the new type of government was a temporary solution to meet a temporary situation and that the Constitution of 1793 would be put into operation as soon as the war and the crisis it engendered was over? and, secondly, how did the new turn to a "revolutionary" government, armed with exceptional powers, affect his own basic beliefs in popular sovereignty and popular democracy? To the first question there can be no generally acceptable answer, as neither Robespierre nor the other main promoters of the law of Frimaire lived long enough to put their promise to the test. Many historians have doubted the sincerity of their pretensions: in so doing, they have invoked the old maxim that "all power corrupts" and, more particularly, they have pointed to the excesses of the Terror and the blood-letting of the summer of 1794. Others have taken a contrary view: they have argued that the Jacobin leaders, though they suspended the Constitution "for the duration", had no intention of abandoning it altogether; in fact, it was not they but their successors (including several of the former terrorists of 1794) who scrapped it in the autumn of 1795. But as dead men can tell no tales, there must always remain an element of doubt.

The second question does not pose similar problems; but before attempting to answer it we must look a little more closely at the way the Revolutionary Government developed and the part that Robespierre played in it. The mainstay of the government, as we have seen, was formed by the two Committees of General Security and Public Safety. The first was, nominally at least, responsible for all matters relating to police and internal security: thus the Revolutionary Tribunal and the local vigilance and "revolutionary" committees were placed under its direct supervision and control. The second Committee had far more extensive powers: to control ministers, appoint generals, conduct foreign policy and military operations, and to purge and direct the work of the departments and communes. It had the further task of drafting laws of every kind for the Assembly to consider. Robespierre had defined this part of its functions shortly before joining it as follows: "To propose decrees or prescribe measures . . . to give the Convention a first impulsion towards the promotion of issues that have already been thoroughly prepared . . . and to aid its discussions with judicious observations and with sound and weighty judgments".[38] So it had wide-ranging powers and responsibilities and added to them, with the approval of the Assembly, as time went by. Thus it took over the direct control of the representatives on mission; it nominated its own suspects for trial by the Revolutionary Tribunal and sent its own instructions to Fouquier-Tinville, the Public Prosecutor; and, in April, it created its own department of police, thus encroaching further, and with consequences that we have seen, on the work of its rival, the Security Committee.

As a member of the senior Committee, Robespierre played an active part in all its activities and deliberations; but the "twelve who ruled" (to use Professor Robert Palmer's phrase) worked together as a team and, formally at least, his part was no more distinctive than that of any of the others. The Committee's orders and decisions (*arrêtés*) – whether they related to military operations, food supplies, the manufacture of arms, security, police, propaganda or the activities of the *représentants en mission* – were signed by those of its members who happened to be present at the meetings at which they were discussed. From the day on which he joined the Committee in July 1793 to the day of his fall a year later, Robespierre signed 544 *arrêtés*, compared with over twice that number by Barère, Carnot and Prieur de la Côte-d'Or; and only Saint-André, Saint-Just and Couthon (the first two frequently absent on missions and the last as often prevented by sickness) signed fewer; and Robespierre signed hardly any at all after 3 July when he began to stay away from the meetings. Moreover, it was Barère, far more than Robespierre himself, who became the Committee's regular *rapporteur* at sessions of the Assembly. More significant perhaps is the number of orders that he personally drafted or on which his signature appears on its own or as first on the list. There are 124 of these, far fewer than those promoted by Barère and Carnot (later to become two of his bitterest critics in Thermidor), which he signed as readily as those initiated by Couthon and Saint-Just. So there is no evidence to suggest that Robespierre was any more assiduous in attendance or in drafting or signing the Committee's orders than the rest of his colleagues. Nevertheless, if we focus our attention on the orders he drafted himself or was the first, or only member, to sign, a certain pattern emerges that gives some indication of what were his major preoccupations at this time. We observe, for example, that he never took the initiative in promoting strictly *military* orders and very few relating to food supplies;

but far more concerning the manufacture of arms, national festivals and propaganda, and even more – and these predominate – that relate to arrests, police and public security. To this we must add the fact that, during the frequent absences of Saint-Just, it was Robespierre who took personal charge of the newly created Department of Police and, during the three months of its existence, presided over its meetings on no fewer than sixty-four consecutive occasions. So there can be little doubt that, even if Robespierre played an altogether secondary role in the great holocaust of June and July, which, mainly on the orders of the Security Committee, sent many hundreds of victims to the guillotine, he played *the* leading part, throughout this period, as a watchdog of the Revolution in ferreting out its enemies and bringing them to justice.[39]

At this point, therefore, it is appropriate to consider what were Robespierre's views on revolutionary justice and how they accorded with his general political ideas. After his fall in Thermidor, it became fashionable, as we have seen, to depict him as a bloodthirsty monster, a *buveur de sang* dedicated to the cult of the guillotine. Albert Mathiez, in leaping to his defence, took a directly contrary view: "Robespierre," he wrote, "represented, within the Terror, moderation, indulgence and honesty";[40] and he appears to suggest that the resort to terror was nothing but a painful duty which he discharged with evident distaste. But perhaps Mathiez protests too much and is inclined to overstate his case. For though Robespierre was a discriminating judge, there is nothing in his record as a revolutionary leader to suggest that he shrank from the use of the harshest methods of justice against those whom he considered to be the enemies of the Revolution. On the contrary: next to Marat, there was no leader who was so constantly on the alert for any signs of treason, "factionalism" and conspiracy and for counter-revolutionary manifestations of every kind. We have seen the role he played as a champion of "public safety" within the Revolutionary Commune of Paris in the late summer of 1792; and historians (and they include Gérard Walter) have severely criticized his public denunciation of Brissot at the height of the prison massacres.[41] Six months later, when the Revolutionary Tribunal emerged from the Dumouriez crisis, Robespierre was immediately ready to spell out its tasks: to proceed not against the Jacobins or the Mountain (as the Girondins would have it do) but against the *émigré* nobles, the inefficient or treasonable generals and the hoarders who were creating an artificial famine; and once this has been done, he adds, "there will be little else to do, for liberty will be assured". But no such moment ever came; and from then on, as crisis followed crisis, he was ever on his guard for any weakness of the Tribunal's judges in meting out swift and exemplary justice. In September, he protests against the leniency being shown to generals who have failed to carry out their tasks, and he notes, "the Tribunal is working badly". But as the first great political trials after the King's – of Bailly and Barnave, of Marie-Antoinette, Brissot and the Girondins – followed each other in rapid succession a few weeks later, his criticisms ceased.[42]

So far, judicial terror had been sporadic, an occasional device directed against a small number of conspicuous offenders; but, with the institution of the Revolutionary Government, it assumed a new dimension as an instrument of policy. As Robespierre told the Convention in his speech in December, "public liberty" had taken the place of "civil liberty": it was no longer a question of "protecting the individual against the abuses of the state", but of "defending the state against the factions that assail it from every quarter". But, as an instrument of government, terror must be institutionalized and, while justice must be swift and merciless, it must be applied only according to the letter of the law. Moreover, for terror to be just it must be tempered with "virtue". Virtue, as we have seen, had been a constant theme of his since his early days in Arras. He returns to it – but in an entirely new context – in his second great speech on revolutionary government, read to the Convention on 5 February 1794. "What," he asks, "is the fundamental principle of democratic, or popular, government; that is, the mainspring that supports and propels it?" And he answers, "It is virtue, and I speak of that public virtue which performed such miracles in Greece and Rome and which is destined to perform even more astonishing miracles in republican France; of that virtue which is nothing other than the love of one's country and its laws." But, he continues, "If the mainspring of popular government in time of peace is virtue, its mainspring in time of revolution is *virtue and terror* combined: virtue without which terror is squalidly repressive, terror without which virtue lies disarmed. Terror is nothing other than swift, severe and inflexible justice; it is therefore an emanation of virtue; and it is not so much a principle in itself as a consequence of the general principle of democracy when applied to the most urgent needs of the nation."

Here again, as in his earlier definition of revolutionary government, Robespierre is breaking fresh ground. There is no precedent in the work of the "philosophers" for this juxtaposition within the same system of government of virtue and terror. As he had noted two years earlier in his journal, *Le Défenseur de la Constitution*, Montesquieu had kept them rigorously apart, seeing terror as the essence of despotism as virtue was that of the Republic. So Robespierre is well aware of the innovation being put forward; and he explains it as follows: "It has been said that terror was the mainspring of despotic government. Does yours then resemble despotism? Yes, as the sword that glitters in the hands of the heroes of liberty resembles the sword that is wielded by the satellites of tyranny. If the despot governs his enslaved subjects by tyranny, as despot he is right to do so; and if you reduce the enemies of freedom through terror, you, as founders of the Republic, will have right on your side as well. The government of the Republic is the despotism that liberty exercises against tyranny. Is force to be used only to shield crime? . . . Indulgence for the royalists, cry some; mercy for the scoundrels! No, I say! Mercy for the innocent, mercy for the weak, mercy for the unfortunate, mercy for humanity!" [43] It was almost a repetition of a phrase he had used in September of the year before, when, in opposing the election to the Committee of Public Safety of the deputy Briez, who had been on mission to Valenciennes at the time of its surrender, he had told the Convention: "It is the weakness being shown to traitors that is the cause of our disasters. You demand indulgence for criminals, for men who surrender their country to the enemy's arms. For me there can be no indulgence but for outraged virtue and injured innocence." [44]

Thus Robespierre's concern for the common people and belief in their virtue remained unchanged; but it was inevitable that his new preoccupation with terror and strong government should have changed the order of his priorities. The Assembly, once tolerated, though with occasional misgivings, as the temporary custodian of the General Will, had become the permanent voice and guardian of the public interest; while the people's share in sovereignty and the direct conduct of public affairs proportionately diminished. "Democracy", he told the Convention in his speech of February 1794, in words which were a direct challenge to the militants in the Paris sections, "is not a state in which the people, split into a hundred thousand fragments, decides the fate of society at large by taking isolated, hasty and contradictory measures: in fact, such a government has never existed; and if it were ever to exist, it would lead the people to despotism." On the contrary, he concluded, "Democracy is a state in which the sovereign people, guided by laws of its own creation, *directly discharges such functions as are within its powers to discharge: those that are not, it delegates to others.*" [45]

So democracy, like terror, was to become institutionalized with the people playing an essential, but subordinate, role as the junior partners of the Convention and its governing committees. "Hasty and contradictory measures" – once condoned and even applauded – were frowned on; insurrection, for the duration at least, was now to be strictly taboo; and the people's "functions" were to attend their sections as docile agents of their Jacobin leaders, to sniff out traitors and intriguers and hand them over for judgment by those "others" to whom their powers had been entrusted. Already in September 1793, sectional meetings had been reduced to two each ten-day "week" (*décade*); and after Hébert's fall in April, popular and "fraternal" societies not under the direct control of the Jacobin Club were closed down, and the Paris Commune, so long seen as "the citadel of liberty" in the struggle against Federalism, had its independence severely reduced. Robespierre either initiated such measures or gave them his active support; and, even after the victory at Fleurus gave some cause for popular celebrations, he joined Barère in denouncing and proscribing the "fraternal banquets" being organized in the sections on the grounds that they were a cover for "aristocratic" intrigue.[46]

Thus all forms of popular initiative and independent activity were discouraged and were even actively suppressed. In large measure, of course, these restrictions flowed directly from the decision to form a government of "a single will", and there is a clear causal pattern that links the law of 14th Frimaire with the closing of popular societies and the banning of banquets in the spring and summer of

1794. But this is not the whole explanation; nor do we need to look for the answer in a "deterioration" in Robespierre's character, as has sometimes been claimed. What emerges clearly from his later speeches, particularly those made after the destruction of the "factions" in April, is a growing disenchantment with the possibilities of realizing the high hopes proclaimed in the great reports of December and February. As new factions arose to take the place of the old, and as the sections reacted with vigour to the removal of once-trusted leaders and to new shortages and rising prices, discordant voices began to be heard in the streets and markets and sectional meetings, and the Jacobin leaders, who had so long basked in popular favour, began to come under fire. Robespierre himself became a target; and in May (to quote one example among many) Hanriot, commander-in-chief of the Parisian National Guard, received a threatening letter, posted in the Faubourg Saint-Marcel, that apostrophized him indelicately as a *"jean foutre"* and a *"foutu satellite* de Robespierre".[47] So the "virtue" of the people could no longer be so implicitly relied on, as, without enlightened instruction, they were all too easily misled. This was certainly not a new idea: he had expressed similar misgivings in his letters and speeches in the early days of the Convention;[48] and in the notes he had drafted in the summer of 1793 he had, as we have seen, deplored the corrupting influence of writers in the pay of "the rich". He had then proposed to tackle the problem by muzzling the venal, reactionary press and by a wider distribution of patriotic pamphlets and journals: *"il faut éclairer le peuple"*. He continued to insist that all writings that undermined revolutionary principles should be vigorously suppressed and their authors sent before the Revolutionary Tribunal. More positively, he went on to urge a far more liberal dissemination of "patriot" ideas of every kind, not only through the press but by every other means of oral and visual propaganda: through theatre, song and music and great festivals and pageants enriched by the artistry of David. Public education, too, must serve a dual purpose: to teach basic skills and to instruct in patriotic principles. For a long time he had been opposed to any national system, fearing that it would provide the government with yet another means to control and mislead the people.[49] But as his views on government changed, his views on education changed with them; and, in June 1793, it was he who drafted the clauses in the Constitution and Declaration of Rights that made education open to all (*"une instruction commune"*). A month later, he presented the Assembly with the Lepeletier report, which proposed that all children of 5 to 12 from every social class should be educated in common schools at the Republic's expense. The plan proposed "to develop the children's bodies by gymnastic exercises, to accustom them to work with their hands, to train them to endure every kind of fatigue, to form their hearts and minds by useful instruction, and to give them the knowledge necessary to every citizen regardless of his occupation".[50] Thus basic instruction and education in bodily health and republican virtues should go hand in hand.

A similar dual purpose informed Robespierre's promotion of a new civil religion. The Cult of the Supreme Being, inaugurated by the Convention in an impressive ceremony on 8 June 1794, corresponded both to his own personal beliefs and to the political needs of the hour. Even at Louis-le-Grand, he had not conformed to the orthodoxy of his Oratorian teachers; and, at the beginning of the Revolution, he shared the general religious views of the "men of 1789". Like them, he believed that Church properties should be put up for public sale; that the clergy should become servants of the State; and, like most of them, he gave enthusiastic support to the Civil Constitution of 1790. He also shared in the general view that religion was a private matter and clergy should be discouraged from meddling over-much in political affairs. But he never subscribed to the opinions of the extreme anti-clerical faction; he had Helvétius' bust broken at the Jacobin Club; and he firmly believed that the soul was immortal and that religion was a necessary stimulus to public virtue: *"Si Dieu n'existait pas, il faudrait l'inventer."* The latter belief was one he could broadly share with Voltairian deists and with the larger body of revolutionaries – Girondins, Jacobins and others – whose adherence to a "natural" religion, stripped of dogma and revelation, may have owed its inspiration to Rousseau. But his belief in the immortality of the soul and in the guiding hand of Providence caused consternation even among patriots and led to a stormy scene in the Jacobin Club in March 1792, when, in the face of angry interruptions, he stubbornly stated his faith: "To invoke the name of Providence and to express an idea of the Eternal Being that guides the destinies of nations and appears to watch with particular vigilance over the Revolution in France, is to give voice not to random reflections but to a sentiment that comes from the heart and is to me of the greatest importance . . . a divine sentiment that has richly compensated me for the lack of the favours that have been lavished on those who have been ready to betray the people's cause." [51] And, in November of that year, a hostile critic wrote in the *Chronique de Paris*: "Robespierre is a priest and will never be anything else." [52]

So when he became a member of the Committee of Public Safety, it was inevitable that his religious views, being held with such conviction, should have played some part in shaping the Government's policy. There were three ways in which they did so. In the first place, he acted, as far as circumstances would allow, as a champion of toleration and insisted that the Assembly's policy of tolerating religious practice should be strictly observed, provided it caused no disorder; and, on several occasions, he protected Catholic believers from persecution. On one such occasion, he wrote: "There are people who are superstititious in perfectly good faith . . . They are sick people whom we must restore to good health by winning their confidence; a forced cure would drive them to fanaticism"; [53] and we have seen how, with embarrassing consequences for himself, he leapt to the defence of Catherine Théot, a fanatical old believer, and had her released from the Public Prosecutor's hands. He also became persuaded that religion – including the practice of the Catholic faith – responded to a deeply felt popular need, was a source of consolation to the old and the poor, and that anti-religious excesses, such as practised by Hébert and the "de-christianizing" movement in the autumn of 1793, would raise unnecessary alarms, prove a dangerous diversion and rebound on the heads of the revolutionaries themselves. In his speech denouncing such excesses in the Jacobin Club on 21 November, he argued that "fanaticism" no longer represented a major threat to the Revolution: "I see only one way of reviving fanaticism among us: it is to affect to believe in its power"; and he added: "Priests have been denounced for saying the Mass. They will continue to do so all the longer if you try to prevent them. He who wants to prevent them is more fanatical than the priest himself." And further: "Atheism is *aristocratic*, whereas belief in a Supreme Being who watches over oppressed innocence and punishes the crimes of the oppressor is *popular*"; and only the rich and the guilty would deny it.[54] He returned to the same theme in his report on 5 February the next year: "To preach atheism is merely another way of absolving superstition and to put philosophy itself in the dock; and to declare war on divinity is to create a diversion in favour of monarchy." Moreover, the "de-christianizers" were "false revolutionaries" who, "having by their violent attacks on religious prejudice, widely spread the seeds of civil war [an evident allusion to the war in the Vendée], will seek to arm aristocracy and fanaticism with the very measures that a sane policy has dictated to you in favour of the freedom of worship".[55]

The next step was to provide a more positive solution: not merely to proscribe anti-religious excess, but to find means to unify the various Republican cults that had mushroomed during the last two years, and to tap the religious feelings, believed (by Robespierre at least) to be held by a majority of Frenchmen, and direct them into channels best suited to serve the Republican cause. This also corresponded to the wishes of many representatives on mission who felt that the existing proliferation of cults caused unnecessary confusion and was completely at variance with official government policy of tightening up administrative controls. In one other respect, too, the ground had been well prepared: it had long been generally understood (and this was by no means an invention of Robespierre's) that any unifying cult that emerged should be dedicated to the Supreme Being, under whose auspices the Jacobin Constitution had already been placed. So the Assembly had, late in 1793, instructed its Committee of Public Instruction to prepare the draft of a suitable decree. The draft came into the hands of the Committee of Public Safety in March; and, on 6 April, Couthon reported to the Convention that the Committee would shortly propose "a plan for a tenth-day festival dedicated to the Eternal Being". This was the nucleus of the Cult which the Assembly discussed and adopted a month later.[56] So it was in no sense a system of Robespierre's invention; yet he had clearly had a great deal to do with the later stages of its preparation; and it was, therefore, appropriate that he should be chosen to present it to the Assembly on 18th Floréal (7 May) and, as current President of the Convention, to deliver the official address at the inaugural ceremony and national festival staged by David on 20th Prairial (8 June).

The decree that Robespierre introduced was composed of fifteen articles, the first three of which gave the substance of the two-fold purpose the Cult was intended to serve:

Article I. The French people recognizes the existence of the Supreme Being, and the immortality of the soul.

Article II. It recognizes that the best way to worship the Supreme Being is to do one's duties as a man.

Article III. It considers that the most important of these duties are: to detest bad faith and despotism, to punish tyrants and traitors, to assist the unfortunate, to respect the weak, to defend the oppressed, to do all the good one can to one's neighbour, and to behave with justice towards all men.

It went on to list the festivals that would be annually held in honour of the Supreme Being and to be named (so ran the fifth article) "after the glorious events of the Revolution, the virtues of which are most dear to men, and most useful, and the chief blessings of nature". The "glorious events" were the fall of the Bastille, the overthrow of the monarchy, the execution of Louis XVI and the expulsion of the Girondin deputies; and the "virtues" and "blessings" numbered three dozen, one for each *décadi*, and ranged over a rich variety of items, including patriotism, the Republic, the hatred of tyrants and traitors, friendship, love, conjugal fidelity, mother-love, filial piety and the benefactors of mankind. In presenting his report, Robespierre told the deputies: "The real priest of the Supreme Being is Nature; his temple, the universe; his worship, virtue; his festivals, the joy of a great people, gathered together beneath his eyes in order to draw close the sweet bonds of universal brotherhood and offer him the homage of pure and feeling hearts"; and he exhorted them: "Let us abandon the priests and return to God. Let us build morality on eternal and sacred foundations; let us inspire in man that religious respect for man, that profound sense of his duties, which is the sole guarantee of social happiness; let us nourish it through each one of our institutions, and let public education, in particular, be directed to this end." [57]

So the Cult, proclaimed at this time, was to be a *political* as well as a *moral* religion. It was designed not merely as a means of channelling worship towards a supreme and omniscient Being; not even as an administrative device for imposing unity on the confusion of religious practices and beliefs that the Revolution had brought about. It was also proclaimed in response to an urgent political need: to attempt to reconcile the conflicting aims of the different factions and groups which were by now, once more, even after the blood-letting of Germinal, threatening to tear the Revolutionary Government apart. But it was already too late. Even the Mountain, so recently seen as the chief repository of public virtue, was now sharply divided into the "pure" and "corrupt", with the "corrupt" showing every indication of taking the upper hand; moreover, it became soon all too evident that the inauguration of the new Cult, far from helping to heal the breach, was threatening to widen it further. The people, too, were no longer a firm bastion of "virtue" but had become similarly divided. Where Robespierre, in June 1793, had broadly drawn his line of separation in terms of class and had summoned the saner portion of the population – the *sans-culottes* – to rally alongside their chosen representatives against the corrupt rich, now such differences had become blurred and the only hope lay in rallying the dwindling band of "virtuous" citizens in every social group. Saint-Just had sensed one side of the problem when, after Hébert's fall and the purge of the popular assemblies, he had noted, *"la Révolution est glacée"*; but, not being a close observer of social realities, he failed to understand how or why. For Robespierre, the festival of the Supreme Being, over which he presided on 8 June, appears to have represented the last great hope of a moral regeneration. Four days later, he was once more in a pessimistic mood when we find him berating the "intriguers" (Bourdon de l'Oise, Tallien and others), while refusing to name them, within the Convention. On 1 July, and again on the 9th, he renewed the attack on "slanderers" and "intriguers" in the Jacobin Club; and, finally, in his swan-song in the Convention, on the 26th (8th Thermidor), he denounced the conspiracy of "the league of scoundrels" and ended with the despairing cry: "If I must remain silent on these truths, then bring me the hemlock . . . Why live in a society where intrigue always triumphs over truth, where justice is a lie? . . . I was made to combat crime, not to condone it. The time has not yet come when men of good will can serve their country unmolested. The defenders of liberty will be so many names for the proscription lists so long as the horde of scoundrels remains in control." [58] And if he failed to defend himself more resolutely against his enemies on the following night, was it perhaps that by now he had had enough and had no stomach left for the fight?

So Robespierre's Republic of Virtue failed. It failed not because he had become a tyrant (as his enemies claimed) where he had been a consistent liberal before. But, basically, both the objective itself and the means by which he hoped to attain it proved to be irreconcilable with the realities of the day – with political tensions caused by war and revolution, with growing conflicts within society that lay beyond his control, and even with the new hopes raised by military victory in the summer of 1794. The year before, he had rightly seen that, if the Revolution was to survive, the wartime emergency called for drastic remedies in the constitution and conduct of government. In the process, it was inevitable that the liberal-democratic Constitution should, temporarily at least, be laid aside and popular initiative be curbed or attuned to the new needs of the State. Did it mean that, in charting such a course, Robespierre had abandoned his old belief in popular sovereignty and democracy and that the Republic of Virtue was a fraud and, as "virtue" became identified with a narrowing political orthodoxy, the cover for a personal dictatorship? Some historians have held this view; yet there is little evidence to support it. There is certainly nothing in his later speeches to suggest that, all other means having failed, he aspired to play the tyrant: in all those made between December and July there is the same insistence on the basic virtue of the common people, the corruptibility of rulers (now more evident than ever), the same profound suspicion of administrators and officials, and the fear that a relaxation of revolutionary government – even after the victory of Fleurus – might lead to a military dictatorship. That he had, since early June, lost confidence in his ability to carry out his aims seems reasonably well established; but this does not mean that he had lost his faith in popular democracy or in the ultimate triumph of the cause he believed in.

We have seen that the survivors of Thermidor blackened his memory; but even during the Thermidorian reaction, there were

Frenchmen who believed that he had loved the people, that he had been a sincere democrat and that, under his rule, equality had been more than an empty sham. Michelet, who was certainly not an unqualified admirer, ends his *History* as follows: "A few days after Thermidor, a man, who is still alive today [Michelet was writing in the mid-1840s] and was then ten years old, was taken to the theatre by his parents and, at the end of the performance, was astonished by the long procession of brilliant carriages that he now saw for the first time. Men in shirt-sleeves, hat in hand, were asking the spectators as they came out, 'A carriage, *master*?' The child did not understand this new expression, and when he asked for an explanation, he was simply told that there had been a great change since the death of Robespierre." [59]

Chapter 2

THE SOCIAL DEMOCRAT

We have seen that Robespierre, as a champion of the Rights of Man, tended to express himself in purely political terms. There were, however, occasions, as in the draft he prepared for the Declaration of Rights and the Constitution of 1793, when he attempted to find social solutions as well. For how reconcile the equality of political rights which he so persistently demanded with the inequalities within the society the Revolution had inherited from the past? How could the poor, whose champion he professed to be, hope to achieve the same rights of citizenship as the rich unless something were done to bridge the economic gap between them?

Although Robespierre's early life was humble enough, there was little in his education or his upbringing to equip him to meet this problem. Under his Oratorian teachers, both at Arras and at Louis-le-Grand, he acquired a solid grounding in Law and the Classics, but no knowledge whatsoever of the social sciences. From the study of Rousseau, it is true, he learned something of the evil consequences that flowed from the unequal distribution of wealth; but, in recognizing and deploring the evil, neither Rousseau nor any other of the *philosophes* offered any practical remedy. Poverty and social inequality were realities that had to be put up with; and they remained an abstraction to whose solution they devoted little attention. So, in this case, his studies were of little use to him; and it was only through his own direct experience of war and revolution, and through the logic of events, that he became one of the handful of Jacobins – Saint-Just and Billaud-Varenne were others – who discovered that democracy had to be fought for in the social as well as the political arena; and it was through such a process of self-education that he became, as Georges Lefebvre has written, not only "the historic leader of political democracy, but of social democracy as well".[1]

The process took time to develop, and there are only occasional glimpses of the results in his early Artesian days and in the two years that he spent as a deputy to the Constituent Assembly. Yet, even at

Arras, he was certainly not unaware that the problem existed; and we noted earlier that, in his first political manifesto, the *Appel à la nation artésienne*, of 1788, he had been concerned that the poor were denied the possibility of making use even of such rights as were open to them by the mere fact that they were poor. At this time, he offered no solution; and, in the Constituent Assembly, he was almost exclusively preoccupied with finding political answers to the innumerable questions he raised about popular sovereignty and "natural" rights. But there were exceptions (some of which have been noted already), as when he proposed that craftsmen and others who discharged their duties as citizens by attending political meetings or parading with the National Guard should be compensated for time lost from work; and, in some of the earlier debates, he defended the actions of peasants who had refused to pay taxes or had protested against the enclosure of land. Such moments, however, were few and far between and even when the opportunity appeared to present itself it was rarely taken up. He intervened, for example, on at least two occasions when the Assembly was discussing food riots: those that took place at Soissons in July 1790 and at Douai in March 1791. But on neither occasion did he attempt to probe the deeper causes of disturbance nor did he excuse or explain the actions of the people most directly involved: on the first, it was rather to argue, on somewhat legalistic grounds, that it was the municipal authority that had the duty, overriding that of others, to place a ceiling on the price of food; and, on the second, that priests, some of whom were accused of fomenting disturbance, had the same rights as other citizens to the protection of the law.[2] In December 1790, he came nearer to the heart of the matter when he opposed a proposal, put forward by Rabaut-Saint-Etienne, that "passive" citizens should be excluded from the National Guard. He refused to accept the argument being advanced that "the enormous disparity in fortunes, which leaves the greater part of the nation's wealth in a few hands", was a valid reason for depriving the poorer citizens of their "inalienable sovereign rights". On the contrary, he argued, this imposed on the Assembly "the sacred obligation" to ensure that, in a society where such inequalities of fortune not only existed but were unavoidable, equality of political rights must be made available to all.[3] So the problem, though recognized, was not squarely faced up to.

In fact, it is rare at this time to find Robespierre arguing a case in other than legal or political terms; and it is therefore not so surprising that he took no part in the discussions which followed the peasant rebellion of the summer of 1789 leading to the first great surrender of the old feudal rights in the countryside; nor did he intervene in the debates on the industrial disputes of the summer of 1791, which culminated in Le Chapelier's law refusing workers the right to combine in defence of wages.

A decisive change in Robespierre's attitude on such matters only becomes apparent, as Jean Massin has pointed out, in the early months of 1792; and it is perhaps no chance that the change coincided with the outbreak of war. The supply and price of food were once more matters of deep concern, and food riots occurred in the Beauce and the Orléanais in the spring of that year as they had, more widely, in the summer and autumn of 1789. In one outbreak in the neighbourhood of Paris, Simoneau, the mayor of Etampes, who had refused to reduce the price of bread, was killed by rioting townsmen. Both the Jacobin Club and the Legislative Assembly, reacting to the event, wished to honour Simoneau as a martyr who had done his duty as a citizen by acting in defence of property. Robespierre opposed such proposals on two occasions in the Jacobin Club; and, more vigorously still, when the Assembly decided to erect a monument to his memory and to organize a festival under the triple device "Liberty, Equality, Property" and supported by a military parade. He saw in Simoneau a grain-speculator who, even if his fate was undeserved, had provoked it by refusing to lower prices and by cornering the market at the people's expense. The incident led him to publish, in his *Défenseur de la Constitution*, the text of a petition and a protest, far stronger than his, written by Pierre Dolivier, the radical *curé* of the neighbouring village of Mauchamps, and to add a commentary of his own. "From the prosperous shopkeeper to the proud patrician," he wrote, in words that were directed as much against the Feuillants and Brissotins in the Assembly as against men like Simoneau himself, "from the lawyer to the one-time nobleman, almost all wish to preserve the privilege of despising that part of humanity that goes by the name of 'people' . . . Let the universe perish or the human race suffer deprivation for centuries on end . . . as long as their wealth increases with their corruption and the

131

people's poverty. Try to preach the cult of liberty to these greedy speculators who know only the altars of Plutus! All that interests them is to know how far our financial system will increase the interest on their capital. Though the Revolution has done service to their greed, it has not been sufficient to reconcile them to it: for that it would have to add further to their wealth and do nothing more." [4] In short, to the rich – and their spokesmen in the Legislative Assembly – the Revolution might go so far, but no further; and where those limits should be drawn would be determined by their property interests and little else.

The problem arose more acutely in the late autumn and early winter, when further disturbances broke out in the grain-growing areas of the Beauce and the department of Eure-et-Loir in November and December. The municipal officers of Chartres, faced with a popular demand for controls on the price of grain, invited the Convention to intervene, and it was decided to send troops. Robespierre, though he showed no sympathy for any "unnecessary" interference with the freedom of the market, objected strongly and proposed an alternative in an important speech that was published in Paris two days later. In it he argued that present remedies for meeting such situations were inadequate to meet the needs: "The value of bounties may be debated; freedom of trade is necessary up to the point where homicidal greed begins to misuse it; the use of bayonets is an atrocity; so the system is fundamentally incomplete because it fails to go to the roots of the problem." He believed that there were two main reasons for these mistakes and omissions:

"1. The authors of the system have treated those commodities most necessary to human existence merely as ordinary merchandise and have made no distinction between trade in wheat and, say, in indigo; they have spent more time talking about the grain trade than they have about the people's needs; and by omitting this factor from their calculations, they have, in practice, falsely applied principles which, in themselves, are self-evident. It is this mixture of truth and falsehood which has given a plausible appearance to an erroneous system.

"2. Still less have they adapted them to the stormy conditions that revolutions bring in their train; and their vague theories, even if they were adequate in ordinary circumstances, would be quite unsuited to the emergency measures which are called for in moments of crisis. They have counted for a great deal the profits of merchants and land-owners, but the lives of human beings they have counted as almost nothing. And why? Because it was the ministers and the men of wealth and social position who wrote and who ruled; if this had fallen to the people, the system would no doubt have been considerably amended!

"Common sense tells us, for example, that such commodities as are not essential to subsistence may be left to unlimited commercial speculation; the momentary shortage which may ensue is, in such cases, a tolerable inconvenience; and, generally, it may be assumed that the unrestricted freedom of this trade will redound to the greater profit of both the State and the individual. But where human lives are concerned we are not justified in taking such a risk. It is not imperative that I should be in a position to buy expensive cloth; but it is imperative that I should have the means to buy bread for myself and my children."

He wound up this part of his speech with a peroration that must have startled his listeners: "*Food that is necessary for man's existence is as sacred as life itself. Everything that is indispensable for its preservation is the common property of society as a whole. It is only the surplus that is private property and can be safely left to individual commercial enterprise.*" [5] Yet, having gone so far, he ended his speech with a number of common-sense proposals that were moderate enough: when necessary, special measures should be adopted to ensure a free and adequate distribution of grain and flour and stern police action should be taken against hoarders and speculators. There was no question as yet of imposing even a partial control on prices; that was a last resort, as later events would show.

Basically, in fact, he still remained wedded to the *laissez-faire* principles that the revolutionaries had inherited from the *philosophes* and *économistes* of the generation before. How strong that attachment was became evident in the next wave of popular disturbance which, in Paris, took the form of riots against grocers, in late February of the following year. This time, the target of protest was not bread or flour, but sugar, coffee and candles and other colonial wares imported from the West Indies and whose prices had doubled or trebled since the outbreak of war. During the two days that the riots lasted, large crowds invaded the grocers' shops in every part of the capital and compelled their owners to reduce prices to their pre-war level. The rioters were condemned by every political party in turn, except the small group of Enragés, led by Jacques Roux who represented the Section des Gravilliers on the council of the Commune. Marat, it is true, proposed, with characteristic venom, that an example should be made by hanging a few grocers from the doorposts of their shops; but he showed little sympathy for the aims and methods of the rioters themselves. Robespierre, too, was far less indulgent than he had been in the previous winter, and he roundly condemned the riots in two speeches to the Jacobins. One reason was that, this time, he was persuaded that the disturbances had been provoked by the aristocracy and were not genuine expressions of popular grievance; and he was all the more willing to believe this as he considered coffee and sugar to be semi-luxuries or "paltry merchandise" ("*de chétives marchandises*") and not to be "essential to subsistence" like bread and flour. He conceded that the people had good reason to feel that they were being "persecuted by the rich, who are still what they always were, hard and merciless," and to believe that, "in default of protective laws, they have the right to take their own measures to satisfy their needs". But, this time, they had been grievously misled; for this was "a plot directed against the patriots themselves"; and, with little supporting evidence, he pointed to the presence in the crowd of aristocrats and Knights of Saint-Louis disguised as *sans-culottes*; and he insisted that the shops of patriots had received more than their share of attention and that the warehouses of the large hoarders had been left untouched. The "true people" of Paris, however, had refused to become involved: "In the Faubourg Saint-Marcel, not a single shopkeeper or merchant was disturbed; and the efforts of the agitators who went into the Faubourg Saint-Antoine were fruitless: they failed completely to rouse the population of that quarter. That is the true people of Paris. They cast down tyrants, they do not invade grocers' shops. The people of Paris have overthrown despotism, but they have not laid siege to the counting houses of the Rue des Lombards." [6]

These speeches are important as they show that, on this occasion as on many others, Robespierre, for all his evident sympathy for popular distress, and his growing realization of its causes, displayed a marked reluctance to encourage the people to seek their own remedies, and least of all in support of economic rather than political ends: it was one thing to "exterminate brigands" (as at the Bastille or the Tuileries Palace); it was quite another to seize sugar or other "paltry merchandise". In such matters, it was far better to leave it to the Assembly or the Jacobins to intervene on the people's behalf and pass "protective laws". He made this clear enough, the following April, in his contributions to the long debate on the new Constitution and Declaration of Rights. As we have briefly noted before, he then took up the question of the rights of property and the need to define it, as the earlier Declaration of 1789 had failed to do. For property, Robespierre argued, could not be an unrestricted right as its individual exercise was a matter of intimate concern to others. In presenting his views in a speech on 24 April, he told the Assembly:

"Ask that merchant in human flesh what property is. He will tell you, pointing to the long bier that he calls a ship and in which he has herded and shackled men who still appear to be alive: 'Those are my property; I bought them at so much a head.' Question that nobleman, who has lands and ships or who thinks that the world has been turned upside down since he has had none, and he will give you a similar view of property. . . .

"But to none of these people has it ever occurred that property carries moral responsibilities. Why should our Declaration of Rights appear to contain the same error in its definition of liberty: 'the most valued property of man, the most sacred of the rights that he holds from nature'? We have justly said that this right was limited by the rights of others. Why have we not applied the same principle to property, which is a social institution, as if the eternal laws of nature were less inviolable than the conventions evolved by man? You have drafted numerous articles in order to ensure the greatest freedom for the exercise of property, but you have not said a single word to define its nature and its legitimacy, so that your declaration appears to have been made not for ordinary men, but for capitalists, profiteers, speculators and tyrants." And he proposed that, "to rectify these errors", the following articles be added:

"1. Property is the right of each and every citizen to enjoy and to dispose of the portion of goods that is guaranteed to him by law.

"2. The right of property is limited, as are all other rights, by the obligation to respect the property of others.

"3. It may not be so exercised as to prejudice the security, or the liberty, or the existence, or the property of our fellow men.

"4. All holdings in property and all commercial dealings which violate this principle are unlawful and immoral."[7]

But we have seen, in the previous chapter, that even the new Jacobin Convention of June 1793 refused to follow his suggestions and that its Declaration, when it emerged from the debate, omitted these clauses as it omitted those relating to the international brotherhood of man. The Assembly also decided that the right to work or to public assistance should not, as Robespierre had proposed, be open to all but only to "*les citoyens malheureux*", or citizens in actual need of support. The principle arose again – though in a different form – and was put to a practical test in September of the same year, when, after a popular insurrection in the streets of the capital, the leaders of the Commune led a deputation of *sans-culottes* to the National Convention. It was during this encounter that the Assembly decided, at Danton's suggestion, to limit sectional meetings to two a week (later, this became two a *décade*) and to compensate "poor citizens" with a payment of 40 *sous* for every day they attended. But the question naturally arose: what was intended by "poor"? Did it mean the poorer citizens, or *sans-culottes*, who lived by the work of their hands; or did it mean only the *indigents*, or indigent poor, who were in need of public relief? In spite of attempts to clarify the issue, the "*loi des 40 sous*", as it finally emerged, left loop-holes for either interpretation; and for several months, each Paris section interpreted the law in the manner that suited it best, until, in June 1794 the Committee of Public Safety finally decided to adopt the less liberal view and ruled that the payment was only due to "*les patriotes malheureux*" who found themselves in need of public assistance. (Their Thermidorian successors, it should be added, proved to be less liberal still and, in August 1794, after Robespierre's fall, they withdrew the payment altogether.)[8]

In this instance, there is no evidence that Robespierre, having lost the earlier debate with his Montagnard colleagues, showed any inclination to reopen it later. But it is one illustration, among others, that he and a small group of his intimate supporters *might*, given the opportunity, have taken a firmer line on a number of "social" questions if the majority had allowed it. Yet as, in such matters, he was inclined to temporize and not to press his arguments too far, we cannot be altogether sure. Moreover, the logic of events and the exigencies of war were eloquent persuaders; and the Jacobin Convention, whatever the natural inclinations and personal reservations of certain of its members, was led to carry through a programme of social legislation that carried them far beyond the earlier *laissez-faire* principles of 1789 and 1791: "The force of circumstance," as Saint-Just aptly declared in February 1794, "may lead us to conclusions that we had not dreamed of before."[9] One example is the remarkable series of laws the Convention carried through to satisfy outstanding peasant demands in the summer of 1793. Almost as soon as the Girondin deputies had been expelled, it adopted a succession of decrees – those of 3 and 10 June and 17 July – which, at long last, completed the peasant "revolution" that had begun, in such dramatic circumstances, in July and August 1789. By these decrees, all feudal dues and obligations were finally abolished and small plots of land were made available for collective purchase by village communities. It is true that many peasant claims remained unsatisfied, such as the total abolition of enclosure and the division of large estates for the benefit of the landless poor, but it was a remarkable achievement and one that, like the new Constitution itself, was rushed through with the greatest possible dispatch; and Professor Manfred, the Soviet historian, has rightly claimed that "the peasants' principal demands . . . were carried through by the Jacobins with a thoroughness without precedent and one that has never been equalled by any other bourgeois revolution."[10]

Where the Jacobins assured themselves of a solid base among the peasants by showing themselves to be far more willing to tear out feudalism by the roots than the Feuillants or Girondins had been before them, they won a similar base among the small consumers – and particularly among the small craftsmen and shopkeepers of Paris – by their adoption of the Maximum law of September 1793. It had a long history (only to be touched on briefly here), which shows that the Jacobins were persuaded to adopt it, as a temporary expedient, more by political necessity than by any ideological conviction; but, in so doing, they displayed once more an ability to adapt themselves to changing circumstance that their Girondin predecessors so signally lacked.

The agitation for a control on food prices went back to the *cahiers de doléances* and the earliest days of the Revolution; it was marked both by peasant and urban riot and by the writings of radical pamphleteers. The Constituent Assembly, as stubborn upholders of *laissez-faire*, had shown little sympathy and, in August and September 1789, abolished such controls as existed and restored freedom of trade in grain and flour. Three years later, following the first wave of rioting in the autumn of 1792, the Convention had consented to revive the old regulations, while emphatically refusing to contemplate a more general system of controls. Meanwhile, however, the needs of war, as well as the clamour of the small consumers, was gradually persuading the Jacobins, even before they came into office, to modify their views. At Lyons, in the spring of 1793, the short-lived radical Commune, directed by Chalier, municipalized the city's bread supply; and, on 4 May, the National Convention, following the Lyons example and that set by the Commune in Paris, imposed a ceiling on the price of bread and flour (the first law of the Maximum). But this first step neither satisfied the small consumers and their spokesmen nor helped to solve the increasingly urgent problems of military supplies. The rioters of 1792 and 1793 had already extended their "taxing" operations far beyond the primary necessities of wheat, bread and flour: in Paris they had imposed lower prices on sugar, soap, coffee, candles, meat and wine; and, in the provinces, on oats, soap, butter, eggs, and even on clogs, timber, iron and coal. Meanwhile, prices in general continued to rise and the *assignat*, having fallen to 36 per cent of its nominal value in June, fell further to 22 per cent in August. The same month, the *levée en masse* caused a problem of its own by calling three-quarters of a million men under arms. To meet the needs of the small consumer, Jacques Roux and the Enragés, the most vocal of the people's champions, had, since January, been campaigning for a General Maximum on prices; and by early September the demand was taken up by nearly every section in Paris. It was voiced by the *sans-culottes* who accompanied their municipal leaders to the Convention on 5 September; and, three weeks later, under the triple stimulus of argument, war-emergency and riot, the Convention yielded, temporarily abandoned its liberal principles, and, through the law of the General Maximum, embarked on a wide-ranging programme of economic controls. The news was received with enthusiasm, as an agent of the Ministry of the Interior reported, by the common people of Paris.[11]

Robespierre had played no distinctive part in arriving at these decisions. He rarely intervened in peasant affairs; we have seen that, in his speech on the food-supply in late November 1792, he had shared his colleagues' reluctance to interfere "unnecessarily" with the free market in grain; and a short speech he made on 31 July 1793 warned that even the first Maximum law could be all too easily abused by "*les malveillants*".[12] He played a more particular and more enthusiastic role, earlier that month, in promoting another part of the Jacobins' social programme, Lepeletier's plan for a national system of education. In the last chapter, we saw that the plan had a dual purpose: both to provide elementary education for all and to form good citizens for the Republic. But it would be a mistake to place too much emphasis on the second at the expense of the first. There seems to be little doubt that Robespierre, in pursuit of his social ideal, was as concerned to provide every child with an equal education as he was "to educate the people" in Republican principles. "Do not let us forget," he told the Convention in presenting his report, "what is the object of this plan for a common primary education for all. We wish to provide the children with physical and moral aptitudes that will, later in life, be useful to all regardless of the station in which they were born. We do not intend to prepare them for any particular destiny: they must be given benefits that will prove equally useful to men of every kind; in a word, we aim, as it were, to shape a raw material of a basic excellence, whose elements we shall develop in such a way that, when it leaves our hands, it may be easily adapted to serve the great variety of occupations of which our Republic is composed." [13]

In the great report on "the principles of political morality" that he presented to the Convention in February 1794, Robespierre returned to a theme that Saint-Just had already broached during the food riots of November 1792: "A people that is not contented has no country of its own." In returning to it fifteen months later, Robespierre re-phrased the theme as follows: "It is only in a democracy that the

State is really the fatherland of all the individuals that compose it and can count as many defenders devoted to its cause as it has citizens within its borders." [14] The meaning is clear enough: it is only by satisfying their basic social and political wants that the common people can become firmly attached to the Republican cause: in fact, as the Jacobins had done through their legislation of the summer of 1793. But, rather surprisingly, he did not elaborate the matter further here any more than he had done in his first report on revolutionary government ten weeks before; nor did he touch on such matters again; and even the abolition of slavery in San Domingo on 3 February 1794 – in itself a momentous decision – passed without comment and appears to have left him unmoved. [15] Yet there had been no change of policy: the social programme of the Jacobin Government continued, though never at the pace that had been set in the previous summer. The last of the great measures adopted was that of 22nd Floréal (11 May 1794), which introduced a system of social security (*"bienfaisance nationale"*) that went far beyond the terms of the clause relating to public assistance in the Declaration of Rights of 1793. It provided not only for relief in case of material distress, but also for medical benefits, pensions for old age and infirmity and grants for large families; in short, it was the forerunner of the social security measures of the modern Welfare State. It may have owed something to Robespierre (though he appears to have played no particular role in its preparation and he did not speak in the debate); but probably more to Saint-Just, who, in the *Institutions républicaines* that he drafted at this time, defined his egalitarian society as one in which "Frenchmen [should] be given the means to obtain the first necessities of life without depending on anything else but the laws and without any mutual dependence between one citizen and another". [16]

It remains to consider the far more contentious Decrees of Ventôse which Saint-Just presented to the Assembly, at the height of the Hébertist agitation, on 26 February and which were adopted on 3 March 1794. What was their significance and what part (if any) did Robespierre play in their formulation? The decrees were in two parts: the first provided that the properties of all *known* enemies of the Revolution should be sequestered; the second that they should be distributed among "indigent patriots" from lists submitted by the communes throughout France. At first sight, it might seem that what was intended was a massive redistribution of property by which the millions of the needy poor (one text speaks of *"tous les malheureux"*) would become the pensioners of the many thousands of suspect rich. Several historians – both friends and critics of the Revolution – have interpreted the Assembly's decision in this way. Among the former, Albert Mathiez hailed the decrees as "the programme of a new revolution" by which "the class of eternal dispossessed" would be "raised to social life"; and he claimed that the Revolution was about to embark on a free and wholesale distribution of the properties of suspects among the "revolutionary proletariat".[17] Thus he saw the measure as one which, by effecting a significant redistribution of property, was intended to have far-reaching consequences for the future of France. Other historians – Albert Soboul, Gérard Walter and Robert Palmer among them – have contested this view. They have argued that a study of the context in which the decrees were put forward will show that they had a far more limited purpose: it was a time when the Hébertist challenge, with its demand for drastic measures of reform, offered a serious threat to the stability of the Government and compelled it, in order to survive, to make concessions to both "advanced patriots" and *sans-culottes*; so it was a measure of circumstance rather than one prompted by a new radical social philosophy. Soboul has shown further that Saint-Just was not putting forward anything new: the question of confiscating the properties of suspects and distributing them among needy patriots had long been in the air and had for some months been the subject of debate in the clubs and sectional meetings. Nor was Saint-Just attacking property as such: patriot property remained sacred and inviolable; nor was there any question of forcing the new rich to disgorge their gains (there were excellent patriots among them, too); in fact, it was only the aristocracy, or those whom the label could be made to fit, who were being called upon to foot the bill. So it was a measure prompted by the political needs of the hour and not really a "social" measure at all.[18] (It also proved to be a dismal failure: not only because it was conveniently forgotten and never put into execution, but because it made little impression on the *sans-culottes*, who were at the time advancing far more radical demands of their own.)

The Ideologue

In any case, it seems unlikely that Robespierre had much to do with it. Mathiez, who believed that he had, bases his case largely on the notes he had drafted in the summer of 1793, when he had proposed to rally "the people" against "the rich" or the bourgeoisie. But this was nine months before; and he does not appear, once he had joined the Committee of Public Safety and once the alliance between the Jacobins and *sans-culottes* had been cemented, to have given such matters more thought: this seems to be borne out by what we have seen of his speeches and activities since July 1793. Moreover, both he and Couthon (whom Mathiez believed to be another principal involved in the case) were absent from all the Committee's meetings at this time: Couthon, as so often, was confined to his bed; and Robespierre had been ill for the past month and no speeches by him have been recorded between 10 February and 13 March. Several other Committee members were also engaged on other duties (Saint-André, Billaud and the Prieurs, for example) and the work of the Committee appears to have fallen largely on Collot d'Herbois and Saint-Just. It was these two, in fact, who most probably drafted the decrees that the Convention discussed on 8th Ventôse and adopted five days later. Perhaps they did so with all the greater relish as they both – though ill-assorted in other respects – had an interest in social measures that were considered radical in their day. Saint-Just was, as we have seen, the author of the *Institutions républicaines* (published posthumously after Thermidor), which proposed to reorganize society on a more egalitarian, Spartan model; and Collot was a co-founder with Fouché of the radical Temporary Commission at Lyons and the friend and confidant of Billaud-Varenne, who had proposed (somewhat vaguely) to re-distribute property in a book, the *Elements of Republicanism*, that he had written the year before.[19]

In fact, if we are to look for the extreme limits of Jacobin social democracy, systematically expressed, we must look for them to works of this kind rather than to Robespierre's own speeches and writings. Moreover, he ceased to debate such matters after he joined the Committee of Public Safety in the summer of 1793; where, as we saw, his main preoccupation was with police and security, government political strategy and the conduct of war.

This is not to say that Robespierre does not deserve the reputation of having been a founder of French social democracy. Far from it: his speeches and writings on the Simoneau affair and on food supplies and property in 1792 and 1793 posed new problems and pointed to their solution with a clarity, vigour and authority that gave the initial stimulus to the Jacobin social legislation of the Year II. They also helped to shape the more advanced views that were later put forward by Babeuf and Saint-Just; and it is probably true to say that no other revolutionary of 1789 – with the possible exception of Babeuf – had so powerful an influence on the great debate on democracy – both social and political – that emerged from the Revolutionary years.

Yet we must recognize the limits of his thinking, circumscribed as it was bound to be by the society in which he lived and the possibilities for change that it appeared to offer. The society in which Robespierre grew up and developed was, as we have already noted, a "pre-industrial" one, in which large-scale capitalist industry and values, though on the ascendant, had not yet come fully into their own. In both towns and villages, the typical producer was still the small independent craftsman and peasant cultivator who owned his own tools and his field or shop and had – or believed he had – a reasonable chance of economic survival. The French Revolution, by destroying the feudal remnants and the old seigneurial system, presented (or appeared to present) two alternative possibilities for social advance: the one through an extension of small-scale production, now rid of the feudal encumbrances of the past; and the other, equally favoured by this surgical operation, by a rapid expansion, in industry, commerce and agriculture, along capitalist lines. Faced with the choice, most of the revolutionaries of 1789, decidedly bourgeois as they were in their habits of thinking, opted for the latter course and many of them gave it a good start by buying up "national properties" (*biens nationaux*) as they came onto the market through the expropriation of Church lands and the properties of *émigré* nobles: this new capitalist-speculative world, thus opened up, was one in which Danton and men like Cambon and Boissy d'Anglas (two of the great survivors of Thermidor) felt thoroughly at home. But this was not Robespierre's world, nor was the society to whose evolution it looked forward one to which he wished to contribute. On the contrary, he pinned his hopes on the other course that he believed it would be possible for the Revolution to follow: to give a stimulus to the small and "middling" independent producer and to keep the development of large-scale enterprise in check. In brief, the society that he hoped the Revolution would help to bring about was one that closely resembled the ideal that he had inherited from Rousseau: "a society of petty producers, each owning a piece of land, a small workshop, or a store, enough to feed his family, and exchanging his produce directly for that of his neighbours";[20] and one, moreover, in which each man's independence would be further assured by the enactment of wise and equitable laws. It was a social ideal that many craftsmen and shopkeepers and small peasant proprietors could readily share with him and helps to explain the popularity that he so long enjoyed among the tradesmen of the "middling sort", who flocked to hear him at the Jacobin Club, and among the petty craftsmen and shopkeepers of the Parisian *sans-culottes*. It also helps to explain why he found it so congenial to spend the three most active years of his life as a member of the Duplay household in the Rue Saint-Honoré. Maurice Duplay was a carpenter of some substance who employed thirty or forty workers of his own. So he was by no means a poor man, not even a *sans-culotte*; and he does not appear to have been on terms of easy social intimacy with the men he employed. But, with his few thousand *livres* a year, his style of living was a modest one, similar to that enjoyed by Robespierre himself; and he, his wife and three daughters represented that degree of comfort, independence and respectability that was fairly typical of the "middling" tradesman of his day.

This, then, was the social *milieu* in which Robespierre chose to live and the social mould in which his ideas on the future "just society" developed. Within these perspectives, the small independent producer and the brash up-and-coming man of affairs – the *capitaliste* or *agioteur*, who was willing to make a "fast buck" at his neighbour's expense, were both social phenomena evident for all to see; Robespierre was drawn to the one and repelled by the other. But there was also a third social phenomenon which largely escaped his notice: the wage-earner or "proletarian", who, in this transitional, "pre-industrial" society, had no recognizable status of his own. To the revolutionaries of 1789 wage-earners did not form a separate or identifiable category: the *ouvrier* was a man who worked with his hands, whether employed by another or not; and when, early in the Revolution, a return was made to the Commune of the number of work-people in every undertaking in Paris, it was done not to distinguish workers from their employers but to establish how great was the need to print *assignats* of small dimensions for the payment of wages.[21] Wage-labour was, in fact, considered – particularly by those who pinned their hopes on the small producer – to be not a permanent but a transitory phenomenon which, while it lasted, tied the worker to his master's apron-strings and denied him his independence and a home and property of his own. Such a status was, therefore, a demeaning one or (at best) a regrettable necessity; and men who were exposed to it were believed to be easily misled, to be likely tools of aristocracy, and to be lacking in the natural "virtue" of the free and independent craftsman. Robespierre, like Marat and Saint-Just and other democrats, broadly shared these views.[22] It is, therefore, not really surprising that he should, like the great majority of his colleagues at the time, have failed to grasp the far-reaching implications of Le Chapelier's law of June 1791, which denied workers the right to combine for higher wages. To him it was largely a question of one group of citizens (a rather unworthy one at that) attempting to usurp a share of sovereignty that was more than their due. For, if wage-labour was a transitory phenomenon and wage-earners were men who were all too easily exposed to "corruption", why should they be allowed the privilege, already denied to others, of forming *corporations* of particular-interest groups which ran strictly counter to Rousseau's teaching on the General Will?

Robespierre, in fact, while a champion of the *menu peuple* who was easily moved to sympathy for the condition of the poor, was oblivious to the existence of a *question ouvrière* and failed to recognize that the wage-earners had any particular problems of their own. It is true that he urged, in his draft Declaration of April 1793, that the State should guarantee a man the right to work, or to subsistence if he could not find it; but this was an attempt to assure to *all* citizens, and not specifically to wage-earners, the right to survive. Nor, on the negative side, does he ever appear to have adopted as drastic an attitude to striking workers as Collot d'Herbois – to take an example from one of the more "advanced" of the democrats – who, in his

Almanach du Père Gérard, a widely circulated publication of 1792, argued that refusal to work was a kind of theft and therefore to be punished as a crime against the State.[23] He rarely intervened on such matters – certainly not in public – during his term of office; but, as a member of the great Committee and one who, within it, was vitally concerned with the recruitment of labour for war production, he must bear his share of responsibility for the numerous *arrêtés* that it issued regulating wages and working conditions and enforcing a rigorous labour code in the Government's own workshops.

The Committee was, naturally enough, concerned to see that the Maximum law, which governed both prices and wages, was reasonably well respected and we should hardly expect it to have conspired with the workers to take such opportunities as were offered to push up their wages in defiance of its own legislation. However, the boot was generally on the other foot, as, in the departments covering the greater part of France, local employers frequently sat on the District committees whose job it was to see that the law was enforced; and they were unlikely to allow workers the better share of the bargain by pegging prices and allowing wages to rise. In fact, it was more usual for the opposite to happen: while the authorities fixed wages in compliance with the law, they were apt to turn a blind eye in the case of prices. In consequence, the proceedings of the Committee for this period are full of complaints from one side or the other of breaches of the law; and it is remarkable how rarely its members, though insisting on the rigorous application of the law, intervened to protect the workers against their employers.[24]

In Paris, the situation was different, as the Commune, which was responsible for applying the law outside the government workshops, was, until their removal in late March 1794, in the hands of Hébert and his lieutenants. As long as they remained in charge, the opposite happened to what happened in the provinces: the law governing prices was fairly rigidly enforced while that governing wages was totally ignored. In consequence, wages rose well above their permissible level: on occasion, to six times that of 1790 where prices, allowed to rise by 50 per cent, doubled at most. So the Committee reacted vigorously, but not until the old Hébertist Commune had, after Hébert's arrest and execution, been thoroughly purged. At first, it set the pace in the workshops coming under its own jurisdiction, tightening up the labour code and placing a firm ceiling on wages; and, next, through the Commune which now acted as its obedient instrument, it fought a series of actions with workers, from both the private and the public sector, who, as price-controls became relaxed in March, went on strike for higher wages. On one occasion, Hanriot, the commander of the National Guard and a devoted supporter of Robespierre, denounced striking port-workers as "egoists" who were exploiting the situation to feather their own nests at the expense of "poor housewives" and *sans-culottes*. Other workers were threatened with the Le Chapelier law, denounced by Barère as counter-revolutionaries, or sent before the Revolutionary Tribunal. And, finally, on 23 July, the Commune decided to apply the law in its full rigour and published new rates of wages which would, overnight, have reduced the earnings of many by one-half or more. It was lawful enough, but an act of incredible folly or miscalculation nonetheless, as the moment chosen was one when the political battle within the Committee was reaching its peak; and there seems little doubt that the estrangement of a large part of the wage-earners (who, in Paris, accounted for nearly half the city's population) contributed to the comparative ease with which Robespierre was overthrown a few days later.[25]

Let us return once more to Robespierre's views on property, as he expounded them in his speeches of December 1792 and April 1793; these, too, were attuned to his social ideal of a community of small and independent producers. "The right of property," he had said, "is limited . . . by the obligation to respect the property of others." Therefore, it cannot be an absolute, inalienable right permitting the unrestrained exploitation of the nation's resources and the unlimited promotion of the interests of the rich while the interests of "ordinary men" are injured or neglected. For "property carries moral responsibilities" and obligations, and it is for the State to define the limits within which it may be safely and justly exercised. Small properties, in fact, and the interests of the small consumers, must be protected against the depredations of "capitalists, profiteers, speculators and tyrants". And he takes the example of food which, "being necessary for man's existence, is as sacred as life itself" and must, therefore, at times of shortage, be subject to such exceptional measures as will ensure that it is available to all: "It is only the surplus that is private property and can be safely left to individual commercial enterprise." Thus private property must be kept within such bounds as correspond to the nation's needs.

But where was the line to be drawn? This was Robespierre's recurring dilemma, as it was that of every revolutionary democrat who wished to create a more egalitarian society. For not only the rich, but the small producer wanted to sell his goods freely on the open market; and if a shortage occurred and prices rose above a certain level, how to reconcile his interests with those of the small consumer? To restrict the free operation of the market by enforcing controls might injure the one but prove advantageous to the other. When faced with this problem – as he frequently was – Robespierre, for all his devotion to principle, was inclined to play it by ear; but, if compelled to make a choice, he was generally more inclined to favour the small shopkeeper and producer than the small consumer. In the provincial riots of 1792, he was able to evade the issue, as small producers were hardly involved and it was possible to direct the limited measures he proposed against "hoarders and speculators" and the larger dealers. In the grocery riots in Paris, however, the problem was a very different one; for now not only the shops of the large wholesalers ("the counting houses of the Rue des Lombards") came under attack, but those of the small and "middling" retailers as well; and this may have largely accounted for his downright condemnation of the rioters' activities and his willingness to believe, with little evidence to support him, that they had been fomented by counter-revolutionary intrigue. It accounts, too, in large measure, for his unwavering hostility to Jacques Roux and the Enragés. The Enragés, in Paris at least, made a special point of defending the interests of the small consumers. In March 1793, Roux urged the Convention to maintain a regular supply of "the essential provisions of foodstuffs to which men have a legal right from the moment they see the light"; and his associate, Jean Varlet, repeated in his journal, *L'Ami du peuple*, that "all men have an equal right to food and to all the products of the land which are indispensably necessary to preserve their existence".[26] So far, they were merely echoing views that Robespierre himself had expressed in the National Convention a few months before. But the remedies proposed were by no means the same: the Enragés were the first, as we have seen, to demand a general control of prices; they were strongly suspected of having instigated the grocery riots in February 1793; and, in June, Roux presented a petition to the Assembly, charging the new Constitution with a failure to provide for firm measures against hoarders. At this point, Robespierre opened his attack and, from then on, gave them no quarter. He had Roux expelled from the Cordeliers Club and denounced him and his partner Leclerc for usurping the name of Marat's famous journal and for preaching "extravagant doctrines". Roux he described as a priest whose main claim to fame was that he had wished to have merchants and shopkeepers massacred "for charging exorbitant prices"; and he had him arrested and thrown into prison, where he died in October of that year.[27]

The agitation over food prices that broke out in early September faced Robespierre with the same problem of how and where to draw the line between the honest merchant or farmer and the hoarder or speculator, or *sangsue du peuple*. Speaking in the Jacobin Club on the day the riots began, he was inclined to blame the disturbances on a handful of "intriguers", in foreign pay, who were misleading the people with false talk of a pending famine: the inference was that, as in February, the patriots and honest merchants would be the victims and the hoarders and profiteers would go unscathed.[28] Two weeks later, we find him rejecting a proposal by Collot d'Herbois, who had recently joined the Committee, to include among officially declared "suspects" all merchants who sold necessities at "exorbitant prices" on the grounds that the law proposed was a general one and that each case must be considered on its particular merits; otherwise the large merchant, with means of corruption at his disposal, might go untouched while the "poor" merchant suffered.[29] The example serves to illustrate how strong was his resistance, to the very last moment, to a general law like that of the Maximum, which, of course, when it passed through the Assembly only a week after, imposed controls on all merchants and shopkeepers, whether large or small, and faced them with fines and imprisonment (or, in extreme cases, with the guillotine) if they broke the law.

But it was only a temporary concession, wrung from the reluctant Jacobins, as we have seen, by the insistence of the small consumers and the compelling needs of war; and both Billaud and Saint-Just admitted as much when the immediate crisis was past. So, for a few months, the small consumers benefited – in Paris, at least, the wage-earners rather more than the rest; while the merchants and farmers (except those, perhaps, who had been compensated by an effective control of wages) felt they were being made to pay the price. The result was a prolonged tug-of-war between producers and consumers, in the course of which the small merchant and shopkeeper eventually passed on to the small consumer the higher prices they were being illegally charged by the larger merchant and producer. Thus a wedge was driven between the merchants and shopkeepers and their customers, the *sans-culottes*, who complained bitterly of the evasion of the law and called on the authorities to intervene by a more effective use of the organs of repression. So the Government, faced with the choice of intensifying the Terror in favour of the small consumer or of relaxing controls in favour of the merchants, whose support was essential for the conduct of the war, chose the latter course. "We had," said Barère, "to revive trade, not to throttle it";[30] and, late in March, an amended Maximum was published, which provided for higher prices and profit margins and, a police agent wrote, seemed "to favour the merchants and not the people".[31]

Meanwhile, Hébert and his associates had stepped into the breach long vacated by the Enragés and, in support of the small consumers, called for sterner measures to be taken against all merchants and shopkeepers. Robespierre, in interpreting their agitation in the Jacobins on 16 March, reported that Hébert had said that "all trade was a form of despotism, that where there was trade there could be no liberty; so trade was a crime and, in consequence, it was impossible to provision Paris and other large cities".[32] It was, no doubt, an exaggeration; but the charge of having conspired to starve the people by an indiscriminate attack on the whole trading community was one, among others, that brought Hébert to the scaffold a few days later.

I have devoted some space to this matter of food supplies because it illuminates Robespierre's views on property and defines and delimits them far better than mere quotations from his speeches. Moreover, it serves to show that he was never a socialist either in theory or performance. Yet some historians have insisted that he was and, in support of this opinion, have pointed to his speeches on property and food supplies in 1792 and 1793: Maurice Deslandres, for example, has written that the articles on property he wished to see added to the Declaration of Rights were "the first manifestation in any French Assembly of a kind of Socialism".[33] Others, more plausibly perhaps, have pointed to the Maximum law and the partially directed war economy of the Year II. But to argue in this way is like arguing that the govermments of the Western Powers were socialist in their conduct of the two World Wars. To be a socialist one must, presumably, believe both in State ownership and in a redistribution of wealth; and Robespierre, as we have seen, though he would not allow unrestricted private enterprise, approached all forms of control – let alone public ownership – with the greatest caution and only accepted them as an ultimate resort. As for plans for an equal distribution of property (what the revolutionaries called the *loi agraire* or "agrarian law"), he strongly disapproved of them and at best, dismissed them as a chimera or visionary's dream. On this point his views were quite explicit on the two occasions when he broached it. On the first, when commenting on Dolivier's petition following the Simoneau affair in June 1792, he described the *loi agraire* as "an absurd bogey created by rogues to frighten fools"; and he added: "as if the defenders of liberty were idiots, capable of conceiving of a project that was both dangerous, unjust and impracticable; as if they could fail to realize that an equality of possessions is fundamentally impossible in civil society, that *it must necessarily be based on community*, which is *still more obviously an extravagant fantasy* in a country like ours; as if there were a single man, *endowed with any skill or ambition*, whose *personal interest* would not be injured by an extravagant plan of this kind".[34] He returned to the subject, in almost identical terms, in his speech on property in April 1793: "You must know that the agrarian law, of which there has been so much talk, is a bogey created by rogues to frighten fools. I can hardly believe it took a revolution to teach the world that extreme disparities of wealth lie at the root of many ills and crimes, but we are not less conscious that the realization of an equality of possessions is a visionary's dream." [35]

It could hardly have been otherwise with Robespierre's own vision of the new society, based on small independent producers, that he hoped to see emerge from the Revolution. He was right to see that, in his day, the "agrarian law" was a chimera or a visionary's dream, which could not possibly win the support of the small peasants or *sans-culottes*, whose social outlook was rooted in small-scale private production and who aspired to own small properties of their own. But what he failed to understand was that his own social ideal, though it was shared by the small peasants and urban proprietors, was also impossible of realization, as it flew in the face of the social and economic realities of the time, which were gradually transforming France into a capitalist country based on capitalist productive relationships and one in which the small producer would enjoy no particular protection and would have to take his chance with the rest. The Revolution had appeared to Robespierre to offer an alternative solution; but it proved, for all his attempts to re-chart the course, to be an illusion. Some of his fellow-deputies whose "corruption" he despised – the Boissys, the Cambons and Talliens – saw the point and proved, in this respect at least, to be more perceptive than he was.

PART IV

The Practitioner of Revolution

Chapter 1

THE POLITICIAN

So far, in discussing the role that Robespierre played in the Revolution, we have been mainly concerned with his philosophical and political ideas: his ideas on the State, religion and society – and how these affected his reaction to events and, after his rise to power, his conduct of affairs. We have given less attention to his tactical handling of problems as they arose, to his qualities as a politician and as a practitioner of revolution. On this point, his critics, as so often in matters relating to his career, have tended to divide into two camps. The more frequent charge has been that he was no politician at all – that he was an unpractical dreamer with his head in the clouds, who lived in a world of abstract speculation and whose reflections on religion, the State and society seldom came down to earth. This view of him, as we have noted more than once already, has been held by admirers and detractors alike. Among his detractors, we have seen that P. Lanfrey, a follower of Taine, wrote him off as a hopeless pedant who never departed, in his political thinking or conduct of affairs, from the strict letter of the *Social Contract*; while J. M. Thompson, who had a high regard for his other talents, believed that he was "at once too visionary, too narrow-minded, and a man of too little worldly experience or tact to be a statesman".[1] On the other side of the fence, there have been those – and they included the Hébertists in his own day and both socialists and conservatives since – who have held that, on the contrary, his much-vaunted devotion to principle was far too easily abandoned when it appeared to promote a political advantage, and they have pointed to such "inconsistencies" as his conflicting views on capital punishment, his ambivalence about the monarchy and war and peace, his adoption of an authoritarian form of government, and his readiness to desert old friends and allies like Danton or the Parisian *sans-culottes*. In short, they have argued that, like any shallow opportunist, he was all too prone to trim his ideological sails to meet each new political wind. In this chapter, it is proposed not so much to enter directly into this debate as to discuss how and why he adapted his ideas to meet new political situations as they arose.

Let us begin with one of the most important problems he had to face, the transition from a monarchy to a republic. Robespierre, as we have mentioned briefly before, was never a Republican *on principle* in the sense of believing that a republic was by its very nature to be preferred to a monarchy; to that extent, he may deserve the charge of having been a *républicin du lendemain*. It would, however, be entirely misleading to argue that by becoming a Republican in August 1792 he abandoned principles held and cherished only a few months before. The point is that with Robespierre the question of opting for a republican as opposed to a monarchical system of government was never a matter of principle at all. The basic principle, to which he remained unswervingly attached, was the sovereignty of the people whose exercise might be favoured, according to circumstances, as well by the one as by the other. But, of course, it was for the politician to study those circumstances as they arose and to decide which system accorded best with that sovereignty and its exercise at any particular time. During the first stage of the Revolution, there is little doubt which system he favoured. "Can it be suggested," he asked rhetorically in an impassioned speech in the Jacobin Club on 10 April 1791, "that I should wish to overthrow the monarchy? As if I were so foolish as to wish to destroy the type of government that best accords with the interests of a great people and can best ensure its rights and prosperity; as if I were more jealous of the government of Poland than of that of Russia or Venice? . . . It is not the King that I fear; it is not the office of king that may prove our undoing; it is the constant tendency to increase the arbitrary power in the hands of the Ministers." [2]

This confidence in monarchy – as long as the King appeared content to remain a *commis*, or agent, of the General Will – was shaken by the royal flight to Varennes in June 1791. For now the King had betrayed his trust and, in the Jacobins, on the night of 21 June, he called for his removal from office. But he had not become a Republican yet; and when the Assembly, having temporarily suspended Louis from office, decided to reinstate him and declared both his office and person inviolable, Robespierre protested but refused to commit himself to one system in preference to the other. "I have been accused of being a Republican," he declared on 13 July; "I am honoured, but I am not one. If I had been accused of being a monarchist, I should have felt dishonoured; but I am not that either." In fact, the terms "monarchy" and "republic" were still "vague and meaningless terms . . . which do not define the particular nature of a government". And, to lend further point to his case, he went on to declare that any free and independent state, with a sense of national pride, may term itself a republic; yet a nation may be free and yet have a monarch: in fact, "the present French constitution is a republic with a monarch; it is therefore neither a monarchy nor a republic . . . it is both at the same time". But he believed that the matter should be referred to the primary assemblies and whether the King should be retained in office or be compelled to resign was for the people to decide.[3]

So there appeared to be two clear alternative courses open: to follow the Assembly's decision to forgive and forget and allow the King to be reinstated in office; or to let the primary assemblies decide the matter for themselves. But it was not so simple; and when, on 15 July, the Jacobin Club decided to draw up a petition, Robespierre reluctantly agreed. The confusion became further compounded when the Jacobin petition, as drafted by Laclos, the novelist, clearly opened the way to a Regency by the King's cousin, the Duc d'Orléans: "to replace the King *by all possible constitutional means*". At this point, the Jacobins' rival, the Cordeliers Club, and its affiliated societies took alarm and produced an alternative petition of their own, which called, quite simply, for abdication and the Republic and a supporting demonstration in the Champ de Mars. Robespierre now changed his mind: the Jacobin petition, couched in such terms, was an Orleanist (and Brissotin) trap; and the Cordeliers' Republican alternative was little better, as it was a dangerous diversion which, under the circumstances of a divided opposition, would play into the hands of an Assembly with all the means of repression at its command. So he persuaded the Jacobins to withdraw their petition; and the Cordeliers, whom he failed to convince, went ahead on their own. The result was the bloody episode, known as the "massacre" of the Champs de Mars, in which fifty citizens, mainly *sans-culottes*, fell under the bullets and sabres of Lafayette's National Guard.[4]

When war broke out, the early defeats and suspected treachery in high places brought the monarchy into further disrepute; and the Republican movement, after a prolonged lull, revived. But Robespierre remained unconvinced. The call for a republic, he declared in a speech on 17 May, was both an irrelevance and a diversion, and a course that had little hope of success. And he added, in a direct allusion to Lafayette, whom he suspected of plotting a military dictatorship: "I would rather see a popular representative assembly and free and respected citizens governed by a king than see a people enslaved and repressed under the yoke of an aristocratic Senate and a dictator. I have no more love for Cromwell than I have for Charles I"; and, returning to the doubts he had expressed a year before, he asked, "Is it in the words *republic* and *monarchy* that we shall find the solution to the main problems of our society?"[5] And even as late as the end of July, when the Republican movement was almost within reach of victory, he still warned against merely substituting one form of government for another. On 29 July, he called for the King's removal or suspension from office; but this was not enough by itself, for if the existing Legislative Assembly remained what would have been gained? For "despotism is still despotism whether it has one head or seven hundred"; and he was horrified at the thought of "an unlimited authority placed in the hands of a great assembly set above the laws, even if it were an assembly composed of sages". Three days later, he defined more precisely what he had in mind: to convene a "national convention" by the direct vote of the primary assemblies from which members of the two preceding parliaments should be debarred.[6]

So the overthrow of the King, which occurred a few days later, was followed, according to Robespierre's precept, not only by the substitution of one form of executive power for another but, through a democratic suffrage, by a considerable extension of the people's authority as well. To Robespierre, in fact, the two were inextricably related: the Republic, which, through military defeats and Louis' treachery, had now become inevitable, would be a hollow victory without a new type of parliament elected by popular ballot and thus more responsive to the popular will. Thus, for the first time, the terms Republic and Democracy went hand in hand: as he told the Convention in February 1794, the two words "democratic" and "republican" government "are synonymous in spite of the abuses of the vulgar tongue".[7] It was a new conception of republic which had little to do with what he had in mind when he had treated it as being almost an irrelevance; and it was the actual experience of revolution that had posed new priorities and brought about the change.

A similar concern for political reality underlay his changing attitude to war and peace. In May 1790, the Constituent Assembly had declared: "The French nation renounces the undertaking of any war with a view to making conquests, and it will never use its forces against the liberty of any people"; and this "no-conquests" formula found its place in the Constitution of 1791. At that stage, a general declaration of the kind was acceptable to all; and, couched as it was, it was, of course, of no embarrassment to Brissot when, in October of that year, he began to bang the drums in favour of an armed crusade of the peoples against their rulers. And Robespierre, as we have seen, was at first attracted by the idea and made a speech in the Jacobin Club in which he threatened the Emperor with a "people's war". But, soon after, he changed his mind, having become convinced that war at this point, whether a war of liberation or any other, would be a disaster and that to provoke it, as Brissot was attempting to do, could only play into the hands of the Revolution's enemies at home and abroad. So, to counter Brissot's arguments, he entered into that long debate which took the form of half-a-dozen speeches made to the Jacobin Club in the winter of 1791-2. The second, and perhaps the most important, of these speeches was one he gave on 18 December. He began by making it amply clear that he was little more of a pacifist than Brissot himself: war, though an evil, might be a *necessary* evil if it could serve to promote the "patriot" cause. "I, too, want war," he declared, "but in a way demanded by the national interest: let us first destroy our enemies within and then march against the enemy without, if any still remains." And he continued: "The Court and the Ministry want war and the execution of the plan they propose to you. The nation will accept the war if it is the necessary price of liberty; but it wants, if possible, both liberty and peace and it rejects any plan for war whose object might be to destroy liberty and the Constitution, even if it is put forward under the pretext of defending them. What is the war that we are faced with? Is it a war of one nation against other nations or of one king against other kings? No: it is a war of the enemies of the French Revolution against that revolution. Are the most numerous, the most dangerous, of these enemies at Coblenz? No: they are in our own midst. Is it [not] reasonable to fear that we might find some of them in the Court and in the Ministry itself?" Moreover, war would strengthen the government and increase the authority of the military command [he already has Lafayette in mind]: "War is always the first object of a powerful government which wishes to increase its power . . . It is in time of war that the executive power displays the most redoubtable energy and that it wields a sort of dictatorship most ominous to a nascent liberty; it is in time of war that a people neglects all discussion concerning its civil and political rights in order to devote itself entirely to external matters and that it withdraws its attention from its lawgivers and magistrates in order to focus all its aims and hopes on its generals and ministers, or rather on the generals and ministers of the executive power . . . In times of factionalism and trouble, army leaders become the arbiters of their country's destiny and tip the balance in favour of the party of their choice." This, however, he continued, "is not the argument employed by those, eager to embark on war, who appear to look upon it as the source of every good, for it is far easier to yield to enthusiasm than to consult the oracle of reason. Thus one already sees the tricolour flag planted on the palaces of emperors, sultans, popes and kings . . . [while] others assure us that no sooner have we made war than we shall see every throne crumble simultaneously before us. For myself, having seen the slow progress of liberty in France, I confess I cannot yet believe in the liberty of people besotted and enslaved by despotism . . . No one loves armed missionaries; and the first advice nature and caution teach us is to repel them as enemies . . . I believe as ardently as any man in the miracles that may be achieved by the courage of a great people which bestirs itself to conquer the freedom of the world; but when I consider the actual circumstances in which we find ourselves, when in place of the people I see the Court and the servants of the Court, when I hear all this prating of universal freedom by men corrupted by the rottenness of Courts, men who, in their own countries, never cease to slander and persecute her; then I demand that one should at least stop to reflect on a matter of such importance." And he concluded: "This is not the moment to declare war. Before all else, this is a moment to manufacture arms, in every place and at every hour; to arm the National Guard; to arm the people, if only with pikes; to adopt severe measures, and not such as have been adopted up to now, so that it will not be left to ministers to neglect with impunity what the security of the State demands: to uphold the dignity of the people and to defend its too long neglected rights. It is the moment to pay faithful attention to our financial resources . . . it is the moment to punish the guilty ministers and to persist in our determination to repress the seditious clergy." [8]

He returned to this theme and repeated these and similar arguments in the speeches that followed. In the Jacobins he probably had the better of the debate and his words were met with thunderous applause; but elsewhere – even among the militants of the Paris clubs and sections – Brissot's arguments were well received and Robespierre's popularity declined. It declined further when he continued his attack on the nature and conduct of the war in the face of the emotions aroused by the first military defeats; and, in May, when he launched the *Défenseur de la Constitution* to state his case, he found himself with few political friends. But, as defeat was followed by crisis and the conviction of treachery at Court, Robespierre appeared to be vindicated and was restored to popular favour; and, as we know, he was able to play a vital part in the overthrow of the King in the summer of 1792.

In September and October, the Republic won its first victories at Valmy and Jemappes; but Robespierre continued to sound the alarm. Now what he feared most was a military dictatorship, a danger that victory conjured up no less menacingly than defeat. Moreover, Jemappes, by opening the road to Belgium, invited further military adventures as well; and, responding to the new opportunities thus offered, the Girondins, as heirs to Brissot, called for the war of liberation to be further pursued among France's neighbours. They were supported by the clubs of foreign "patriots" established in Paris, whose spokesman was Anacharsis Cloots; and, under this combined pressure, the Convention adopted two decrees in November and December 1792, which placed the newly "liberated" territories under French military occupation and prepared the way for extending France's own "natural frontiers" and for the creation of like-minded "sister republics" beyond.

Robespierre opposed each of these measures in turn, believing that they opened up prospects of unlimited war; and, in their place, he argued the need to respect existing treaties and the rights of small nations and neutrals: the most that France should promise to the "patriots" across her borders was to assist a revolution that was already under way and not import one of their own from outside. His caution is reflected in the four clauses on war and peace which he tried, unsuccessfully, to persuade the Convention to accept in April 1793. The first read: "Men of all countries are brothers, and the different peoples ought to help one another according to their ability, like citizens of a single state"; and others went on to abjure wars of conquests and to denounce kings and tyrants as "slaves in rebellion against the human race". It was clearly a challenge to Brissot's expansionist aims; and it was probably also intended, as J. M. Thompson has put it, "to take the wind out of Cloots's sails".[9] Yet, unlike Danton, he was not proposing that the revolutionary war should be brought to an end; on the contrary, as far as the "tyrants" were concerned, it must be prosecuted with all the means at the Republic's disposal.

It was a similar policy of friendship towards the people but of "war-to-victory" against "tyranny" that he presented to the Convention on the Committee's behalf on 27th Brumaire (17 November 1793). It took the form of an eloquent plea for friendship and cooperation between France and "non-allied" countries with histories and interests somewhat similar to her own, such as Switzerland and the United States of America. The Convention accepted his report and took a number of decisions, of which the first two read as follows:

"I. The National Convention declares, in the name of the French People, that the constant resolution of the Republic is to appear terrible to her enemies, generous to her allies and just to all peoples.

II. The treaties that bind the French People to the United States
of America and to the Swiss Cantons shall be faithfully
observed."[10]

But, long before this, since the previous spring, the Republic had
been driven back from the Low Countries and the Rhineland and
was, once more, facing foreign invasion and a defensive war. So,
for a year or more, the question of expansion through "liberation"
could be one for the future alone; moreover, the Girondins, the
main advocates of expansion, had by now been driven from the
Assembly and their leaders sent to the scaffold. In the following
spring, however, the Republic's fortunes revived and when her
armies entered Catalonia in April, Robespierre's policies and those
of his critics could, once more, be put to the test. The Committee, in
this instance, decided on a compromise: while rejecting a proposal to
annex the province outright, it adopted a plan for turning it into
an independent republic under French "protection". Meanwhile,
Cloots' plan – which was also the Commune's – for a universal war
of liberation had been abandoned; all foreigners, even foreign
"patriots" fell under suspicion; and Cloots himself, implicated in
a so-called "foreign plot" (*complot de l'étranger*), went to the
guillotine.

Fleurus followed three months later and, once more, put expansion on the order of the day. For the last time, Robespierre sounded
the alarm; and, in addressing the Assembly on the day before his
fall, he issued the warning: "Victory serves merely to give arms to
ambition, to lull patriotism to sleep, to arouse false pride and, with
its glittering hands, to dig the grave of the Republic. What does it
avail us that our armies drive before them the armed satellites of the
kings if we recoil before the vices that destroy our public liberty?
What does it avail us to conquer the kings if we are conquered by the
vices that lead to tyranny?"[11] It was an argument he had used
against Brissot nearly three years before: war, whether it leads to
victory or defeat, carries within it the seeds of a threat to liberty. It
was not a plea for the rejection of war as an evil in itself; but war
was an instrument of policy to be judiciously handled and whose
conduct could not safely be left in the hands of the personally ambitious or "corrupt". In this sense, victory might present a greater

danger than defeat. Once more, in the scale of values, it was the interest of the Revolution that was paramount; all other considerations must be subordinated to that.[12]

He brought similar political considerations to bear in his attitude to capital punishment. There is perhaps no issue on which he appears to have changed his mind so sharply as between his total rejection of the death penalty when the matter came up for debate in the Constituent Assembly, and the initiative he took in bringing the King to trial and execution in December 1792; and, we might add, the role that he played, in the Year II, as the leading exponent and practitioner of the Terror. In his first speech on the question, on 30 May 1791, he reveals himself as a man of the Enlightenment, a student of Beccaria's *Of Crimes and Punishments*, to whom capital punishment is utterly repugnant on both moral and philosophical grounds. Yet, even here, he appeals not only to a moral absolute but also to what best serves society and the State. This dual concern is apparent in his opening words: "I have come," he said, "to beg the legislators to efface from our penal code the bloody laws that sanction *judicial murder*, laws which are repugnant to the Frenchmen's way of life and to their new constitution. I wish to prove to them: first, that the death penalty is *fundamentally unjust*; secondly, that it is *not the most effective of penalties* and that far from preventing crimes it increases them." Then, having cited chapter and verse to prove his point, he ended with the peroration:

"The legislator's first duty is to form and to preserve public morality, which is the source of all liberty and of all social well-being. When, in pursuit of a particular goal, he departs from this basic and general aim, he commits the most vulgar and the most disastrous of errors.

"The laws must, therefore, always afford peoples the purest model of reason and justice. If for the august severity and the moderate calm that should distinguish them they substitute anger and vengeance; if they shed human blood that they have the power to prevent and that they have no right to shed at all; if they display before the people scenes of cruelty and corpses bruised by torture, then they pervert in the citizens' minds all idea of what is just and unjust, and they give rise within society to terrible prejudices which engender others in their turn. Man is no longer so sacred a concern, his dignity is rated of lesser worth when public authority sets little store by his life. The idea of murder inspires far less terror when the law itself sets the example of it for all to see. Horror of crime diminishes when its only punishment is by another crime. Beware of confusing the efficacy of punishment with its excessive severity: the one is fundamentally opposed to the other. Moderate laws win the support of all; savage laws provoke a general conspiracy." [13]

But, of course, the social-utility argument admits of no absolutes and must, by implication, leave the door open to the exceptional case. There were no such cases, in Robespierre's view, in the early summer of 1791: capital punishment was a barbarous survival from a "despotic" past and it needed to be rejected with all the greater vigour because its typical victims were not the powerful and rich, but the ordinary common-law offenders whose physical destruction could not, under any foreseeable circumstances, be of any advantage to society and the State. But, with the King's treachery and over-throw the following year, the situation had radically changed: first, Louis was no ordinary criminal but a ruler on whom the people had, by their insurrection, already passed judgment; and, secondly, his death, under these conditions, would, far from being injurious to the State, be essential for the Republic's survival. But it would still be an exception to a general principle that remained unchanged. As he told the Convention on 3 December 1792:

"For myself, I abhor the penalty of death that your laws so liberally impose, and I have neither love nor hatred for the King; it is only crime that I hate. I demanded the abolition of the death penalty in the Assembly that you still call the Constituent Assembly; and it is not my fault if the first principles of reason appeared to that Assembly to be moral and political heresies. But if you never thought to invoke them on behalf of so many wretches whose crimes are not so much theirs as those of the government, what prompts you now to remember them in order to plead the cause of the greatest of all criminals? You ask for an exception to the penalty of death for the one man in whose case it would be justified! Yes, *the death penalty in general is a crime, and for this one reason: that, according to the indestructible laws of nature, it can be justified only in cases where it is necessary for the security of the person or the State.* Now public security never warrants that it be invoked in respect of ordinary common-law offences, because society can always prevent them by other means and render the culprit harmless to injure further. But when a king is dethroned in the midst of a revolution whose laws are still in the making, a king whose very name draws the scourge of war on to a nation in tumult, neither prison nor exile can destroy the influence that his existence continues to exert on the public welfare; and *this cruel exception to the ordinary laws* that justice prescribes can be imputed only to the nature of his crimes. It is with regret that I utter this baneful truth . . . But Louis must die in order that our country may live." [14]

The Terror, of course, was something else. It was not just an extension of the "ordinary laws" under which Louis, as "a cruel exception", was sent to his death. Now the government itself, as he stated in his speech of December 1793, had become "exceptional", and both the Revolutionary Tribunal and the justice it meted out were "exceptional", too. So the principle by which the death penalty was to be generally condemned had, like the Constitution itself, been put into cold storage. For, far from being considered a barbarous relic from the past, it was now to become a constant weapon in the Republic's armoury; as terror, once the monopoly of despotism, was now to be wielded by democracy as well. But for what purpose? Not to strike down the common-law offender (here the principle remained unchanged), but to impose "swift, severe and inflexible justice" on all the enemies of the people, now no longer a small handful, as in the summer of 1792, but a growing number of "assassins", "intriguers" and "traitors" to the Republic's cause. In his report on 25 December, he briefly expounded the new principle: "To good citizens revolutionary government owes the full protection of the State; to the enemies of the people it owes only death." [15] Six weeks later, he elaborated it as follows:

"Society affords protection only to peaceful citizens: *in the Republic there are no citizens other than Republicans.* Royalists and conspirators are, to her, strangers, or rather they are enemies. Is not the terrible war that liberty wages against tyranny indivisible? Is not the enemy within the ally of the enemy without? The assassins that rend the country from within; the intriguers that buy the conscience of the people's mandatories; the traitors that sell it; the mercenary scribblers hired to discredit the people's cause, to kill republican virtue, to stoke the fires of civil discord and to prepare the way for political counter-revolution through the corruption of morals; are these people less guilty or less dangerous than the tyrants they serve?" Yet terror must not be an open-ended instrument for the settling of old scores; it must be tempered with "virtue" – and mercy for those who have simply been led astray: "Therefore, I say, cursed is the man who dares to inflict on the people the terror that is intended for the people's enemies! Cursed is the man who, mistaking the un-avoidable errors of which even the best of citizens are guilty for the calculated errors of villainy or for the crimes of conspirators, pursues the peaceful citizen while leaving the dangerous intriguer to go free!" [16] In practice, this led him to call for the speeding-up of the leisurely procedures of the Revolutionary Tribunal to deal with the "dangerous intriguers", while he showed a far greater indulgence than many of his colleagues for those whom he thought to have been merely misled. A case in point is the contrast between his handling of the law of 22nd Prairial and his consistent opposition to taking stern measures against the 73 rank-and-file Girondin deputies who had protested against the expulsion of their leaders from the Assembly in June 1793.[17] (In fact, they survived to join in the general chorus of denunciation of the "tyrant" after Thermidor.)

Another quality of Robespierre's as a revolutionary politician was his sense of timing, his concern to choose the right moment for marshalling his forces in order to carry through policies once they had been generally agreed. The importance he attached to this "tactical leadership" (as later revolutionaries have termed it) is another feature of his long speech of 17th Pluviôse (5 February 1794). "I may add," he told the deputies, "that I have no wish to justify excess. The most sacred of principles may be abused, and it is a measure of the wisdom of government that it *should take careful note of circumstance, seize the right moment* and *choose the means*, for the manner of preparation of great deeds is an essential part of the ability to see them through, just as wisdom itself is a part of virtue." [18] To take careful note of circumstance, seize the right moment and choose the means: these were, in fact, qualities that marked his political conduct as surely as violent response, vigour of expression and impetuosity marked Marat's. It explains why he was so admirably cast to be a man of government as well as of opposition, which

Marat, even if he had been given the opportunity, so patently was not. It explains, too, why the two men found it hard to get on and why Marat, after the first long interview they had together, wrote of him "that he combined the intelligence of the wise legislator with the integrity of the man of honour and the zeal of the true patriot; but that he *lacked both the vision and the audacity* of the statesman".[19]

We have already noted this element of caution – this lack of "audacity" – in his handling of the Champ de Mars affair ten months before this interview took place: it sprang inevitably from his concern to take careful note of circumstance and avoid precipitate action as long as the democrats' flanks were dangerously exposed.[20] We shall find a similar preoccupation with the choice of the moment and the means in the part he successively played in the overthrow of the monarchy, the expulsion of the Girondin deputies and the destruction of the factions in the early months of 1794.

The armed attack on the Tuileries and the King's surrender have so often been presented as an inevitable and premeditated act that it might seem that the whole affair was a foregone conclusion which it only needed a few bold spirits – Marat, Santerre and the Marseillais battalions – to see it through. It might seem so; yet it was not so at all. Even after the two *faubourgs* had invaded the Tuileries, in a preliminary dress-rehearsal, on 20 June; even after the Marseillais and the other federal volunteers had come to Paris for the 14 July celebration and been fêted by the radical and Republican groups; and even after the more militant sections had begun to call for the King's removal (as they had already done a year before); even after all these preliminaries, a successful assault on the Tuileries was not inevitable at all. The King still held too many trump-cards in his hand: as witness the stream of resolutions that poured in to the Palace pledging provincial support; the offensive being taken against "patriots" by the "loyalists" in Paris; and the defection of the Girondins who, after leading the campaign for the King's suspension, drew back in support of monarchy in mid-July. So the objective, though desirable, was fraught with problems which it was wise for responsible leaders to take account of before committing their troops to the affray.

No one was more aware of these problems than Robespierre and, with characteristic caution, he waited for a favourable moment to

strike. He had, as early as 11 July (that is, before the Jacobins took
over the direction of events from the Gironde), posed the question
of an insurrection and even suggested a tentative date; and, soon
after, he was in touch with Marat, who had for some time been
calling for an armed uprising which the majority of the Paris sections
were likely to support. Moreover, as we have seen, Robespierre
called for the King's abdication in the Jacobins on the 29th. Yet, a
full week later, on 7 August, he appears to have been visited by
Pétion, an old friend but now committed to the Girondin cause; and
it may be that even then he was prepared to play a mediating role
between the Assembly's majority and the Republican groups, if
only to avert an immediate confrontation. But, the next day, there
was a new and unwelcome development when the Legislative
Assembly took a decisive turn to the Right by deciding, by a large
majority, to reject a proposal to arrest Lafayette and bring him to
justice; and, on the 9th, Robespierre wrote to Couthon, who was out
of Paris, that the die was cast and that the "final act in the constitutional drama" was likely to be played that night. On the next
morning, as the Marseillais and the battalions of the Parisian National
Guard were storming the Tuileries, Robespierre (like Marat and
Danton) was not to be seen; but this does not mean, as Vergniaud,
the Girondin leader and one of his principal critics, later averred,
that he was hiding in a cellar. And that evening, as we have seen, he
joined the Revolutionary Commune in the City Hall and played a
major part in guiding its operations in the weeks that followed.[21]

Robespierre has so often been called a legalist, a man always
over-anxious to resort to constitutional means, that it is perhaps
worth adding here as an appendix to his role in August the speech
he made in the Convention in November to justify his conduct and
that of the Revolutionary Commune in whose "illegal" activities
he had become so deeply involved. "Why don't you," he asked his
Girondin accusers, "why don't you set up a commission to receive
the complaints of the aristocratic and royalist writers? Why don't
you reproach us for having dispatched all the conspirators to the gates
of the city? Why don't you reproach us for having disarmed all
suspects, for having driven out of our meetings, in which we were
considering measures of public safety, the known enemies of the
Revolution? . . . For all these things were illegal, as illegal as the

Revolution, as the overthrow of the throne and the Bastille, as illegal as liberty itself! Citizens, *did you want a revolution without a revolution* . . . Who can determine, after the event, the precise point at which the flood of popular insurrection should have stopped?" [22]

He showed a similar concern to choose the right moment and the right means when the question arose of expelling the Girondins, or "disloyal" deputies (*les députés infidèles*, or *corrompus*), in the late winter and spring of 1793. The proposal was first put forward in a petition from the patriotic societies of Nîmes and Marseilles, which demanded the recall of all those deputies who, two months before, had voted for a popular referendum (*l'appel au peuple*) to determine the fate of the King. In the Jacobin Club, where the matter came up for discussion at the end of February, Robespierre applauded the petitioners' sentiments but believed the moment to be badly chosen for the action proposed: for one thing, it would prove a dangerous diversion at a time when France had just entered the war with England. [23] But, soon after, the demand for expulsion gained momentum when it was taken up by the Paris sections and clubs, many of whom called for a popular insurrection to impeach Roland, the Minister of the Interior, and purge the Assembly of the Girondin leaders. The Enragés, as ever responsive to popular demand, had already been drawing large crowds at the gates of the Assembly and provoked an abortive uprising on 10 March. But, at this stage, it had little chance of success as it encountered the resolute opposition of the Faubourg Saint-Antoine, the Commune and the Jacobin leaders.

For, guided by Robespierre, the Mountain and Jacobin leaders, although they approved of the objective, were in no immediate hurry to act. They were already reaching the point of an open breach with their Girondin opponents and were perfectly willing, provided the moment were favourable, to harness the popular movement to their own political ends. But they had no intention whatever of allowing its direction to fall into the wrong hands – either to the Enragés or to Hébert, whose influence was steadily increasing in the Cordeliers Club and the Paris Commune. Besides, they feared that a premature rising would entail too drastic a purge of the Convention, whose Rump would be powerless to resist the economic demands of the *sans-culottes*; that it would be accompanied by a new outbreak of prison massacres and leave Paris dangerously exposed to the hostility of the provinces, where the Gironde could count on a considerable body of support.[24] So it was important to pin-point the target more exactly and point the accusing finger not at the "corrupt" or "disloyal" deputies in general, but at the leaders whose removal could be more safely carried through, while still leaving the Jacobins with a majority in a purged Assembly. Robespierre, no doubt, had this in mind when, in the Jacobins on 3 April, he insisted that the majority of the *députés infidèles* were "nothing but a stupid flock of sheep who had been carried away by the eloquence of their leaders"; and it was against these, and against these alone, that action should be taken.[25]

By this time, it appears that, after a month's hesitation, the moment and the means had been decided. For, two days later, Augustin Robespierre chose the rostrum of the Jacobin Club to invite the sections to present themselves at the bar of the Convention and "compel us to arrest the 'disloyal deputies'". The response was almost immediate: on 8 April, a deputation of the Bon Conseil Section called on the Convention to bring to justice the best-known Girondin leaders, including Vergniaud, Guadet and Buzot; and, the day before, the Section of the Halle au Blé had begun to circulate an address, couched in more comprehensive and militant terms, which castigated the majority of deputies as "corrupt" and demanded that criminal proceedings be opened against the most guilty. On the 10th, Robespierre carried the attack into the Convention and drew up a formidable list of charges against his Girondin opponents: specifically, he named Brissot, Guadet, Vergniaud, Roland and Gensonné and hinted at several more. But the Halle au Blé petition still had to be dealt with; and, in the Jacobins that evening, he pledged his support to the action demanded provided the target was more precisely defined.[26] Eventual agreement was reached by the naming of twenty-two (later they became twenty-nine). Thus both parties were satisfied: the sections with the prospect of the purge of a discredited Assembly; and the Jacobins with the knowledge that such an operation, while not so drastic as to be uncomfortable, would assure them of a working majority. And it was around this slogan and on this understanding that the detailed preparation for the May–June insurrection now went ahead. They were given an added impetus by the arrest of Marat, at this time the idol of the Parisian *menu peuple*, and the Girondin attempt to have him condemned by the Revolutionary Tribunal. On 26 May, Robespierre gave the insurrection his formal blessing. "It is," he told the Jacobins, "when all the laws are violated, when despotism is at its height, when good faith and honour are trampled underfoot that the people must rise. That moment has come." [27] He played no direct part in the uprising that followed five days later; but he had, as in the greater uprising of the year before, played an essential part in its preparation, in its timing and in the choice of the means whereby it was carried through.

He applied similar talents to his handling of the bewildering series of events that culminated in the deaths of the associates of Hébert and Danton. The "war on the factions", as we have already seen, threatened the stability and survival of the Revolutionary Government from opposing quarters and lasted from Brumaire (October 1793) to Germinal (April 1794). As we look back on these events, it may seem obvious that a government of the kind, caught between two fires and seeing its authority threatened, should have acted as it did and removed both groups of opponents almost at a single stroke. But to Robespierre and his colleagues, who could only see the crisis unravel stage by stage, it did not seem as simple as all that. So they handled each stage as it arose and the executions of Germinal were only the final act in a six-months' drama.

It began in Brumaire (late October), when Fabre d'Eglantine, a friend of Danton's, who was dabbling illegally in India Company stock, to turn attention away from his own activities denounced (among others) Hérault de Séchelles, a member of the Committee of Public Safety and one-time aristocrat with Hébertist leanings, as an agent of the so-called "foreign plot" (*complot de l'étranger*). Paris was full, at this time, of visitors and refugees from other countries; they included "patriots", like Tom Paine and Anacharsis Cloots, and bankers and men of affairs, like the Englishman Boyd, the Swiss-Prussian Perrégaux, the Belgians Proli and Walckiers, the Spaniard Guzman, the Dutchman Kock, and the Austrian Frey (alias Schoenfeld). Some of these were active in "patriot" clubs, others in business operations (often involving revolutionaries like Danton, Fabre, and Hérault himself); and, at this stage of the war when the air was thick with rumours of Pitt's Gold, all foreigners were suspect. So Robespierre believed Fabre, and Hérault, though a member of the Committee, was put under close observation. And, as the Fabre revelations roughly coincided with the stage in the anti-religious activities of the de-christianizers that was causing the Jacobin leaders the greatest alarm, the first blow against the "factions" was directed against the Left. This took the form of Robespierre's famous speech in the Jacobins on 21 November, when, as we saw, he denounced "de-christianization" as a harmful diversion and one calculated to give comfort to the Revolution's enemies abroad. Such being his conviction, it is not surprising that he should have linked the activities of Hébert and the "de-christianizers" with those believed to be involved in the Foreign Plot; and, at the same session, Proli and Pereyra, a Bordelais Jew, were driven from the Club. Three weeks later, on 12 December, Cloots, who was doubly suspect as having dabbled in both "de-christianization" and relations with "patriots" abroad, was driven out in turn. "Can we," Robespierre asked the Jacobins on this occasion, "can we consider a German baron as a patriot? Can we regard as a *sans-culotte* a man with an income of over 10,000 livres? Can we believe a man to be a Republican who only frequents bankers and the counter-revolutionary enemies of France? No, citizens, let us beware of foreigners who set themselves up to be more patriotic than Frenchmen themselves." [28]

Up to now, the Jacobins' fire had been directed almost exclusively against the Left and the Dantonists, the Government's critics from the Right, had emerged almost unscathed. Yet Danton himself had already returned from his property at Arcis to conduct the Indulgents' operations in Paris, and Camille Desmoulins, his principal lieutenant, had begun to publish *Le vieux Cordelier*, which pleaded for clemency for the many thousands of "suspects" in gaol. Yet preoccupied with the Hébertist opposition, Robespierre at first remained unmoved and was even willing to use the Right against the Left, as when he allowed Vincent and Ronsin, two of Hébert's principal supporters, to be placed under arrest. And, in two speeches he made on 3 and 14 December, he defended Danton and Desmoulins in turn against their accusers. In the first, he described Danton as a patriot who had deserved well of the Republic and was now being slandered by its enemies; and, in the second, he spoke of Desmoulins, with condescending affection, as one who had done the Revolution great service, but was something of a spoilt child and should be more careful in his choice of friends.[29] But the tide was already beginning to turn: Fabre's forgeries of India Company documents came to light on 19 December; and, on the 21st, Collot, the friend of Hébert and Ronsin, returned from his bloody mission to Lyons, began to marshal the Left for a counter-stroke against the Indulgents, and secured the release of Ronsin and Vincent. Under this impact, Robespierre, who feared that the attacks on the Left were losing the Government support among the militants and *sans-culottes*, now changed his tune; and, in his speech of 25 December, he assailed both factions at once. The Revolutionary Government, he said, "must sail between the twin reefs of weakness and temerity, of moderation and exaggeration whose resemblance to energy is like that of dropsy to good health . . . We have to avoid the two abuses, for by one the Republic would be threatened with death from internal dislocation, and by the other it would inevitably perish from failure to adopt energetic measures". Yet, having condemned both factions, he showed clearly where, if he had to choose between them, his sympathies now lay: "If we have to choose between an excess of patriotic zeal and the empty shell of bad citizenship, or the morass of moderation, we will not hesitate. A vigorous body suffering from an overabundance of sap is a richer source of strength than a corpse." [30]

So the main danger was now seen as coming from the Right; all the more as Desmoulins, undeterred by Robespierre's admonitions, had stepped up his campaign against the Government's repressive measures in subsequent issues of *Le vieux Cordelier*. At the Jacobins, on 7 January, when the 4th number was read aloud, Robespierre, while still offering Camille a limited protection, reproached him for giving comfort to the "aristocracy" and proposed that the offending issue should be burned on the floor of the Club; and Desmoulins and Fabre, like Cloots and Proli before them, were expelled a few days later. Moreover, Fabre, as well as Hérault and a mixed bag from both Left and Right, were sent before the Revolutionary Tribunal which was instructed to speed up its work. Thus the pendulum was now swinging strongly – perhaps too strongly – to the Left. Sensing the danger, Robespierre struck a more even balance between the two when he returned to the theme in his report of 17th Pluviôse (5 February 1794). The two factions were, once more, presented as being two sides of the same coin:

"France's enemies from within have divided into two factions, as though they were two army corps. They march under banners of different colours along different roads; but they march towards the same goal. The goal is the disruption of popular government, the ruin of the Convention, in short the triumph of tyranny. One faction drives us towards weakness, the other towards excess. The one has the aim of converting liberty to bacchanalia, the other to prostitution." Both *ultras* and *citras* can, in fact, be given the common label of "false revolutionary": "The false revolutionary is perhaps more often he who falls short of rather than he who goes beyond the sound aims of revolution: he is a moderate or an exaggerated patriot according to the situation at hand"; and with evident allusions to Cloots and Hébert on the one hand and Danton and Desmoulins on the other, he castigated both types of "false revolutionary" in turn as insidious enemies who were both endangering government and leading innocent patriots astray.[31] Yet, this time, the most bitter shafts were reserved for the Left; and, on 8 February, Carrier, a friend of Collot and the Hébertists, was recalled, at Robespierre's instigation, to account for his excesses – the notorious *noyades* – at Nantes.

Two days later, Robespierre fell ill and stayed, on sick-leave, at the Duplays' until 12 March. So he was only kept in close touch with further developments in the month that intervened by his friends on the Committee. The period was marked, in particular, by an intensification of Hébertist activity, not only in pursuing the Dantonists with relentless hostility but, as the food crisis became worse, with bloodthirsty threats against all shopkeepers and merchants. And, as has been argued already, it was against this background of Hébertist agitation – which solicited a sympathetic response in the Paris sections – that the Decrees of Ventôse were submitted to the Convention by Saint-Just on 26 February and adopted on 3 March. So the Left now, once more, moved into the position of Enemy no. 1; and, on 13 March, the day Saint-Just presented his main report to the Convention on "the factions of foreign inspiration and the conspiracy plotted by them in the French Republic", Robespierre appeared at the Club from his sick-bed to denounce Hébert and his associates as the authors of a "new conspiracy" that called for speedy vengeance.[32] The next evening, the Cordeliers Club, the stamping-ground of Ronsin, Vincent and Momoro, all leading Hébertists, reacted sharply to these events, damned Robespierre as an *endormeur* and a lukewarm patriot, threw a black veil over the Declaration of Rights and, with precedents of June and September 1793 in mind, proclaimed a state of insurrection. One solitary section – the Section Marat – responded; but Hébert, Ronsin, Vincent and two others were seized during the night, charged with conspiring to cause famine in Paris, and, for these and other crimes, were executed ten days later.

So it was more or less by chance that the faction of the Left had been the first to be destroyed; but once Hébert and the Cordeliers Club leaders had gone to the guillotine there could be no question of showing mercy to their opponents. It has been argued that such situations have a logic of their own and that a government like that of the Committee of Public Safety could not tolerate opposition from whichever quarter it came. (Had not Saint-Just declared in his indictment of both factions on 13 March that "what constitutes a Republic is the total destruction of all that is opposed to it"?) Yet it was not lógical formulae of the kind that prompted Robespierre and his colleagues to deal as harshly with Danton as they had with Hébert: it was sheer political necessity. It was perhaps not so much the comparatively minor irritations of Desmoulins' propaganda in *Le vieux Cordelier* that tipped the scales – until in his last (and unpublished) number he openly called for peace with England; but Danton's efforts to end the war were proving a serious embarrassment to the Government's military operations. And most important of all: as every move against one or the other of the factions had, ever since November, tended to throw the Committee into the arms of its rival, so the survival of the Dantonists after Hébert's removal would, inevitably, have made the Government a prisoner of the Right. In addition, there were Robespierre's (and Saint-Just's) moral scruples against "corruption", which made it easier for him to turn against Danton (*l'idole pourrie*), as he did in a final denunciation before the Jacobins on 31 March. Fabre d'Eglantine and other *corrompus* had already been rounded up and sent for trial a few days before. With Desmoulins, for whom Robespierre felt a close personal tie, it was another matter; and it may well be that it was only on the insistence of Saint-Just, Collot and Billaud that he was persuaded to overcome his misgivings and append his name, with theirs, to the death-warrant. So Danton and his associates – both Indulgents and *corrompus* – were sent to the guillotine, with Hérault and Fabre, on 5 April (16th Germinal).[33]

We argued, in our first chapter, that there was no inexorable sequence of events that led from Germinal to Thermidor as though Robespierre's own fate was already sealed by what happened to Danton and Hébert: this would, for one thing, reduce the victory of Fleurus to an event of secondary political importance. Yet the end of the "war on the factions" does mark a vitally important turning-point in Robespierre's career as a political leader and politician. With the exception of Mathiez, all the most reputable of his defenders have recognized that, at some stage during these months, his old sureness of touch and sense of political reality appeared to desert him, possibly through disillusionment or, possibly, through sheer physical exhaustion (it has been left to his detractors to opt for a deterioration of character). Massin seems to draw this line somewhere in late April or early May, with his promotion of the Cult of the Supreme Being; and Walter and Lefebvre a few weeks later: they are both severely critical of his handling of the law of 22nd Prairial (10 June). In Massin's view, it was the show-down with the Cordeliers Club in March which, by severing his ties with the *sans-culottes*, was mainly responsible for the change. From then on, he writes, "everything happened as if, despairing of maintaining much longer the coalition between bourgeois Montagnards and *sans-culottes*, he was trying to transcend their antagonism by appealing to a common moral order. The emphasis on abstract virtue is here far more in evidence [Massin is referring to his report on the new Cult on 7 May] than in the report of 17th Pluviôse [5 February]." [34]

Perhaps Massin attributes too much importance to the single factor of the breach with the Cordeliers Club leaders; perhaps, too, he allows his own lack of sympathy with the Cult of the Supreme Being unduly to colour his judgment of the speech of 18th Floréal (7 May). But, whatever the causes, or combination of causes, that brought about the change, the change itself appears to be real enough. The man who appealed to moral absolutes in Floréal, who played into the hands of his enemies by his mishandling of the law of 22nd Prairial and who, in Messidor-Thermidor (July), abandoned the field to his critics on the Committee of Public Safety and retired to his solitary refuge in the Rue Saint-Honoré; that man was no longer the political realist who so adroitly handled the crises of the two previous years.

Chapter 2

THE POPULAR LEADER

In earlier chapters, we have seen that to Robespierre, as a revolutionary democrat, the interests and welfare of the people were matters of continuous concern. These interests, as he saw them, were that they should be assured of their proper share of sovereignty through the exercise of the vote and other rights of citizenship, a share in common happiness (*le bonheur commun*), and the provision of cheap and plentiful bread. To realize such aims was a primary task of the people's mandatories; and to fail to do so would be to neglect a sacred duty, as it would spell the failure of the Revolution itself.

But the French Revolution was not only a political revolution fought out "at the top" by the nation's mandatories in the National Assembly or the "Patriots" of the Jacobin Club. It was also a great social upheaval in which many thousands of common people – the peasants and *sans-culottes* – became involved; and they became involved not merely as passive agents responding to the directions of leaders or as passive recipients of such favours as the revolutionary Assemblies would be willing to hand them. Their involvement in revolution was prompted by, and coloured by, their own social interests and aspirations as well. In consequence, it took the form not only of participation in the great political "events" such as the capture of the Bastille and the assault on the Tuileries, but also of food riots and industrial disputes, and of other activities in which their own particular interests were more directly engaged. In short, they developed a popular movement of their own which sometimes accorded with, and sometimes ran counter to, the wishes and interests of even the most democratic and enlightened of the predominantly middle-class leaders who spoke in the Assemblies and the Cordeliers or Jacobin Club.[1] It is Robespierre's attitude to this movement and the challenges it imposed on him that it is proposed to consider, in rather more detail than we have before, in the chapter that follows.

In doing so, we shall find it convenient to draw a distinction between one type of popular activity and another – between, say, a food riot and an assault on the Bastille or the Tuileries; and also between the period when Robespierre was in opposition and when he was a member of the Revolutionary Government. But it is perhaps best to start by stating one simple principle of his that has some relevance for his attitude towards the popular movement as as a whole: that the people did not always know what was good for it and that it was always (whether in 1789 or in 1794) a duty of the most enlightened of the people's mandatories to help it to find it. He stated this principle very clearly indeed in a speech he made to the Jacobins on 2 January 1792. The occasion was one where he was defending his own conduct against the charge that, by refusing to accept Brissot's arguments in favour of a "people's war", he was belittling the people's capacity to play a decisive and particular role. Having first proudly asserted his claim to have been the only consistent champion of the people's rights in the Constituent Assembly, he went on to say: "The best way to show one's respect for the people is not to lull it to sleep by vaunting its strength and independence, but to defend it by making it aware of its own faults; *for the people has its faults*"; and he cited Rousseau's authority: "The people always wishes the good, but it does not always see it"; and added in words of his own: "The people's mandatories often see the good, but they do not always *wish* it." So there should be a sort of division of labour between the two, whereby the people, with its solid good sense and natural instinct for virtue, would help to keep the mandatories on the straight path of "justice and humanity", while they, in their turn, would keep the people on its guard against the intrigues of their mutual enemies. For the people, being innocent of guile, was easily exposed to the guile of others; as "its natural goodness inclines it to be the dupe of political charlatans who know it and turn it to their own advantage".[2]

Thus popular action, if not guided and directed into proper channels, might all too easily degenerate into licence or be exploited by the Revolution's enemies or false friends. In the early days of the Revolution, when "aristocracy" and "tyranny" were more evident for all to see, this was less likely to happen. In 1789, when one bastion after another fell before the popular onslaught, it was apparent that the danger of diversions was not so great; moreover, in several of these events, as in the siege of the Bastille, the reins were tightly held by the revolutionary leaders or their trusted lieutenants. So the craftsmen of the *faubourg* Saint-Antoine, who "exterminated brigands" on 14 July, were heroes who had performed a signal service in the cause of liberty; and, as we noted before, the lynching of an enemy of the people, like Foullon, while it might be regrettable in itself, could be condoned on the grounds that he had been "sentenced by the people". It was for the same reason that he was also prepared to defend the rioters who, during that week, killed a miller at Saint-Germain, while a farmer at Poissy escaped a similar fate by the skin of his teeth.[3] In the debates that followed the great peasant rebellion of that summer, he had little to say; but he most certainly approved of the destruction of *châteaux* and manorial rolls as a blow against "feudalism"; and when the disturbances revived in the south and south-west in the early months of the following year, Robespierre leapt to the rioters' defence. He refused to call them "brigands" when challenged to do so by deputies of the Right, and he opposed the proposal that troops be sent to suppress them. It was not that he approved of the rioting itself; but he considered that the peasants, under the circumstances, had shown commendable restraint; it would, therefore, be both unjust and inexpedient to reduce them by force; moreover (and this was a characteristic observation), it would be extremely unwise to put arms into the wrong hands. In reporting the last of these debates – on 22 February 1790 – Camille Desmoulins' paper quoted him as saying: "You have seen a great people, which has taken its destiny into its own hands, return to calm and order midst the general collapse of the authorities that have oppressed it for centuries on end ... The people will soon once more submit to the law, and of its own accord, once it has seen that the law will protect it and prove to be to its advantage. Let us not allow armed soldiers to oppress good citizens on the pretext of defending them. Let us not put the fate of the Revolution into the hands of military leaders."[4]

The rural disturbances of 1790 were a comparatively minor interruption of the long period of social peace that attended the deliberations of the Constituent Assembly after its removal to Paris in October 1789. The next popular intervention of any significance was at the Champ de Mars in the summer of 1791. It was, as nearly as any event of its kind ever was, a purely political affair, inspired by the Republicans and democrats of the Jacobins' rival, the Cordeliers Club. Robespierre was, as we have seen, broadly in sympathy with the petitioners' objective: to bring pressure on the Assembly "to replace the executive by other means". Yet he showed extreme caution for reasons we have noted: he feared a trap, baited by the Orleanists or the Feuillant leaders of the Constituent Assembly, and therefore persuaded the Jacobins to withdraw the support they had previously pledged. Moreover, he was not happy that the movement should have fallen into the hands of the Republican groups; and there is no indication that he allowed himself to be involved in any way in defending the many hundreds of democrats and *sans-culottes* from all over Paris who were arrested in the weeks preceding and following the Massacre itself.[5]

His attitude towards the armed insurrections that led, successively, to the overthrow of the King and the expulsion of the Girondins was, as we have seen, of a different order. In both cases, admittedly, he showed great caution and refused to be drawn into precipitate action; and, on the first occasion, he gave no support or approval whatever to the invasion of the Tuileries by the Faubourgs Saint-Antoine and Saint-Marcel on 20 June, for the very sound political reason that it was almost certainly inspired by the rival Girondin group. It was only when the Republican movement came under the direction of the Jacobins themselves, as it did about three weeks later, that he was willing to give the insurrection his blessing, as in his speech to the Jacobins on 29 July. The performance was repeated in the spring and summer of 1793: at first, extreme reluctance to countenance any popular action as long as there was any danger of its being directed by Hébert or the Enragés; then, after careful preparation by the Jacobins, the blessing given in early April to an action that eventually took place at the end of May. In both cases, of course, unlike the Champs de Mars affair, the action itself, when it came to the point, was in safe and reliable Jacobin hands.

However, it was not quite so simple as that. Even the most carefully prepared and directed of popular movements might get out of hand. Here the September Massacres served as a warning and example. Even today, after the patient scholarship of Pierre Caron, who left few stones unturned to arrive at the truth, considerable mystery surrounds their origins and the nature and identity of their participants and promoters.[6] And even though Robespierre was willing to lend them a certain justification after the event (*"Citoyens, vouliez-vous une révolution sans une révolution?"*), it seems extremely unlikely that he had any direct part in their preparation himself: this was not his style at all. But they certainly continued to haunt him and made him doubly cautious of popular movements unless carefully contained and used with the greatest caution and circumspection. So we find him, during the trial of the King, expressing grave concern that the episode, for which he had been more responsible than any other person, should not be allowed to provoke any sort of public commotion, as it might be used by Brissot and others not well-disposed towards the Revolution to discredit the whole affair. "The people," he told the Jacobins in a speech on 23 December, "must remain calm and preserve its dignity"; and even if the Convention decided to postpone Louis' execution, this must be accepted without demur, for "the laws must be obeyed". And it is significant that, in the same speech, he referred back to the Champ de Mars affair, arguing that his caution at the time was doubly justified as the commotion then stirred up by the democrats played into Lafayette's hands; for "two months of calm would have spelled his ruin".[7] He called for calm again in the days following the expulsion of the Girondins. He rejected further measures, proposed by Barère, to consolidate the popular victory of 2 June lest they should serve as a provocation and lead to more disorders at a time when war and civil war were threatening the Revolution from within and without. "All is calm in Paris," he told the Jacobins, "so leave things as they are. What was done in the last revolution has had no disastrous results and no blood has been shed." [8] *The people must remain calm.* Popular commotion, even when promoted to serve the cause of liberty, was a delicate and uncertain instrument that must at all times be handled with caution and discretion.

So popular movements, when geared to radical political solutions, might be viewed with cautious sympathy or even, on occasion, be actively sponsored or encouraged. But it was a different matter, even in the early years of revolution, when the people took matters into their own hands and acted on their own account, either as small consumers in pursuit of lower prices or as wage-earners in support of higher pay, as in the food riots of 1792 and 1793 and the wages movement of 1791. To these Robespierre tended to be unsympathetic or indifferent, at least. To industrial protest movements, in particular; and we do not need to repeat what has been said already about his silent acceptance of the Le Chapelier law in restraint of "coalitions" or his failure to respond, with any sympathy at all, to the claims for higher wages put forward by journeymen carpenters, hatters, locksmiths, farriers, cobblers and others in the summer of 1791. This indifference, or hostility, was shared by other democrats – but not by all. The Cordeliers Club, for instance, put a meeting-hall at the carpenters' disposal; and François Robert, the secretary of one of the Cordeliers' committees, argued their case in his paper, the *Mercure national et étranger*. And Marat, though not generally a wage-earners' champion (he viewed the unemployed workers in the National Workshops with the greatest suspicion as ready tools of aristocracy), on this occasion opened the columns of *L'Ami du peuple* to workers' correspondence and published a violently-worded letter, purporting to represent the views of the building workers employed on the construction of the church of Sainte-Geneviève, in which the contractors were assailed as "vampires" and "ignorant, rapacious and insatiable oppressors".[9] This, again, was not Robespierre's style at all. Yet there appears to have been at least one exception to this attitude of total indifference to workers' particular problems, though it was one in which other, wider, issues had become involved. In early July that year, Camille Desmoulins claimed that he had Robespierre's support for the text of a petition he presented to the Assembly on behalf of the workers in the Bastille workshop for the unemployed whose closure had been ordered. The petition made two demands: first, that subsistence should be seen as a citizen's right; and, second, that the workshops should be maintained from profits made available by the sale of Church lands.[10] Robespierre's sponsorship seems plausible enough, as the reader may remember that he made similar proposals himself on two widely separated occasions.*

In the case of food riots, his attitude was rather more ambivalent and was strongly influenced by the circumstances in which they took place. In 1789, food riots and the peasant destruction of *châteaux* became closely related and were treated in a common context of

*See pages 18 and 149 above

anti-feudal rebellion. (We noted his reaction to the riots at Poissy and Saint-Germain.) We have seen also that he did not condemn the crowd that killed Simoneau at Etampes in March 1792 or the villagers who rioted for cheaper grain and bread in the Orléanais at the end of that year. On the contrary: he chose both occasions to direct his attack against the large wholesalers and merchants for withholding supplies from the market and, in consequence, robbing the people of their basic means of existence. But he does not appear to have responded to food riots with equal indulgence later. The circumstances attending the Paris riots of February 1793, which we have considered before, were admittedly different: it was no longer a question of bread and flour but of sugar and coffee (therefore of "luxuries" that were not "sacred as life itself"), and there were rumours (though ill-founded) of an aristocratic provocation. But Robespierre's comment on them is worth repeating as it draws so neat a distinction between the type of rioting in which the people may (with certain safeguards) legitimately engage and that in which they may not. "When the people rise," he asked contemptuously in the Jacobins, "should they not have an object worthy of themselves? Should they be merely concerned with paltry merchandise? . . . The people, indeed, must rise, but to exterminate brigands"; and later (referring to the revolutionary bastions of Saint-Antoine and Saint-Marcel): "that is the true people of Paris. They cast down tyrants; they do not break into grocers' shops." [11]

A similar failure to understand a genuine popular movement marked Robespierre's response to the small consumers' protest and bread riot in Paris on 4 September of that year, which led to the enactment of the Maximum law a few weeks later. When told of it (he was in the Jacobin Club at the time, a bare mile from its outbreak), he described it as "a plot to starve Paris and to plunge it into blood and despair"; and he added that "trouble-makers and scoundrels have joined the groups at the doors of the bakers' shops" and that he had been told that "Pache [the mayor] is besieged not by the people but by a handful of intriguers who are harassing, insulting and threatening him"; and that Brissot and his accomplices were at the back of it all.[12] And the next day, when Hébert and Chaumette, the leaders of the Commune – and not the long discredited Brissot – escorted the rioters' deputation to the Convention, it was decided, from a long list of proposals, to pay needy *sans-culottes* for attendance at sectional meetings; but also (and this was the rub!) to forbid the old "permanent" sessions and reduce them to two a week. When Varlet, four days later, presented a petition of protest, Robespierre rejected it on the grounds that "permanent" sessions favoured aristocratic intrigue. "Is it not true," he asked, "that, when the sections met *en permanence*, the people did not discuss their own interests? In fact, who were they who were able to devote time to attend the meetings? Were they the labouring and highly respected class of artisans? Were they citizens who work to earn a living? No, they were the rich, the intriguers and *muscadins* [young bourgeois]. The people at most spent two days a week, which they took off from their work, to exercise their right of sovereignty and to ensure their liberties; and when they appeared in the political assemblies, the *muscadins* stayed silent and the aristocracy was reduced to impotence." [13] It was a familiar argument and almost an exact repetition of that used by Marat in a letter to the Convention nearly three months before, and it had a great deal to recommend it. But the outcome – and no doubt the intention – was to subject the sections more easily to government control.

In the notes that he traced in June or July 1793, Robespierre had, as may be remembered, argued the case for a government of "a single will" and, to bring this about, to establish a firm alliance between the Jacobins and the *sans-culottes*: "the people must ally itself with the Convention and the Convention make use of the people". So there was to be a bargain struck that would be of advantage to both: the people under arms (as in the June "days") would assure the Jacobins of their political ascendancy and they, in turn, would educate the people and "give them bread". Broadly, the bargain was carried out in the weeks that followed: the Jacobins secured their majority and their subsequent dictatorship; and the people were rewarded by a long list of social measures ranging from the final abolition of feudal dues and the control of prices to a system of national education and far-reaching plan for social security. But these were, of course, benefits that the Jacobins bestowed on the people "from above". As junior partners in revolution, who had helped their allies to power, they were now expected to play a quiescent role. Apart from the regular military units and the battalions of the National Guard, there was to be no more question of "the people under arms"; and the "sacred right of insurrection", though enshrined in the Constitution of 1793, was, like the Constitution itself, held strictly in abeyance: we saw what happened to the Cordeliers Club leaders when they invoked it in March 1794. Indeed, popular political initiative of any kind became discouraged – far more than it ever was before the Jacobins came to power – as soon as preparations were under foot (as they were in October 1793) for transforming the sketchy project of a government of a "single will" into the reality of the Revolutionary Government of Frimaire. In fact, after the September "events", there were no more popular political *journées* of any kind, whether Jacobin-directed or not, until many months after Robespierre's fall.

In the sense of *journées*, or large-scale street demonstrations, then, we have exhausted the record of Robespierre's relations with the popular movement. But, if, during the period of Jacobin ascendancy, there was little or no public agitation in the markets and streets, there was plenty of activity in the sections and in the Commune of Paris, in which the *sans-culottes* and their representatives, as part of their "bargain" with the Jacobins, became firmly installed in the late summer of 1793. By this time, too, the *sans-culottes*, in addition to filling posts in the lower organs of government, had begun to create political institutions and to formulate political and social programmes of their own; and it is to this part of the popular movement – the most advanced and sophisticated in the history of the Revolution – and to Robespierre's relations with it that we must now devote some attention.[14]

But first we need to consider rather more closely than we have before who the *sans-culottes* were, what they expected from the Revolution, and how they came to play so important a role within it. First of all, we must reiterate that they were not a working class in the modern or nineteenth-century industrial sense of the term, and not even a proletariat in embryo, as Daniel Guérin, a French historian, has made them out to be.[15] In fact, they did not constitute a single social class at all; but rather an amalgam of social groups of petty producers and consumers – of urban craftsmen, small shop-keepers and traders, journeymen, labourers and city poor – who, under the Old Régime, were generally known as the *menu peuple*.

There were obvious differences between them: wage-earners and masters, for example, were in occasional dispute over wages; but, in the social and economic conditions of the times, these tended to be eclipsed by a common concern for the supply of cheap and plentiful bread. In addition, these groups were distinguished from the more elegant and prosperous classes by their speech, by the houses and tenements they lived in, by the taverns they frequented and their style of dress: in fact, it was the use of trousers, instead of the more fashionable knee breeches, that won them, early in the Revolution, the name of *sans-culottes*.

Basically, then, the *sans-culottes* were bound together by social and economic ties – in particular, as small consumers with a common interest in the price of food and in such administrative controls as would keep it in cheap and plentiful supply; and, in addition, they entered the Revolution with a simple political philosophy – a hatred of "aristocracy" – which they shared with the revolutionary bourgeoisie. But, as the Revolution progressed, through their own direct experience and their indoctrination by the middle-class radical groups, they acquired other political interests as well: they demanded the right to vote and a share in that popular sovereignty of which Robespierre and the other democrats so eloquently spoke. They became members of the National Guard and of popular societies and study groups, many of them sponsored by the Cordeliers Club; some of them read papers like Marat's *L'Ami du peuple* and Loustalot's *Révolutions de Paris*; and by the time of the Champ de Mars affair, two years after the Revolution began, they were already a political force to be reckoned with and one that could not be ignored by the parties contending for power. Their importance became the greater when, armed with full rights of citizenship, their presence began to be felt in the Paris sections in the summer of 1792; and, after the expulsion of the Girondins the following year, the moderates and *honnêtes gens* were driven out of the sectional assemblies and it was the *sans-culottes* who took over. In fact, by the late autumn of 1793, they formed the backbone of the local administration; for, by then, their militants dominated not only the assemblies and committees of the majority of the forty-eight sections, but the general assembly and executive council of the Commune itself. The extent to which they did can be seen in figures that emerge from recent scholarly research: these show that no fewer than three in four of the members of the "revolutionary" committees in Paris in the Year II and two in three of the general councillors of the Commune were *sans-culottes*.[16]

By this time, too, the *sans-culottes* had greatly enlarged their horizons and had found their own spokesmen to give them expression. They had realized their primary aim of acquiring cheap (if not always plentiful) bread through the Maximum laws; but their social requirements were no longer confined to the basic necessities of life. They were now also concerned with what Félix Lepeletier, a Jacobin leader, had called *l'égalité des jouissances*, or equality of social benefits: such matters as the right to work or public relief, education for all and the progressive taxation of the rich; and some of these – but not all – had, as we have seen, become part of Government's own programme of reform. But they went further: as small producers and consumers, they were (like Robespierre himself) opposed to the unrestricted exercise and expansion of private industry and commerce. So they demanded not a general sharing-out of property through an "agrarian law" – this would hardly have accorded with the interests of the small owners, or would-be small owners, among them – but a limitation of the size of properties. It was a view that found expression, in its extreme and classic form, in a resolution passed by the Jardin des Plantes Section in Paris on 2 September 1793, which, after demanding a general control of the supply and price of food (a measure not yet conceded), added:

"Let the maximum of wealth be fixed;
Let no individual possess more than this maximum;
Let nobody rent more land than can be tilled with a specific number of ploughs;
Let no citizen own more than one workshop or more than one shop." [17]

It was perhaps not a typical case; but it showed that *sans-culotte* thinking on property rights went far beyond the shadowy limits prescribed by the Declaration of Rights of 1793; and, even, it may be added, beyond those envisaged by Saint-Just in his Ventôse Decrees (March 1794).

In addition, the *sans-culottes*, conscious of their new-found authority and of the positions they had won at the grass-roots of administration, were, by now, formulating political demands of their own which were by no means acceptable to their Jacobin allies and mentors. For one thing, they wanted their sectional meetings to be fully autonomous, without government supervision and control, and that they should remain in "permanent" session instead of being confined, as the Convention had decreed, to two meetings a week. They also claimed the right, through their primary assemblies, to have a preliminary say in all legislative measures, to brief their elected representatives by an "imperative mandate" and to recall, at short notice, any deputies who ignored their constituents' instructions. Moreover, if the Assembly or the Government behaved unjustly or ignored the people's wishes (or, more precisely, the wishes of the people of Paris), they should have both the right and the obligation to stage an insurrection and overthrow the constituted authorities by force. In short, the *sans-culottes* held views on "direct democracy" which owed a great deal to Rousseau, but a great deal more to their own experience and aspirations.

In any event, it is not surprising that such views as these, whether expressed in social or in political terms, should find little favour with the men in authority, even with the most advanced democrats among them such as Robespierre or Saint-Just. In fact, the *sans-culotte* idea of democracy was almost exactly what Robespierre, in his speech of 17th Pluviôse (5 February 1794), said it was not. "Democracy," he then declared, "is not a state in which the people, continuously assembled, directly controls all public affairs; still less is it one in which the people, split into a hundred thousand fragments, decides the fate of society at large by taking isolated, hasty and contradictory measures."[18] Admittedly, his view of the sort of society he hoped would emerge from the Revolution had a great deal in common with theirs; but as a government leader, charged with the responsibility of conducting a protracted war and, therefore, faced with the need to maintain the largest possible degree of national unity, the methods proposed were hardly likely to be commendable. Moreover, such measures as price-control which, to him, were only temporary expedients, were to many *sans-culottes* essential and permanent steps towards a more egalitarian society.

So a clash between them was inevitable, and it was all the more likely to occur after the Revolutionary Government was firmly installed and when the war had reached a critical stage, as in the spring of 1794. Hébert, as we have seen, proved a serious obstacle as he both played up to the *sans-culottes'* egalitarian demands and their claim to local autonomy and acted as a brake on the operation of the wages provisions of the Maximum law. But when Hébert and Chaumette and the Cordeliers Club leaders had been removed, the Government felt free to deal more decisively with partners whose activities had become an embarrassment. The operation, however, was a protracted one and began some six months before. It went back to September 1793, when, as we saw, the meetings of the sectional assemblies were restricted and subjected to closer government control; and it was partly to offset this blow to their independence that the *sans-culottes*, or sectional militants, set up new local societies of their own, the so-called *sociétés sectionnaires* (or *sociétés populaires*). The Government took alarm, all the more so as the new societies were most often established outside the aegis of the parent-Jacobin Club (*"la Société-Mère"*). So the societies were first invited to submit to a rigorous purge. Supporting the measure in the Jacobins on 9 November, Robespierre gave the characteristic warning that the societies had become a refuge for "aristocratic" intrigue. "If [he said] one popular society has been shown to harbour assassins of the Champ de Mars and agents of Lafayette . . . how much greater must be our concern to see 45 sectional clubs established, particularly in those sections which have always had the reputation of having been seduced, corrupted and influenced by the large number of the people's enemies that are found within them." On 26 December, as the purge continued, he sharpened the attack: "These societies," he claimed, "were founded by aristocrats to weaken the attachment of good citizens to the parent-societies [Jacobin clubs]." [19] At this stage, the societies could still redeem themselves by seeking affiliation to the *"Société-Mère"*; but, after the Ventôse crisis, even this avenue was denied them and thirty-nine of them were dissolved between mid-April and late May, while a general proscription followed soon after. The vigilance, or "revolutionary", committees of the sections – another bastion of militant popular democracy – fared little better. When launched in the spring of 1793, they had been elected by the sections' general assemblies. In the autumn, as plans for a revolutionary government began to take shape, they were placed under the (still benevolent) tutelage of the Paris Commune; in the winter, control passed to the Committee of General Security; and, with the Ventôse crisis, they lost all initiative and independence when the senior Committee took over, appointed their members and dictated their policy. The General Council of the Commune suffered a similar fate. Following the execution of Hébert and Chaumette, the Council was drastically purged and several of its members were sent before the Revolutionary Tribunal; Payan, a nominee of Robespierre's, was appointed to the new post of "national agent"; and, under his direction, the Commune became a rubber stamp for the Government's decisions. To fill the gaps left by the purge, new members were appointed without consulting the sections, and the sections themselves were placed under the Commune's direction and forbidden to vote by acclamation or by open ballot. So, by one means or another, the wings of *sans-culotte* democracy had, by the early summer of 1794, been fatally clipped.

Meanwhile, the Revolutionary Government's economic measures had, as we have seen, further estranged the *sans-culottes* as small consumers; and to the wage-earners the *coup de grâce* was given by the Commune's decision to impose a drastic reduction in their rates of pay. The *sans-culottes* and the militants had their revenge, though it hardly turned out to be to their advantage. By refusing to rally in large numbers in support of their former leaders and allies, they undoubtedly contributed to the comparative ease with which the Robespierrist group was overthrown. It would, of course, be absurd to attempt to explain the Thermidorian crisis and its *dénouement* purely – or even largely – in such terms: there were too many other issues and stresses involved. But the disillusionment of the common people was certainly a factor that affected the outcome. Old loyalties, it is true, still lingered on; and, at one time during that fateful night, when Robespierre and his supporters were deliberating in the City Hall, 3,000 National Guardsmen, who had responded to the Commune's summons, were drawn up in the Place de Grève outside, waiting for instructions that never came. So, for lack of leadership and purpose, they gradually melted away and, like the

The Jacobin Club

The members of the former Breton Club began to meet in the old *couvent des Jacobins*, off the Rue Saint-Honoré, in October 1789. The Club was the scene of many of Robespierre's most important speeches, including those he made in reply to Brissot's advocacy of a "revolutionary" war in December 1791–May 1792 (p. 26).

The top picture shows the closing of the Club soon after Robespierre's overthrow in Thermidor (July 1794).

The Tennis Court Oath

On 20 June 1789, the members of the Third Estate, locked out of their usual meeting place, took over a nearby tennis court, where they swore not to disperse until they had given France a constitution (p. 18).

Fifty of the deputies in this picture have been identified, of whom a dozen are

mentioned in this book. Of these, *Bailly* is shown administering the oath, with right arm upraised, in the centre of the picture, with the *Abbé Sieyès* in the centre foreground with a monk and a priest. *Mirabeau* is the squat figure, with face upturned, in the right foreground; *Pétion* is shown next to the seated figure, his left arm outstretched and almost touching Bailly; while *Robespierre* stands between Pétion and Mirabeau with arms clasped to his chest.

Robespierre

Both portraits date from the time of the Convention: the first is by an admirer and the second by a critic. The more unusual portrait is the first, where he is shown to bear a strong resemblance to Danton.

Couthon and Saint-Just

Couthon (from a painting by Ducreux, engraved by Vérité) and Saint-Just (drawn and engraved by Bonneville), Robespierre's closest associates on the Committee of Public Safety, who shared his fate in Thermidor.

The Festival of the Supreme Being

The inaugural ceremony was designed and staged by David in the Champ de Mars on 8 June 1794. Robespierre, as president of the Convention, headed the procession of deputies (shown in the first picture) and gave the official address (p. 125).

Thermidor: the fall of Robespierre

The scene in the Place de Grève outside City Hall, where Robespierre, Couthon, Saint-Just and their colleagues had taken refuge, on the night of the 9th-10th Thermidor (27-28 July 1794). The mounted figures in the left foreground are the two deputies sent by the Convention to read the proclamation of outlawry recently issued against the fallen leaders (p. 52).

Thermidor

Robespierre is shown lying wounded in the ante-chamber of the Committee
of Public Safety after his arrest by Barras in the City Hall.

Thermidor

Two versions of the wounding of Robespierre in the City Hall in the early hours
of 10th Thermidor: the first showing him
being deliberately shot by soldier Merda,
the second being shot (though with Merda's
help) by his own pistol. A third version
(not shown here) is that he attempted to
take his own life as the soldiers burst in
(p. 52).

Thermidor

The execution of Robespierre and his associates in the Place de la Révolution on the morning of 10th Thermidor (28 July), as represented by a hostile witness. Robespierre is shown seated in the middle of the tumbril nearest to the foot of the guillotine, while Couthon's head is being displayed to the crowd.

majority of the sections, who had more decidedly declared for the Convention, left the fallen leader to his fate.

How far this defection of the *sans-culottes* was due to the Government's attacks on the popular political movement and how far to its economic policies is, for lack of precise evidence, a matter of conjecture. But it seems certain that disillusionment with the Maximum was a factor of some importance: in particular in the case of the wage-earners. We know, for example, that, that same afternoon, a large number of workers assembled for a protest meeting outside the City Hall, and it was variously explained by observers that it was "a revolt against the Maximum", that the protesters were about to march on the Convention, and even that they had assassinated Robespierre.[20] Another pointer to popular attitudes is the further report that, two days later, when the councillors of the Commune were, in their turn, being driven to the place of execution, workers (*ouvriers*, as the report says) are said to have shouted as they passed, "*foutu Maximum!*"; while others, in a group of brush-makers, celebrated the occasion of Robespierre's fall with the remark, "*et voilà le Maximum dans le panier!*" (meaning roughly, "that puts paid to the Maximum"), and put in hopefully for a 33 per cent rise in wages.[21] To some small consumers, at least, experience of the Thermidorian "reaction" brought second thoughts and a change in the order of their priorities; and from a later police report we learn that a carpenter by the name of Richer was arrested in the following May for having said: "Under the reign of Robespierre blood flowed but we did not lack bread; today blood no longer flows but we have no bread; so blood must flow again for us to have it."[22] It was perhaps a back-handed compliment but, broadly speaking, the observation was a just one: whatever the Terror had failed to do, it had fulfilled Robespierre's pledge of a year before and given the people bread.

Now, finally, to return to the main theme of our chapter. From the Constituent Assembly onwards, Robespierre was the recognized champion of popular sovereignty and the people's "liberties", rights and aspirations. Moreover, his ideal of a society of small and independent producers corresponded closely to that of the craftsmen and shopkeepers who formed the backbone of the *sans-culottes*; he also shared with them a deep suspicion of commercial capitalism and a hatred of "feudalism" and aristocracy. Therefore, it is not surprising that, as he held such views and voiced them day in and day out from the rostrum of the National Assembly and Jacobin Club, he should have evoked an enthusiastic response among the common people of Paris. So he was, in a real sense of the term, a *popular* leader and, moreover, one whose popularity was quite unique. Yet, while he identified himself so closely with the people's hopes and needs and won their affection and admiration, he remained remote, spoke and dressed in a different style, and was never, in spite of his boast (*"je suis peuple moi-même"*), really one of them. He was, in fact, a leader from outside – from the elevation of the Jacobin Club, the National Assembly or the journalist's desk – who never took part in a demonstration or descended to the level of the market or street. This clearly distinguishes him from Marat, whose popularity at times (as in the spring and summer of 1793) may have eclipsed his own, who wore the trousers of the *sans-culottes*, lived in a garret and was carried shoulder-high by the people (as Robespierre never was) after his release from the Revolutionary Tribunal in April 1793. It distinguishes him, too, from Jacques Roux, the "red priest", who mingled freely with the *sans-culottes* – in their *ateliers* and shops – in his own Section des Gravilliers; from the Cordeliers Club leaders, who made a special point of drawing wage-earners into political discussion and activity in the spring and summer of 1791; and, certainly, from Hébert, who, though no *sans-culotte* himself, affected the popular manner of speech in his *Père Duchesne*, which, in the later months of 1793, probably had the largest circulation of any paper in France.

Moreover, as Robespierre tended to see the people from outside, he had a corresponding tendency to know what was best for them without being over-concerned to enquire what they had to say about it themselves. For, as we have seen, the people "has its faults"; above all, the fault of allowing itself to have the wool pulled too freely over its eyes by the "aristocracy" and those masquerading as its own best friends. Such being his view, he was naturally wary of allowing a free rein to popular movements or popular activity, unless these were rigorously circumscribed and channelled to achieve goals prescribed for them by the people's trusted mandatories or the patriots of the Jacobin Club.

This suspicion of independent popular activity naturally became the greater with the problems arising from war and political crisis in the early months of 1794; and it led to an inevitable confrontation with the *sans-culottes*, who, by this time, had acquired a programme and a degree of independence incompatible with the needs of a revolutionary government charged with the conduct of a revolutionary war. And the real tragedy – and irony – of Thermidor was that two of the contenders – the Jacobins and *sans-culottes* – fell together; and that those who survived and reaped the rewards were the moneyed men who had done well out of the Revolution, the up-and-coming commercial bourgeoisie, who were the enemy of both.

Chapter 3
THE REVOLUTIONARY LEADER

The most important question still remains. What were Robespierre's qualities as a revolutionary leader – his strengths and his short-comings – and how do these compare with those of other leaders of the Revolution of 1789 and, in a wider context, with those of leaders of other revolutions both before and since his day?

Having posed the question, "Where did his greatness lie?" J. M. Thompson answers, in a phrase that sounds remarkably like Michelet, "In the thoroughness with which he embodied the main ideas and experiences of the Revolution, from the enthusiastic liberalism of 1789, through the democratic aspirations of 1792, to the disciplined disillusionment of 1794".[1] As far as it goes, this judgment is likely to be fairly widely acceptable today. If the test of a man's greatness is to be the impact he makes on the events of his time, then no other figure can seriously challenge Robespierre's reputation as the outstanding leader to emerge from the Revolutionary years before the advent of Napoleon. At times, it is true, there have been other contenders put forward to dispute the title. In the first year of the Revolution, none had the prominence and prestige of Mirabeau, the great tribune of 1789 and the leading spokesman against aristocracy and privilege in the first National Assembly; but the impact he made was shortlived and he died, almost totally discredited, in April 1791. Marat, perhaps more than any other of the Revolution's leaders, had the capacity for voicing the moods of the people; he was the great proponent of Revolutionary vigilance and, though he did not live long enough to see it, the real founder of the Terror of 1793. So he acted as a spur and a conscience, but he never stood at the centre of events. Saint-Just, Robespierre's closest companion in the Committee of Public Safety and its youngest member, combined, to a remarkable degree, a capacity for action with cool and logical thought: an arch-exponent of the Terror, whose moral rectitude was as great as that of the Incorruptible himself; but his impact was a brief one, and he lacked those qualities of tactical leadership which Robespierre so evidently possessed.

Carnot can claim a particular distinction as the man whom Napoleon termed the "organizer of victories" of the Republic. And, finally, Danton, who, more than any other leader, was the incarnation of national revolutionary defence in the critical months of August–September 1792, when the Prussians were driving towards Paris, and whose reputation, as we have seen, long eclipsed Robespierre's own in the eyes of posterity as the Revolution's most illustrious son. Yet Danton's reputation has depended too much on rabble-rousing oratory – a quality greatly admired in the early days of the Third Republic; his reputation as the great Corruptible has never recovered from Mathiez' probing enquiries; and today, when other qualities are looked for in leaders of revolution, he appears somewhat of a tarnished hero and a pricked balloon. In short, none of these other contenders can measure up to the test prescribed by J. M. Thompson. None held the Revolutionary stage as long as Robespierre; none left his mark, as he did, on each one of the Revolution's main phases: from its inception in May 1789 to the drama of Thermidor (July 1794); and none other can claim that when he fell from power, the Revolution itself appeared to come to an end.

Yet this judgment, however plausible and however valid as far as it goes, is a somewhat superficial one: it tells us a great deal about Robespierre's capacity for political survival, but comparatively little about his qualities (including his shortcomings) as a leader of revolution. Moreover, if we are to arrive at a judgment of him as a figure in history, we must attempt to set these qualities within a wider perspective than the events of 1789–94 in France alone.

To begin with the *positive* qualities of his leadership. The first point to note is the boldness of his promotion of new ideas and as a strategist of revolution. Though this quality of his has been muddied and confused by later controversy, it was widely accepted at the time and explains why it was nearly always he – with the occasional substitution of Couthon or Saint-Just – who was chosen by his colleagues on the great Committee to present their views to the Convention when important new decisions had to be taken. So it was with the great reports of 17 November 1793 on the conduct of diplomacy and war; on the principles underlying the Revolutionary Government in December 1793 and February 1794; and on the Cult of the Supreme Being on 7 May of the same year. On each of these occasions, he revealed himself not merely as a spokesman for the Committee's collective views but as an innovator who was charting a new course and inviting the National Convention to attune its policies to meet a new strategic situation. The most remarkable of these reports were, as we have suggested more than once already, the two concerned with the principles of revolutionary government. "The theory of revolutionary government," as he told the Assembly on 25 December, "is as new as the Revolution itself." It was no idle boast: Rousseau had laid a broad theoretical foundation with his ideas on popular sovereignty and equality; but for the particular situation in which the Republic found itself in the autumn of 1793 he had provided no recipe at all. Here one is reminded of Lenin, with his genius for adapting the teachings of Marx to the circumstances attending the Russian Revolution of 1917; and, in particular, of his adoption of the Soviet form of government and of the bold experiment of the New Economic Policy following the devastation of war and civil war. These were feats which more doctrinaire, or orthodox, socialists, like the Mensheviks, would have been incapable of accomplishing; in the same way as the Girondins were incapable of adapting themselves to meet new situations in the spring of 1793, whereas the Jacobins proved themselves able to do so a few months later. But Lenin had one considerable advantage over the revolutionary leaders of 1793: although there were no ready-to-hand answers to be read in Marx, he could learn from the Jacobins' experience of 130 years before. Robespierre and his colleagues were not so fortunate; they had no model to fall back on (the Cromwellian example, which they misunderstood, would, in fact, have been of little use to them). So they had to start from scratch and devise a brand-new model of their own. And this model of a "revolutionary and democratic dictatorship", as the Bolsheviks later called it, was precisely the one that Lenin proposed to apply in Russia in 1905 and, again, at an early stage of the Revolution of 1917.[2] It was for this reason – and not because they saw him as a forerunner of socialism – that Russia's new rulers gave Robespierre a monument near the Kremlin soon after they took power.

Another quality that marks Robespierre as a revolutionary leader was the extraordinary persistence and tenacity with which he communicated his ideas. Opinions have varied as to his virtues as a public speaker; and he certainly lacked the oratorical flamboyance of Mirabeau or Danton, or of Lamartine or Ledru-Rollin in the Revolution of 1848. Nor was he a rabble-rouser who chose to address an audience from a chair in the Palais Royal, the balcony of the City Hall or a platform on the Terrasse des Feuillants, like Desmoulins in July 1789 or Jean Varlet, the Enragé, at the time of the still-born insurrection of March 1793. His was a more carefully rehearsed and sedate performance, delivered from the rostrum of the Jacobin Club or the National Assembly. A German visitor to Paris in the early summer of 1794 described his manner as follows: "When he mounts the rostrum, it is not with a studied indifference or exaggerated gravity, nor does he rush upon it like Marat; but he is calm, as though he wished to show from the outset that this is the place which, without challenge, is his by right." The same observer noted his remarkable physical stamina, which made it possible for him, after a month's illness in February and March, to attend almost every session of the Convention as well as being in regular attendance at the Jacobin Club and the Committee of Public Safety.[3] By this time the Revolution had been going on for nearly five years; and, all this time, with few intermissions, he had been making speeches, almost as often as he could catch the President's eye, in both the Jacobins and National Assembly. The volume of his contributions to public debate was, therefore, very considerable indeed. In the Constituent Assembly alone, he is reported as having spoken 68 times in 1789, 125 times in 1790 and, in 1791, no less than 328 times before the Constitution was adopted at the end of September. Meanwhile, he had already spoken on 35 occasions in the Jacobin Club, a number that rose to 100 in the first seven months of 1792 (when he was no longer a member of the Assembly) and to another 144 by the end of the year. It was a remarkable feat of endurance, all the more as, after September, he often spoke in the Jacobins and the Convention on the same day. It was in reference to this stage of his career that Jaurès wrote of him: "What a harsh and exhausting life it was for him to attend a popular assembly, often rowdy and unresponsive, on almost every night of the week to render an account of his day's work."[4] To this must be added a further 300 speeches and observations made during the twenty-two months that he was a member of the National Convention (for twelve of which he belonged to the Committee of Public Safety as well). In all, a staggering total of 900 reported speeches in five years; and this is without taking account of the many nights spent in editing – almost single-handed – the copy of his two papers, the *Défenseur de la Constitution* and the *Lettres à ses commettants*, that followed one after the other between May 1792 and April 1793.[5] When we consider that the public galleries of the Jacobin Club and the revolutionary Assemblies were daily crowded with spectators, we can imagine the total impact made on the Frenchmen of his day by such a volume of words.

Robespierre's persistence in conveying his views to the public was matched by his persistence as a watchdog of revolution and his determination to uproot all relics of the past and build the Republic on entirely new foundations. To him there was no question of the Revolution being safely established once a constitution had been signed or a military victory won. Danton was only too willing to settle down to a peaceful life in the country when he retired from the Committee of Public Safety in July 1793; for him the main battles of the Revolution had been won and it was now time for men of good sense – particularly for those who had acquired a stake in the new society by the purchase of *biens nationaux* – to relax and enjoy its fruits. Robespierre's perspectives were entirely different. He neither accepted Danton's *République des possédants* as a desirable objective, nor did he believe that it had been fully secured. For each stage of the Revolution created new problems and each new problem had to be tackled afresh. Above all, a revolutionary must never lower his guard; once he relaxes, old institutions, old ideas and old habits revive and threaten to engulf the Revolution and to push it back to the point from which it started. So, without continuous vigilance, the Revolution will be lost. He expounded this idea, among so many others, in his speech of February 1794. "The first concern of the legislator," he told the deputies, "must be to strengthen the principles on which the government is founded. Thus, it is your duty to promote or establish all that tends to arouse a love of country, to purify manners, to elevate the spirit and to direct human passions towards the general good. Conversely, you must reject and suppress all that tends to direct these passions towards a love of self or to arouse infatuation with what is petty and contempt for what is great. In the system we have created all that is immoral weakens the body politic, all that corrupts is counter-revolutionary. *Weakness, vice, prejudice are so many sign-posts leading back to monarchy.*" [6] In short, old habits die hard; and, unless vigorous measures are taken to uproot them, they will disrupt and destroy the Revolution from within. In Buonarroti's words (he was writing in 1837): "In the Convention, it fell to Robespierre to combat at once the remnants of royalism, bourgeois greed and the immorality of public men. His constant thought was to reform both manners and the social order by creating institutions that would serve as a base for the majestic edifice of equality and the people's Republic." [7] Here, too, Robespierre takes his place in a long line of revolutionary leaders for whom the revolution can only be won if it is fought for, long after the seizure of power, every inch of the way. Gerrard Winstanley, the spokesman for the Diggers, or True Levellers, of the English Revolution of the seventeenth century, held similar views. "Kingly power," he wrote in one of his tracts, "is like a great spread tree; if you lop off the head or top bough, and let the other branches and root stand, it will grow again and recover fresh strength." [8] It is an idea expressed, in a more directly political form, by Marx when, after the experience of the Paris Commune, he insisted that the new socialist, or proletarian, State could only be built on the ruins of the State power of the bourgeoisie. Lenin returned to the same theme in his *State and Revolution* nearly half a century later; and he elaborated it further, now in an economic guise, with his warnings against the survival, within the emerging socialist State, of "the anarchy of the petty proprietor" and such capitalist remnants as private ownership of goods and freedom of trade. [9] Mao used a similar argument, though again in a different form, when, in launching his Cultural Revolution, he urged the need to uproot the dangerous survivals within the Party and State of bourgeois habits and methods of thought.

Robespierre's insistence on the need for vigilance to protect the Revolution from disruption from within went back, of course, far further than the days of the National Convention. In the Constituent Assembly, as we have seen, he was constantly alerting his colleagues of such dangers, often to their intense irritation and annoyance. But, as Dubois de Crancé, a later enemy and never more than a lukewarm friend, wrote of him: "He was never discomfited by slander or hostile interruption; I have seen him resist the whole Assembly and demand with calm dignity that the President call it to order." [10] A constant refrain of his at that time was the danger that public servants would unlawfully usurp the sovereignty that properly belonged to the people or, by delegation, to their elected representatives. This, too, was a theme that he returned to in his two great speeches on revolutionary government. In the second, he declared that "once the people has set up a representative body and vested it with full authority, it is for this body to watch, punish and control all public servants";[11] and it was, as we have seen, with this object in view that he persuaded the Committee of Public Safety to set up a police department of its own. This, again, was a preoccupation that he shared with other spokesmen for revolution both before and since. One method that Winstanley recommended, over a century before, for uprooting the remnants of "kingly power" was for the wielders of State authority to be kept under constant democratic surveillance.[12] Lenin, too, was continuously exercised, after the Bolshevik seizure of power, by the insidious infiltration by bureaucracy of every nook and cranny of the political machine. "We have now a vast army of government employees," he told the Fourth Congress of the Communist International in 1922, "but lack sufficiently educated forces to exercise real control over them"; and he had previously complained that "our worst internal enemy is the bureaucrat" and that what they had in Russia was not simply a "workers' state", but "a workers' state with bureaucratic distortions".[13] It was an intractable problem and one that neither he nor his successors have ever been able to solve; and, in China, Mao, who was determined to learn from the Soviet example, made the uprooting of bureaucracy within the Party a primary aim of the Cultural Revolution. (With what success it is perhaps still too early to judge.)

Another quality of Robespierre's that we have noted was his capacity for tactical leadership, his responsiveness to new situations as they arose and his concern to choose the right moment for putting decisions into operation and for attack or withdrawal. It is with such considerations in mind that we saw how he handled the Champ de Mars affair, the expulsion of the "disloyal deputies" from the National Convention and the elimination of the warring factions of Hébertists and Indulgents. At the risk of wearying the reader with constant repetition, it is perhaps appropriate, as an example of this quality, to refer once more to his exposure of the disruptive activities of the "de-christianizers" in his speech of February 1794: "To preach atheism is merely another way of absolving superstitition and putting philosophy in the dock; and to declare war on divinity is to create a diversion in favour of monarchy." [14] In short, to make war on religion at this stage of the Revolution was a luxury the revolutionaries could ill afford: it was to lend grist to the enemy's mill by antagonizing the peasants, not to mention such would-be allies as the Belgian Catholics across the Republic's borders. One is reminded of Lenin's strictures against his critics from the Left in *Left-Wing Communism: An Infantile Disorder*. There are also memories of Robespierre's earlier prescription for "choosing the right moment" in Lenin's careful tactical planning and his choice of the appropriate moment for advance or retreat. Referring to the former (as in the autumn of 1917), he wrote: "Never *play* with insurrection, but when beginning firmly realize that you must *go to the end* . . . The defensive is the death of every armed uprising." [15] At other times, like Robespierre, he was equally insistent in advocating a tactic of retreat: as at the time of the Stolypin reforms following the revolution of 1905; during the peace negotiations at Brest-Litovsk; and the decision temporarily to abandon socialist planning in the New Economic Policy of 1921 – a retreat that would (as he explained) make it all the more possible to resume the advance when a more favourable occasion arose. "It is not enough," he wrote at this time, "to be a revolutionary and an adherent of Socialism or a Communist in general. One must be able at each particular moment *to find the particular link in the chain* which one must grasp with all one's might in order to hold the whole chain and to prepare firmly for the transition to the next link. At the present time . . . this link is the revival of internal trade under proper state regulation. Trade – that is the 'link' in the historical chain of events, in the transitional forms of our Socialist construction in 1921–22, which we . . . must grasp with all our might." [16] It was a similar type of argument, though couched in less precise and sophisticated terms, that Robespierre had used, on more than one occasion, to persuade his listeners to alter course over a century before.

Among Robespierre's other qualities, there is one that has been less disputed than any other: his incorruptibility. It is a virtue that many political leaders, both in Robespierre's time and in our own, have found it possible to do without; and its absence has not, in the short-term at least, meant a necessary forfeiture of public esteem. In the French Revolution, we may cite the names of Mirabeau and Danton as obvious examples of widely respected leaders who, when the opportunity arose, did not hesitate to feather their own nests or help themselves from the public till; and, for the present day, the reader will no doubt be able to find examples of his own. Perhaps, however, posterity has been inclined to show more favour to those leaders who have lived relatively simple lives, and have not played too blatantly to the gallery or made personal fortunes from the holding of public office. Robespierre was, quite decidedly, of this latter kind; and it has generally been accounted to his credit. We referred earlier in this book to his refusal to accept financial rewards and to his modest style of life. A year after his death, Babeuf, a one-time critic, wrote that his "goods and chattels" had been sold by the State, in late January 1795, "for the sum of thirty thousand francs in *assignats*, or three hundred francs in coin." [17] This confirms the opinion held of him by William Augustus Miles, who, in reporting back to his superiors in London a few months before "the tyrant's" fall, wrote: "I tell you again, he is beyond the reach of gold. I do not think he could have been bought at any period of the Revolution." [18] And the German visitor to Paris, whose testimony we quoted a few pages back, describes the simplicity of his style of life in the Duplay household when he was still at the height of his popularity in the early summer of that year: "His household is one of extreme simplicity; he has about him only the family of the carpenter in whose house he has lodged since his arrival in Paris . . . In the carpenter's family he is like the son of the house." [19] But incorruptibility in a public figure, as Miles pointed out to his London correspondent, may take other forms as well: not only scrupulous honesty in financial matters and simplicity in one's style of living, but also firm attachment to political principle and indifference to the vagaries of public opinion. On these two counts as well Robespierre may be said to have deserved the reputation he has been given. His attachment to principle was generally applauded; but his political rectitude – and this was a not particularly amiable quality – on occasion bordered on the self-righteous and won him rather more enemies than friends. On the other hand, his refusal to court popularity at times when he believed the public was being misled attests to his moral and political stamina. This was evidently the case in the early months of 1792, when his refusal to follow Brissot in welcoming a war of "liberation" lost him a large part of the following he had built up through his public conduct the year before.

So much for Robespierre's virtues as a revolutionary leader; but what of his shortcomings? These would seem to be evident enough if we were to accept at their face-value all the charges made against him by his successors, or for that matter the verdict of conservative and liberal historians during the century that followed his fall from power. Let us first return briefly to the once familiar charge that he was a *buveur de sang* or a bloodthirsty tyrant devoted to the cult of the guillotine. This would perhaps not, in itself, be a serious indictment of a revolutionary leader who was concerned for the safety of the State, unless it could be shown that his use of terror was carried to excess, that it was *unnecessary* for achieving the purposes intended or, by discrediting the system that was being built, rebounded on the head of the practitioner himself. Was this the case with Robespierre? His Thermidorian successors and critics, who patently had their own axe to grind, obviously thought it was: we have but to read the testimony of men like Fouché and Merlin de Thionville. Merlin wrote of him: "In those days so rotten had the condition of France become that a bloody mountebank without talent or courage, whose name was Robespierre, made every citizen tremble under his tyranny" (he added that history would say little else of "this monster"); while Fouché, more specifically, observed that "he had an unquenchable thirst for the blood of his colleagues".[20] Such an indiscriminate indictment has, of course, not stood the test of time and, soon after, two other contemporaries, Napoleon and Levasseur de la Sarthe, argued that, on the contrary, the critics had been more bloodthirsty than "the tyrant" himself and that Robespierre, far from being an advocate of intensified terror, had been overthrown because he wanted the blood-bath to end. In presenting his case, Levasseur made a careful distinction between the "legal" use of the guillotine against the proved enemies of the State, such as Girondins and Dantonists, and its "illegal" and indiscriminate use against the Lyonais, Bordelais and Nantais and the victims of the Great Terror in Paris: "There is a vast gulf separating these acts of legal vengeance, whose necessity they [the Jacobins] believed to be established, from the bloody holocausts that horrified all France; it is the gulf dividing the legal punishment of crime from the murder of innocent men in the bosom of their families." [21]

It may, in fact, be readily conceded that the charges made by the Thermidorians were not only fantastic and exaggerated but were intended to serve as a smoke-screen to cover up their crimes. Robespierre, as later evidence has shown, was at no time a blood-thirsty maniac, revelling in terror for its own sake, such as Collot and Fouché appear to have been at Lyons, Tallien at Bordeaux and Carrier at Nantes. Moreover, he showed, both by his speeches and by his performances as a member of the great Committee, that he always carefully discriminated between those whom he considered to be active counter-revolutionaries and "intriguers" and those who had merely been "misled". This is clearly the message of that part of his speech of 5 February that deals with Virtue and Terror: "Virtue without which Terror is squalidly repressive; Terror without which Virtue is disarmed." It emerges, too, in the distinction he made in the same speech between "peaceful citizens" (however much inclined to be misled) and "royalists and conspirators": "Indulgence for the royalists, cry some [an obvious allusion to Camille's plea for the release of "suspects"]; mercy for the scoundrels! No, I say! Mercy for the weak, mercy for the unfortunate, mercy for humanity!" And, in his last speech, he made a long indictment of his critics on the Committee of Public Safety for the excesses perpetrated during the Great Terror in Paris: "They are giving the revolutionary government a hateful name in order to destroy it." [22] Further, we have Buonarroti's judgment, which is shared by Levasseur: "Far from demanding, as has been claimed, an end of revolutionary government, he counselled that it be maintained, while insisting that it be purged of the rogues and traitors who had crept into its ranks.

As for the Terror, he wished, while lightening its burden on the people, to make it both more just and more severe in dealing with aristocrats and enemies of civic virtue."[23] This is a balanced judgment which broadly appears to accord with the facts: there was no question, on Robespierre's part, even after the victory at Fleurus, of ending the Revolutionary Government or of dismantling the Terror; but it must be used with discrimination, and with proper attention to legal process, against the "intriguers" and the "corrupt", including a small number of powerful men strongly entrenched within the Convention itself. But some apologists, reacting against the exaggerated charges made by others, have been inclined to carry their white-washing to ludicrous proportions; as with Ernest Hamel in France in the 1860s; while, in England, Bronterre O'Brien, as a "moral-force" Chartist, refused to allow Robespierre any part in the Terror at all. On the contrary, his responsibility for the Terror, even for that of the summer of 1794, was greater than Buonarroti's or Levasseur's judgment would appear to admit. For, with Couthon, he had promoted the law of 22nd Prairial, which whatever the precise intentions of its authors, provided the legal sanction for the very excesses he deplored.

Other common charges made against Robespierre were that he was vindictive and mean to his opponents and over-sensitive on all matters touching his personal dignity. Among historians, Michelet and Aulard have made a great deal of these failings, and even Jaurès reports them with evident disapproval. Some critics among his contemporaries were more charitably inclined. Dubois de Crancé, for example, though he had no great affection for him, referred to his tendency to be stubborn and self-opinionated (as well as being proud and jealous of his reputation) as one of a number of "minor blemishes" that often injured his cause; and Barère, who later repented of the part he played in his overthrow, praised him as "a man of purity and integrity, a true Republican", while still insisting that "it was his vanity, his irascible sensitivity, and his unjust suspicions of his colleagues that were the cause of his downfall".[24] In this case, the charge, even allowing for post-Thermidorian prejudice, seems to be well enough established; yet these were indeed "minor blemishes" that do – or should do – little to affect one's judgment of Robespierre as a revolutionary leader. More important is the criticism that has often been made that he was no activist or mass-leader and that when rapid decisions were called for he allowed legalistic scruples to stand in the way. Such failings may or may not be related, so we will consider them apart. That he was not an activist in any real sense of the term, and more of "a leader by intellect alone" (as John Reed wrote, not quite so appositely, of Lenin in 1917), we have already seen in the previous chapter. Here we may contrast his manner and style with those of a breezy extrovert like Danton, who was ever willing to raise his loud voice on the hustings; a grass-roots activist like Jacques Roux, who wandered freely among his constituents of the Section des Gravilliers to test their opinions first-hand; or Marat, who always had a direct contact with the people and did not have to reach them, indirectly, from the rostrum of a Club or an Assembly. It distinguishes him, too, from Saint-Just, who was both a theorist and a man of action and played a decisive role, as representative with the Army of the Sambre et Meuse, at the battle of Fleurus. In other revolutions, we may contrast him with Blanqui, the great activist of the consecutive workers' rebellions and insurrections of 1839, 1848 and 1870–71; and, in our own day, with leaders of a more "rounded" stature like Mao or Ho Chi Min. The contrast with Lenin, with whom he had much in common in other respects, is here equally striking. Robespierre, as we have seen, played no direct part in the uprisings of 10 August and May–June 1793; whereas Lenin, in October 1917, directed the day-to-day operations of the Bolshevik take-over from the Smolny Institute with almost military precision.[25]

So of Robespierre's personal remoteness from direct action and from direct contact with the crowd there can be no question at all. More questionable, perhaps, is the charge that he allowed action to be paralysed by excessive concern for legal and constitutional procedures. Marat, whose temperament was so different from his own, certainly believed that this was so: this appears clearly enough from his report of their meeting in late 1791 or early 1792. Robespierre then reproached him (so he writes) for having destroyed "the prodigious influence" of his paper "by dipping [his] pen in the blood of the enemies of liberty and by talking of ropes and daggers" against what he presumed was his better judgment. Marat replied that to use "closely reasoned arguments" was not at all his style; and, to prove it, he told him: "If, after the massacre of the Champ de Mars, I could have found 2,000 men filled with the anger that tore my heart, I would have placed myself at their head, stabbed the general* to his death in the midst of his battalions of brigands, burned the despot within his palace, and impaled our odious representatives on their benches, as I told them at the time." He added: "Robespierre listened to me in horror, paled and for a while remained silent." [26]

Marat, it may be remembered, drew from this episode the conclusion that while Robespierre was a "wise legislator", he lacked "the vision and *audacity* of the statesman"; and many historians have followed suit by contrasting his strength as a man of theory with his weakness as a man of action. Frequently, they have cited the example of his hesitation to take a rapid decision on the fatal night of Thermidor to prove their point. This failure to act, even in self-defence, was dictated, it has been argued, by legal scruples: by a refusal to defy the National Convention, the supreme interpreter and executor of the General Will, once it had decided to proscribe him. The argument is plausible enough and there is plenty of circumstantial evidence to support it. We have seen that, at the time of the Champ de Mars affair, he refused to be involved in the Cordeliers Club's petition once the Constituent Assembly had decided to restore the King to office; again, in December 1792, at the time of Louis' trial, he called on the people to keep calm and respect the law, and even to accept a postponement of his execution if the Assembly should so decree; and, once more, in the spring of 1793, he insisted that the expulsion of the Girondins should be limited to little more than a score of leaders. In each case, respect for the dignity of the office of deputy and concern for the integrity of parliament were matters of prime concern, as they most certainly would not have been for Marat; and, on the very eve of the Thermidorian *débâcle*, had he not told the Assembly, when he addressed it for the last time, "As for the National Convention, my first duty, as it is my first inclination, is to show it boundless respect"? [27]

So it would be strange indeed if such a concern did not influence the decision he had to take, only twenty-four hours later, when to make war on the Convention was his only hope of survival. Yet, even so, the argument is not conclusive. On the night of 9th Thermi-

*Lafayette

dor, as in the Champ de Mars affair and the insurrection of May–June 1793, there were other factors involved: we have noted already his bitter disenchantment and physical exhaustion as possible alternative explanations. More generally, this charge of an excessive concern for constitutional proprieties does not accord with the boldness of the decisions he took at other times and in other places. We may remind the reader that it was he who told the Convention that the action taken by the Revolutionary Commune in August and September 1792 was as "illegal" as the Revolution itself; and Alfred Manfred, the Soviet historian, has ample evidence to support his view that the bold, and highly *illegal*, decision to suspend the Constitution and create a "revolutionary" government in the autumn of 1793 was prompted by the urgent necessities of war and civil war and only received its theoretical justification in the months that followed.[28]

Other critics have pointed to Robespierre's ambivalent attitude towards the poorer classes and his failure to come to terms with the social realities of his day. It is true enough, as we noted in earlier chapters, that while a champion of social, as well as political, democracy, he often failed to appreciate the economic problems of the common people, tended to confuse food riots with aristocratic conspiracies and showed a total incomprehension of the wage-earners' basic needs. Moreover, as Dr C. L. R. James, the historian of the "black Jacobins" of San Domingo, has argued, his attitude to the abolition of Negro slavery was less than enthusiastic: he championed the rights of the free men of colour, or mulattoes, but for the black slaves he had little or nothing to say.[29] In addition we have seen how he pinned his hopes on a social ideal impossible of realization: on the survival and continued evolution of a society of small and independent producers, which would be able to keep the expanding forces of industrial and commercial capitalism at bay. It proved, of course, to be an illusion, as Robespierre's Thermidorian successors were only too willing to emphasize; and we have noted how Marx, in his early writings, dismissed the whole notion of the Republic of Virtue as a hopeless anachronism, based on a model drawn from the past and turning its back on the realities of a newly emerging industrial society. And, here again, we may contrast Robespierre's perspectives with Lenin's: where Lenin based his policies on a new and expanding class, the proletarians or industrial workers (even though they formed a small minority in the Russia of his day), Robespierre based his on a large, but declining, class whose hopes of independent survival, let alone of setting the pace for others, proved to be a chimera.

But it is somewhat unreal, and certainly unfair to Robespierre, to attempt to draw up a sort of balance-sheet of virtues and failings without placing them in a more precise historical context. "Great men make history," it has been said, "but only such history as it is possible for them to make. Their freedom of achievement is limited by the necessities of their environment."[30] Seen in this light, Robespierre has as much right as any other historical figure to be judged according to the opportunities offered and the limitations imposed on him by the times in which he lived. As a man who grew up in the pre-industrial society of late eighteenth-century France – a society, moreover, that only through revolution shook off the despotic and semi-feudal institutions of the Old Régime – some choices were evidently open to him, while others equally evidently were not. In the autumn of 1793, for example, he and his Jacobin colleagues had the choice between following the *laissez-faire* policies of the former Girondin majority or of striking out on the new course of revolutionary government with terror to enforce it. They chose the latter course and, as it proved the more fruitful of the two, they thereby "made history". Though later historians appear sometimes to have regretted it, they did not have a further choice to fall back on: that of behaving like English nineteenth-century Liberals in settling their internal political disputes. It was not so much that they had not read John Stuart Mill as that they had no similar parliamentary tradition to guide them. Equally, Robespierre might have chosen differently when he pinned his social and political hopes on the small producers. He could, like Danton, Cambon and others, have put his money on what Babeuf called the Republic of the Rich; or he could opt, as we know he did, for what, under the conditions of the time, still *seemed* to be a viable alternative: the small producer and the Republic of Virtue. It is easy enough now to argue that he thereby doomed himself to failure and should have struck out more boldly and looked to the future and not to the past. The trouble is that, for him, the options were severely circumscribed. It is true enough that his own "petit-bourgeois" upbringing and temperament inclined him to show greater sympathy for small proprietors than for wage-earners or *sans-culottes*; but this was not really the crux of the problem: when it came to the point, he did not have Lenin's option of making a clear choice between a rising industrial bourgeoisie and an emerging proletariat. Neither of these two classes had fully emerged in France in Robespierre's day; and even in England, where the process had gone much further, the main social divisions of the future industrial society were still only faintly discernible. In France, Babeuf, alone of the revolutionaries of 1789, devised a system of equality that had any particular relevance for a future society of "proletarians"; but its promotion was throttled at birth and it is significant that it only evoked a response, among those it was intended to protect, in the early 1830s, when France herself was going through the first stage of an industrial revolution.

This, however, is not the whole story and does not alone account for Robespierre's dilemma and the tragedy of Thermidor. A leader, placed as he was, was not entirely a prisoner of his times, as though every decision taken and every choice made were determined by the compelling pressure of actuality, or by what Saint-Just called *"la force des choses"*. Some choices, as we have seen – and they included some of the most important – were of this kind, while others were not. At what point, then, does the "force of circumstance" cease to be an adequate explanation and personal inclination or an ideological *parti pris* or, for that matter, some psychological "hang-up" from one's past take over? Or how, more exactly, to strike a balance between the two? Let us allow that Robespierre and his colleagues, placed as they were and holding the views that they did in the crucial year 1793, could not resist the pressures of war, civil war, economic crisis and counter-revolution which imposed on them solutions that were inevitable if they wished to remain in power and to keep the Revolution on its course. So, faced with only two alternatives, they had virtually no choice but to act as they did. But there were other occasions in Robespierre's political career where the range of choices was not so circumscribed and the decision to adopt one course rather than another cannot be explained in such terms. Why, for example, did he choose to stay away from the Committee of Public Safety and the Convention during those critical weeks in June and July 1794 and stubbornly refuse to listen to Saint-Just's advice to be a little more accommodating towards his critics on the Committees? This cannot be explained, even in its broadest essentials, in terms of the "force of circumstance" or of basic political or philosophical beliefs. So, inevitably, some element of purely personal choice (or a physical factor like sickness, fatigue or a breakdown in normal responses) must be brought into play to determine why, at that moment, he made that choice and no other. Such matters are of obvious concern to the biographer; but, whatever the explanations put forward, the historian has the right to judge the result rather than the intention; and he can hardly avoid the conclusion that Robespierre's behaviour in the weeks preceding Thermidor was almost unbelievably foolish and, by lending credence to the suspicion that he was engaged in behind-the-scenes intrigues with a cabal of his intimates, played right into the hands of his opponents.

But these, like his vanity and "irascible sensitivity", are relatively minor matters and, in terms of the role he played in history, do little to alter the score. The French Revolution was one of the great landmarks in modern history. No other single event did so much to destroy the aristocratic society and absolutist institutions of Old Europe and to lay the groundwork for the new societies – both bourgeois and socialist – that, on every continent, have risen from their ashes since. To this transformation Robespierre made a signal contribution: not only as the Revolution's outstanding leader at every stage of its most vigorous and creative years; but also as the first great champion of democracy and the people's rights. And this, essentially, is what establishes his claim to greatness.

APPENDICES

GLOSSARY

BIBLIOGRAPHICAL NOTE

NOTES

INDEX

APPENDIX I

Chronology of Main Events in the Revolution and in the Life of Robespierre

Year	The Revolution	Life of ROBESPIERRE
1758		May 6: Birth of ROBESPIERRE at Arras
1765–9		School at Arras
1769–81		At Collège Louis-le-Grand in Paris
1781–9		Lawyer (*avocat*) at Arras
1787	Feb–May: Meetings of Notables; fall of Calonne; Brienne	
	Aug–Sept: Exile & recall of Parliament; riots in Paris	
1788	May: Lamoignon edicts	
	May–Sept: "Aristocratic Revolt"	Aug: First published work: *Appel à la nation artésienne*
	Sept: Recall of Parliament; riots in Paris	
	Dec: Royal Council decrees "doubling" of Third Est	
1789	Feb: Abbé Sieyès' pamphlet, *Qu'est-ce que le tiers état?*	
		April: Elected deputy for Third Estate of Artois
	Apr 27–28: Réveillon riots in Paris	May: Joins Breton Club (later Jacobins)
	May 5: Estates General assemble at Versailles	
		June 6: Criticizes wasteful luxury of Bishops
	June 17: National Assembly declared	
	June 20: Tennis-Court Oath	
	June 23: Royal Session	
	June 27: King orders 1st & 2nd Estates to join 3rd	
	July 12–14: Paris revolution and fall of Bastille	July 17: Accompanies King to Paris
	July–Aug: Peasant revolt and "Great Fear"	

Year	The Revolution	Life of ROBESPIERRE
	Aug 4–11: Decrees abolishing "feudalism" Aug 25: Declaration of Rights of Man & Citizen Oct 5–6: Women's march to Versailles; King returns to Paris Oct 21: Martial Law decreed Nov–Dec: Secularization of Church lands & issue of *assignats* Dec 22: Property qualifications decreed for voters & deputies	Aug 24: Speech in favour of liberty of Press Sept 7: Opposes royal Veto Oct–[July 1791]: Lodges at 30, Rue Saintonge in Paris Oct 21: Opposes Martial Law Oct 22: Opposes exclusion of "passive" citizens from Primary Assemblies Dec 23: Demands civil rights for Jews, actors, Protestants
1790	 June 19: Abolition of nobility and titles July 12: Civil Constitution of the Clergy July 14: Feast of the Federation	*Speeches in Assembly*, Jan–May— Jan: Opposes ban on export of corn Feb: Opposes repressive measures against rioting peasants March: Opposes enclosure of land April: Defends autonomy of Paris Sections May: Opposes King's right to declare war; supports clerical marriage *Speeches*, July–Nov— July: Supports civil rights for Jews Aug–Sept: Defends mutinous troops at Nancy Oct: Supports creation of Supreme Criminal Court Nov: Urges annexation of Avignon
1791	April 2: Death of Mirabeau April 3: Papal Bull condemns clergy's "constitutional" oath April 18: King's aunts stopped visiting St Cloud	*Speeches in Assembly*, April–May— April: Opposes *marc d'argent* qualification for deputies; defends freedom of speech; demands citizen membership of National Guard; defends rebellious Avignonnais

Chronology

Year	The Revolution	Life of ROBESPIERRE
		May: Defends right to petition and freedom of Press; champions free men of colour in Colonies; proposes "self-denying ordinance" for deputies to out-going Assembly; opposes death penalty
	June 14: Le Chapelier law banning workers' organizations	June 10: Elected Public Prosecutor in Paris
	June 20: King's flight to Varennes June–July: Feuillants (Moderates) secede from Jacobins July 17: Massacre of Champ de Mars Aug 27: Declaration of Pillnitz Sept: Avignon annexed to France; constitution of 1791 voted by Assembly	June 21: Calls for deposition of King in Jacobins end July: Moves to Duplays', 366 Rue Saint-Honoré
	Sept 30: Dissolution of Constituent Assembly Oct: Meeting of Legislative Assembly Nov: Pétion elected mayor of Paris	Sept 30: Popular ovation in Paris Oct–Nov: Final – and triumphant – visit to Arras
		Dec 1791–May 1792: *Speeches against war* (in Jacobin Club)
1792	Jan–Feb: Food riots in Paris	*Speeches in Jacobin Club*, Feb–April— Feb: Defends mutinous soldiers of Châteauvieux March: Declares belief in God
	April: English democrats fêted by the Jacobins April 20: Declaration of War against Austria June 13: Dismissal of Girondin Ministers	April: Opposes honour to Simoneau, mayor of Etampes, killed in a food riot May–Aug: Edits *Défenseur de la Constitution*
	June 20: Popular invasion of Tuileries July 20: Brunswick Manifesto	July 29: Calls for deposition of King Aug 1: Calls for election of National Convention

Year	The Revolution	Life of ROBESPIERRE
	Aug 10: King driven from Tuileries Sept 2: Surrender of Verdun Sept 2–6: Prison massacres in Paris Sept 20: Prussian defeat at Valmy Sept 21: Meeting of National Convention Nov 6: Victory of Jemappes Dec 1792–Jan 1793: Trial of Louis XVI	Aug 10: Member, Gen. Council of Revolutionary Commune Sept 5: Elected deputy for Paris to National Convention Oct–April 1793: Edits *Lettres à ses commettants* Dec 2: Speech on regulation of food supplies Dec 3: Calls for execution of King Dec–Jan: Speeches on trial and execution of King
1793	Jan 21: Execution of King Feb 1: Declaration of war on U.K. and Holland Feb 25–26: Food riots in Paris March 10: Attempted popular insurrection in Paris March: Revolt of the Vendée Revolutionary Tribunal April 15–16: Treason of Gen. Dumouriez; Committee of Public Safety set up May: First law of Maximum; revolt at Lyons May 31–June 2: Girondin deputies driven from Convention June 24: Adoption of Constitution of 1793 July 10: Danton removed from Committee of Public Safety July 13: Assassination of Marat July 17: Remaining feudal obligations abolished without compensation	Feb 25, March 1: Condemns food riots in Paris March 10: Calls for strong central government April 10: Denounces Brissot and Girondins April 24: Presents draft of new Declaration of the Rights of Man May 12: Demands arming of *sans-culottes* May 26–31: Speeches against Girondin leaders June 2: Proposes government of "a single will" June 25: Denounces Jacques Roux, the "red priest" July 27: Appointed to Committee of Public Safety July–Aug: Presents Lepeletier's plan for Public Education July 31: Defends first law of Maximum

Year	The Revolution	Life of ROBESPIERRE
	Sept 4–5: Popular insurrection in Paris; law of Suspects; beginning of Terror	Sept 17: Supports restriction of meetings of Sections to two per week and "law of 40 *sous*"
		Sept 18: Defends merchants against Hébertists
	Sept 29: Law of General Maximum, putting a ceiling on food prices and wages	Oct 8: Supports suspension of Constitution of 1793
	Oct 10: Constitution declared suspended until end of war	
	Oct: Lyons revolt suppressed; execution of Marie-Antoinette; "de-christianization" campaign	
	Oct 31: Execution of Girondins	Nov 17: Speech on the conduct of diplomacy and war
		Nov 21: Condemns "atheism" (in Jacobin Club)
	Dec 4: Revolutionary Government established	Dec 6–7: Speech on freedom of worship
		Dec 25: First speech on principles of revolutionary government
1794	Feb 26–March 3: Laws of Ventôse	Feb 5: Second speech on principles of revolutionary government
	March 15: Arrest of Hébertists	Feb 10–March 12: Illness
	March 25: Execution of Hébertists	March 16: Speech condemning Hébertists
	March 30: Arrest of Dantonists	March 31: Speech against Danton Indulgents
	April 5: Execution of Dantonists	April 4, 5: Speeches against Dantonists
		May 7: Speech on Cult of Supreme Being
	June 8: Festival of Supreme Being	June 8: Heads procession at Festival of Supreme Being
	June 10: Law of 22nd Prairial	June 10: Defends law of 22nd Prairial
		June 12: Attacks "intriguers" in Convention
	May–June: Affair of Catherine Théot	June 26: Advocates mercy for Catherine Théot
	June–July: The Great Terror	end June–end July: Absence from Committee of Public Safety

Year	The Revolution	Life of ROBESPIERRE
	June 26: Victory at Fleurus	July 1, 9: Further speeches against "intriguers" (in Jacobin Club) July 16: Opposes "popular banquets"
	July 26–29: Conspiracy and crisis of Thermidor; fall of Robespierre; execution of Robespierrist members of Paris Commune Nov: Jacobin Club closed Dec: Repeal of Maximum laws	July 26: Last speeches in Convention and Jacobin Club July 27, 28: Refused hearing in Convention, arrested and executed

APPENDIX II

The Revolutionary Calendar

The Revolutionary (or Republican) Calendar was in use between 22 September 1793 (1st Vendémiaire of the Year II) and the end of 1805 (11th Nivôse of the Year XIV).

The year was divided into twelve months of thirty days, called after the seasons or seasonal activities, leaving five days ("jours sans-culottides") at the end of the year which were treated as holidays. Each month was further divided into three "weeks" of ten days, called décades, of which the last day, the décadi, took the place of the former Sunday as a day of rest.

In leap-years (1796, 1800, 1804), which do not concern us here, 11th Ventôse corresponded to 29 February and the extra day of the Republican year was "found" by adding a sixth "jour sans-culottide" to the five shown below.

	Sept.–Oct. Vendémiaire	Oct.–Nov. Brumaire	Nov.–Dec. Frimaire	Dec.–Jan. Nivôse	Jan.–Feb. Pluviôse	Feb.–March Ventôse	March–April Germinal	April–May Floréal	May–June Prairial	June–July Messidor	July–Aug. Thermidor	Aug.–Sept. Fructidor	September Jours sans-culottides
1	22	22	21	21	20	19	21	20	20	19	19	18	17
2	23	23	22	22	21	20	22	21	21	20	20	19	18
3	24	24	23	23	22	21	23	22	22	21	21	20	19
4	25	25	24	24	23	22	24	23	23	22	22	21	20
5	26	26	25	25	24	23	25	24	24	23	23	22	21
6	27	27	26	26	25	24	26	25	25	24	24	23	

7	24	7	25	7	25	7	26	7	26	7	27	7	25	7	26	7	27	7	27	7	28	7	28
8	25	8	26	8	26	8	27	8	27	8	28	8	26	8	27	8	28	8	28	8	29	8	29
9	26	9	27	9	27	9	28	9	28	9	29	9	27	9	28	9	29	9	29	9	30	9	30
10	27	10	28	10	28	10	29	10	29	10	30	10	28	10	29	10	30	10	30	10	31	10	1
11	28	11	29	11	29	11	30	11	30	11	31	11	1	11	30	11	31	11	1	11	1	11	2
12	29	12	30	12	30	12	31	12	1	12	1	12	2	12	31	12	1	12	2	12	2	12	3
13	30	13	31	13	1	13	1	13	2	13	2	13	3	13	1	13	2	13	3	13	3	13	4
14	31	14	1	14	2	14	2	14	3	14	3	14	4	14	2	14	3	14	4	14	4	14	5
15	1	15	2	15	3	15	3	15	4	15	4	15	5	15	3	15	4	15	5	15	5	15	6
16	2	16	3	16	4	16	4	16	5	16	5	16	5	16	4	16	5	16	6	16	6	16	7
17	3	17	4	17	5	17	5	17	6	17	6	17	7	17	5	17	6	17	7	17	7	17	8
18	4	18	5	18	6	18	6	18	7	18	7	18	8	18	6	18	7	18	8	18	8	18	9
19	5	19	6	19	7	19	7	19	8	19	8	19	9	19	7	19	8	19	9	19	9	19	10
20	6	20	7	20	8	20	8	20	9	20	9	20	10	20	8	20	9	20	10	20	10	20	11
21	7	21	8	21	9	21	9	21	10	21	10	21	11	21	9	21	10	21	11	21	11	21	12
22	8	22	9	22	10	22	10	22	11	22	11	22	12	22	10	22	11	22	12	22	12	22	13
23	9	23	10	23	11	23	11	23	12	23	12	23	13	23	11	23	12	23	13	23	13	23	14
24	10	24	11	24	12	24	12	24	13	24	13	24	14	24	12	24	13	24	14	24	14	24	15
25	11	25	12	25	13	25	13	25	14	25	14	25	15	25	13	25	14	25	15	25	15	25	16
26	12	26	13	26	14	26	14	26	15	26	15	26	16	26	14	26	15	26	16	26	16	26	17
27	13	27	14	27	15	27	15	27	16	27	16	27	17	27	15	27	16	27	17	27	17	27	18
28	14	28	15	28	16	28	16	28	17	28	17	28	18	28	16	28	17	28	18	28	18	28	19
29	15	29	16	29	17	29	17	29	18	29	18	29	19	29	17	29	18	29	19	29	19	29	20
30	16	30	17	30	18	30	18	30	19	30	19	30	20	30	18	30	19	30	20	30	20	30	21

GLOSSARY

Accapareur. A hoarder (most frequently used of a real, or suspected, hoarder of food).

Armée révolutionnaire. A citizen army of *sans-culottes* (see below), raised in various regions in the autumn of 1793 and primarily intended to ensure the grain-supply of Paris and other cities.

Assembly. (See *National Assembly.*)

Assignat. Revolutionary paper-money, at first issued to finance the sale of Church lands, but in general use after the summer of 1791.

Biens nationaux. Confiscated properties of Church, aristocracy or "suspects" (see below), nationalized and sold by auction during the Revolution.

Bourgeois, bourgeoisie. A generic term more or less synonymous with urban middle classes – bankers, stockbrokers, merchants, large manufacturers, and professional men of every kind.

Brissotins. Followers of Jacques-Pierre Brissot, journalist and deputy for Eure-et-Loire, at the time of the Legislative Assembly. (See also *Girondins.*)

Buveur de sang. A term of abuse applied to Jacobins in general and to Robespierre in particular after Thermidor (see below). Variations on this theme are *septembriseur* and *terroriste.*

Cahiers de doléances. The lists of grievances drawn up by each of the three "orders" or estates in towns, villages and guilds in preparation for the Estates General of May 1789.

Champ de Mars. The military parade-ground (where the Eiffel Tower now stands) and scene of the "massacre" of 17 July 1791. Also the scene of the main civic festivals and pageants during the Revolution, e.g. Festival of the Federation on 14 July of each year and of the Supreme Being on 8 June 1794.

Comités révolutionnaires, or "revolutionary" (or "vigilance") committees. The local committees attached to the Sections (see below) created in April 1793 and made responsible for police and internal security.

Committee of General Security. One of the two main government committees of the Year II (see below), specifically charged with responsibility for police and internal security.

Committee of Public Safety. The more important of the two leading govern-

225

Glossary

ment committees of the Year II. Generally responsible for the conduct of both internal and external affairs, its powers overlapped with those of the Committee of General Security in police and judicial matters.

Commune. Title given to the Paris local government that emerged at the City Hall (Hôtel de Ville) after the fall of the Bastille. The so-called "Revolutionary Commune" temporarily usurped its powers in the crisis of August–September 1792. The Commune itself was abolished shortly after Thermidor.

Complot de l'étranger. The "foreign plot" which Pitt and his agents were widely believed to be hatching against the Republic in 1793–4.

Cordeliers Club. The more "plebeian", and generally the more radical, of the two major clubs of the Revolution in Paris. The best known of its leaders were (at various times) Marat, Danton, Hébert, Vincent and Ronsin.

Dantonists. Basically, the friends of Danton (e.g. Desmoulins, Legendre, Merlin de Thionville, Fabre d'Eglantine); but, by extension, the term "Dantonist" was also applied to the Indulgents, or opponents of the Terror (e.g. Bourdon de l'Oise, Delacroix, Thuriot), and certain business-operators (Fabre, Basire, Philippeaux), all of whom formed the opposition from the Right in the "factional" crisis of the spring of 1793. (See also "*Factions*".)

Décade. The 10-day periods into which the Republican 30-day month was divided.

De-christianization. The attack on Christian clergy and religion (both Catholic and Protestant) mounted by Hébert and his supporters (see *Hébertists*) in the autumn of 1793. It took the form of closing churches, stripping clergy of their vestments and offices and of promoting the cult of the Goddess of Reason. The "de-christianizers" came under government censure after Robespierre's speech denouncing them on 21 November 1793.

Emigrés. Nobles, clergy and others who emigrated from France from July 1789 onwards.

Enragés. The extreme revolutionary party, led by Jacques Roux, Jean Varlet and Théophile Leclerc, who, while condemned by the Jacobins and Cordeliers alike, had considerable influence on the Paris *sans-culottes* in 1793.

"Factions". Term applied, in particular, to the two opposing factions of Dantonists (the Right) and Hébertists (the Left) in the political crisis that reached its climax in March–April 1793.

Faubourgs. Literally "suburbs", originally, as in Paris, lying outside the old city walls but gradually enclosed within the modern city as it grew.

Glossary

In the Revolution, the term is more particularly applied to the great popular *"faubourgs"* of Saint-Antoine and Saint-Marcel.

Feuillants. Name given to the large group of royalist deputies and journalists who broke with the Jacobins to form their own Club in protest against the campaign to depose the King or suspend him from office after the Flight to Varennes in June 1791.

General Will. Rousseau's term for the collective will of the community at large.

Girondins. Name originally given, as an alternative to *Brissotins* (see above), to a group of Left-wing deputies in the Legislative Assembly, who supported Brissot's policy of a "revolutionary war" in the autumn and winter of 1791 and several of whom came from the south-western region of the Gironde. Later applied to a wider group, emanating from the first, who shared a more-or-less common political and social programme in opposition to that of the main body of Jacobins.

Hébertists. A convenient but imprecise term originally applied to the followers and associates of Jacques-René Hébert, editor of *Le Père Duchesne.* By extension, Hébertism came to be applied to all groups taking part in the Left opposition to the Revolutionary Government in the autumn of 1793 and the spring of 1793. By this time, the term was applied equally to Hébert's associates on the Paris Commune and in the Ministry of War (Chaumette, Vincent), the "de-christianizers" *en bloc*, the proponents of "universal war" (Cloots), and the leaders of the *armée révolutionnaire* and Cordeliers Club (Ronsin). (See also *Dantonists* and *"Factions".*)

Jacobins, Jacobin Club. Name assumed by the members of the former Breton Club when they established themselves in the former Couvent des Jacobins in Paris in October 1789. The Club went through a series of transmutations – through the secession of the Feuillants (June 1791) and the successive purges of Girondins, Dantonists and Hébertists – and ended up in the summer of 1794 as the group within the original Jacobin Club who remained devoted to Robespierre. The Club was dissolved by the Thermidorians in November 1794. (See also *Mountain.*)

Journée (or *journée révolutionnaire*). A day of revolutionary struggle in which crowds, generally composed of *sans-culottes*, participated, e.g. capture of Bastille, overthrow of monarchy, expulsion of Girondin leaders from Convention.

Levée en masse. Law of 23 August 1793 mobilizing the whole French nation for war.

Livre (or *franc*). In 1789, roughly equivalent to 1s. 8d. sterling. There were 20 *sous* to the *livre*.

Glossary

Mandat impératif. The specific instructions to which, according to Rousseau's theory of representation, the legislators, elected by the people, should be bound by their constituents. Hence, *mandataire* or "mandatory" as a term for a deputy or representative.

Marc d'argent. A silver mark worth 52 francs. This was the annual amount that had to be paid in direct taxes in order to qualify as a deputy to the National Assembly (see below) by a law of December 1789. Following protests by Robespierre and others, the qualification was changed, in August 1791, to one of "active" citizenship.

Maximum. There were two laws of the Maximum: that of May 1793, imposing a limit on the price of grain only; and that of September 1793, extending price-control to most articles of prime necessity, including labour (*maximum des salaires*).

Menu peuple. The common people: wage-earners and small property-owners. (See also *sans-culottes.*)

Mountain. Name acquired by the Jacobin deputies for Paris, led by Robespierre, who, after their election to the National Convention in September 1792, sat in the upper seats of the Chamber. By extension, term later applied to similarly-minded deputies from all over France. Hence, *Montagnards.* (See also *Jacobins.*)

National Assembly. The term is here used for each of the successive parliaments of the Revolution: Constituent Assembly (June 1789–September 1791); Legislative Assembly (October 1791–August 1792); National Convention (September 1792–October 1795).

National Guard (or *milice bourgeoise*). Citizens' army, or militia, originally raised by the Paris Districts (see *Sections*) in July 1789.

Noblesse de robe. Wealthy magistrates of the Old Régime who, by purchase or inheritance of public office, had acquired the status of nobility.

Ouvriers. Term applied in eighteenth-century France to all town-dwellers who worked with their hands, whether as small manufacturers, independent craftsmen, or wage-earners.

"Patriots". Generally used at this time in the sense of a radical reformer rather than a "nationalist". In this context, often synonymous with "Jacobin".

Plain (or Marsh). The Centre group of deputies in the National Convention, who had no continuous commitment to either the Girondin or *Montagnard* (Jacobin) cause.

Privilégiés. The privileged orders, i.e. the clergy (though generally applied only to the higher clergy) and nobility, on the eve and at the beginning of the French Revolution.

Representatives on mission. Deputies sent to the provinces, after March

Glossary

1793, to impose the policies of the Convention and Committee of Public Safety.

Révolte nobiliaire. The revolt of the nobility and Parlements (higher courts of law) of 1787–8, which served as a curtain-raiser to the Revolution of 1789.

Revolutionary Government. The strongly centralized government, first proposed by Robespierre, Saint-Just and their associates on the Committee of Public Safety in October 1793 and adopted by the Convention in the law of 14th Frimaire (4 December 1793).

Revolutionary Tribunal. High court of justice created in March 1793 to try all offences against the State by new and "revolutionary" procedures.

Sans-culottes. An omnibus term (literally, those who wore trousers and not knee-breeches), sometimes applied to all the poorer classes of town and countryside; but, more particularly (as here), to urban craftsmen, small shopkeepers, petty traders, journeymen, labourers and city poor. By extension, attached as a political label to the more militant revolutionaries of 1792–5 regardless of social origins.

Sections. The 48 units into which Paris became divided for electoral (and general political) purposes, in succession to the 60 Districts created in April 1789, by a municipal law of May–June 1790.

Sociétés populaires (or *sectionnaires*). General term applied to the local clubs and societies after the summer of 1791. Many were affiliated to the Jacobin Club; but, after the "law of the 40 *sous*" (see pages 109, 136 above), many, to avoid the Parent-Club's surveillance, set up independently. In consequence, these societies came to be frowned on by the Committee of Public Safety; many were closed down after the fall of Hébert; more were closed shortly before and shortly after Thermidor; a few stragglers, however, managed to survive until the early months of 1795.

Suspects. Persons suspected of harbouring treasonable designs against the Revolution; term in use from August 1792 on. Several "suspects" were rounded up and gaoled at this time but there was no general Law of Suspects, entitling such persons to be arrested and brought before the Revolutionary Tribunal, until 5 September 1793. It marked the official opening of the Terror and filled the prisons in the months that followed.

Taille. The principal direct tax paid by all commoners (*roturiers*) before the Revolution, usually levied on personal income (*taille personnelle*), more rarely on land (*taille réelle*).

Taxation populaire. Reduction of food prices by riot (examples here given: in the Orléanais in November–December 1792; in Paris in February 1793).

229

Glossary

Terror. Here used in two senses: "terror" (with a small "t") as a mode of compulsion, either official or "popular" (such as in September Massacres, 1792); and "Terror" (with a capital), which generally applies to a period rather than to a method: the period September 1793 to July 1794, when the Jacobin (or Revolutionary) Government imposed its authority by varying means of compulsion – military, judicial and economic. Hence, also, the "Great Terror" of June–July 1794.

Thermidor. The month in the Revolutionary Calendar running from 19 July to 17 August. Here applied, in particular, to the two days in Thermidor (9th and 10th) of the Year II, which saw the overthrow of Robespierre and his associates and the end of the Revolutionary Government. Hence, *Thermidorians*, i.e. Robespierre's immediate successors. (See also Appendix II.)

Third Estate (or *tiers état* or *tiers*). Literally, the representatives of the non-privileged of the three estates summoned to attend the Estates General. More generally, used to denote all social classes other than the aristocracy, upper clergy or *noblesse de robe* (see above) – i.e. *menu peuple* (see above) as well as bourgeoisie.

Virtue. Here generally used, as by Robespierre, in the sense of civic virtue (e.g. love of country or loyalty to the Jacobin cause) rather than in that of private morality or virtuous conduct in personal relations.

Year II. The second year of the French Republic, i.e. from 22 September 1793 to 21 September 1794. Most often, as here, applied to the period of office of the great Committee of Public Safety (27 July 1793–27 July 1794). (See also Appendix II.)

BIBLIOGRAPHICAL NOTE

There has been a rising interest in Robespierre as a world-historical figure in the past half-century, particularly since the series of modern revolutions began with the Russian Revolution of 1917. New books about him or relating to him have appeared in several European countries: in Russia, Austria and East Germany, as well as in France and Italy; in North and South America and Japan. For a discussion of Robespierre as seen by historians in a number of countries (including France, England, Belgium, Spain, the U.S.A., Hungary, Germany and Russia), the student is referred to *Actes du Colloque Robespierre* (Société des Etudes Robespierristes, Paris, 1967), pp. 165–238. As very little of this work has been translated into English (and much of it not into French), it will have to be largely ignored in this Note. An exception, has, however, to be made in the case of the bi-centenary volume dedicated to Robespierre, published in the German Democratic Republic in 1958: W. Markov, ed., *Maximilien Robespierre 1758–1794*, Berlin: Rütter & Loening, 1958; rev. edition (1961), with an introduction (in French) by G. Lefebvre and articles (in German) by French, English, Italian, Polish, Hungarian, Czech, German, American and Russian historians.

The manuscript sources relating to Robespierre are almost as abundant as those relating to the Revolution itself, particularly for the period September 1792 to July 1794; so it would be invidious to attempt a sample. (The reader is, however, referred to that made by J. L. Carr in his *Robespierre. The Force of Circumstance* [1972],* pp. 221–3.) Among published memoirs and reminiscences of relevance are those of Laurent de l'Ardèche (1818–21), Napoleon (as interpreted by the Count de las Cases, 1823), Levasseur de la Sarthe (1828), and Charlotte Robespierre (edited by Laponneraye, 1835). But by far the most valuable source-materials are undoubtedly his own writings and speeches, above all the 10-volume complete edition – *Oeuvres de Maximilien Robespierre* – compiled from a large range of journals and newspapers by the Société des Etudes Robespierristes, begun in the 1930s and completed in 1967. Other collections of extracts from Robespierre's speeches in French are to be found in A. Vermorel, *Oeuvres de Robespierre* (1865); H. M. Stephens, *The Principal Speeches of the Statesmen and Orators of the French Revolution, 1789–1795,*

*French titles may be assumed to be published in Paris and English titles in London, unless otherwise stated.

Bibliographical Note

2 vols. (Oxford, 1892); and, in English, R. T. Bienvenue, ed., *The Ninth Thermidor: the Fall of Robespierre* (Oxford, 1968). In addition, speeches or extracts are to be found in some of the collections of documents relating to the Revolution as a whole: e.g. in Buchez and Roux's *Histoire parlementaire de la Révolution française*, 40 vols. (1834–8); and in A. Aulard's *La Société des Jacobins*, 6 vols. (1889–97) and *Recueil des actes du Comité de Salut public*, 26 vols. (1889–1923). Unfortunately, very little of this has appeared in English (as will be evident from the footnotes to the present volume).

For historians' views of Robespierre, in addition to those included in the *Actes du Colloque Robespierre*, see Lord Acton, *The Literature of the Revolution* (Appendix to his *Lectures on the French Revolution*, 1910); G. P. Gooch, *History and Historians of the Nineteenth Century* (1931); H. Ben-Israel, *English Historians of the French Revolution* (Cambridge, 1968); P. Farmer, *France Reviews Its Revolutionary Origins*, (New York, 1963); and, above all, the 35-page Introduction to J. M. Thompson's *Robespierre*, 2 vols. (Oxford, 1935). For views of Robespierre by his contemporaries, see L. Jacob, ed., *Robespierre vu par ses contemporains* (1938), of which some use has been made in my last chapter, and G. Walter, *Robespierre*, 2 vols. (1938, 1961), II, 334–55. There are also contemporary sketches of him in *The Correspondence of William Augustus Miles, 1789–1817*, 2 vols. (1890); in J. M. Thompson, ed., *Witnesses of the French Revolution* (Oxford, 1939); and in B. C. Davenport, ed., *A Diary of the French Revolution by Gouverneur Morris*, 2 vols. (1939).

For general bibliographies of Robespierrist literature, see the works of Carr, Markov, Thompson and Walter cited above.

Among biographies of Robespierre in French, one of the earliest and longest is E. Hamel's *Histoire de Robespierre*, 3 vols. (1865); but this is a solemn piece of hagiography rather than a critical work of history (see also J. B. O'Brien's work below). In fact, the English-speaking reader may reasonably confine his attention to a number of recent French biographies, of which the most important and one of the two best in any language is G. Walter's (see above); while J. Massin's *Robespierre* (1956) and M. Bouloiseau's (1961) are both excellent short studies. But he should also consult some of the numerous studies of Robespierre by his great rehabilitator, A. Mathiez, such as *La conspiration de l'étranger* (1917), *La corruption parlementaire sous la Terreur* (1918), *Robespierre terroriste* (1921), *Autour de Robespierre* (1925), *Girondins et Montagnards* (1930), *Etudes sur Robespierre* (1958), and the collection of essays translated into English as *The Fall of Robespierre and Other Essays* (London, 1927). Reference may also be made to G. Lefebvre's *Etudes sur la Révolution française* (1954) for portraits of Danton and Robespierre; and students should read A. Soboul's *The Parisian Sans-culottes and the French Revolution 1793-4* (Oxford, 1964) and his article "Robespierre and the Popular Movement of 1793-4", in *Past and Present*, May 1954. For a critical view of Robespierre from a "Trotskyist" standpoint, see D. Guérin, *La lutte de classes sous la Ière République: bourgeois et "bras-nus" (1793-1797)*, 2 vols. (1946). For other special aspects, see G. Michon, *Robespierre et la guerre révolutionnaire 1791-1792* (1937); A. Latreille, *L'église catholique et la Révolution française* (2 vols. 1946-50); A. Mathiez, "Robespierre et le culte de l'Etre Suprême", in *Etudes sur Robespierre*, 1958 ed. pp. 157-84; G. Lenotre, *Robespierre et la "Mère de Dieu"* (1926); and A. Ording, *Le bureau de police du Comité de Salut public* (Oslo, 1935); and for Robespierre in literature, see the brief list in Walter, II, 522-4.

In addition, specialists may wish to consult the index of the *Annales historiques de la Révolution française*, or the general histories of the Revolution by G. de Staël (1818), A. Thiers (1824-5), F. A. M. Mignet (1815), J. Michelet (1847-53), L. Blanc (1847), E. Quinet (1865), A. Aulard (1910), J. Jaurès (1901), A. Mathiez (1927), G. Lefebvre (1962, 1965); and A. Soboul's *Précis d'histoire* (1962), now available in English as *The French Revolution 1787-1799*, 2 vols. (1974).

Scholarly work on Robespierre by English and American historians has been scanty and much of it has been undistinguished. Of that done up to 1914, only one piece is still of interest: J. W. Croker's 130-page essay on "Maximilien Robespierre", which first appeared in the conservative *Quarterly Review* in 1835 and was republished in the author's *Essays on the Early Period of the French Revolution* in 1857. There is also J. B. O'Brien's *Life and Character of Maximilien Robespierre* (1837) and his *Dissertation and Elegy on the Life and Death of Maximilien Robespierre* (1859), both glowing tributes lacking in scholarly merit; and, on the eve of the First World War, Hilaire Belloc's *Robespierre: A Study* (1901); and C. F. Warwick's *Robespierre and the French Revolution* (New York, 1909). For other nineteenth-century work the student may perhaps confine himself to consulting the general histories or published lectures of W. Smyth (1846), G. H. Lewes (1849), H. Morse Stephens (1886, 1891); and P. Kropotkin (1909); and – most worthwhile – Thomas Carlyle (1837) and Lord Acton (1910).

More recent biographies of Robespierre in English include R. Korngold's *Robespierre and the Fourth Estate* (New York 1941); J. L. Carr's *Robespierre: The Force of Circumstance* (1972) [see above]; and N. Hampson's *The Life and Opinions of Maximilien Robespierre* (1974). But by far the most complete and the most perceptive biography of Robespierre

Bibliographical Note

in English – and perhaps one only equalled by Walter's in French – is J. M. Thompson's *Robespierre*, 2 vols. (Oxford, 1935; rev. ed. 1 vol., 1939), which is essential reading for every student. There is a shorter biography by the same author entitled *Robespierre and the French Revolution* (1952); and there is a useful portrait in his *Leaders of the French Revolution* (Oxford, 1928). In addition, there are two "psycho-biographies": Reginald Somerset Ward's *Maximilien Robespierre and the French Revolution* (1934), based on extremely dubious historical research; and Max Gallo's well-meaning but naïve *Robespierre the Incorruptible* (New York, 1971). For special aspects, see R. R. Palmer's *Twelve Who Ruled: The Year of the Terror in the French Revolution* (Princeton, 1941), the only scholarly account in English of the collective work of the members of the great Committee of Public Safety; two excellent articles by A. Cobban: "The Fundamental Ideas of Robespierre," and "The Political Ideas of Robespierre during the Convention," both from his *Aspects of the French Revolution* (1971), pp. 137–91; G. H. McNeil, "Robespierre, Rousseau and Representation," in R. Herr, ed., *Ideas in History* (Durham N.C., 1956), pp. 135–56; J. L. Talmon, *Origins of Totalitarian Democracy* (1952); Joseph I. Shulim, "The Youthful Robespierre and his Ambivalence toward the Ancien Régime," in *Eighteenth-Century Studies* (Berkeley, California) V, (1971–2), 398–420; and R. T. Bienvenue, ed., *The Ninth Thermidor: the Fall of Robespierre* (Oxford, 1968).

NOTES

PART I – THE MAN AND THE EVENTS

1. M. Gallo, *Robespierre the Incorruptible: A Psycho-Biography*, New York, 1971, p. 25.

2. Yet J. L. Carr, Robespierre's latest biographer in English, writes of the episode: "The grooming of the martyr had begun already in that rain-soaked Paris street and the young man never quite forgot the shame he felt during those terrible moments of despair" (J. L. Carr, *Robespierre, The Force of Circumstance*, London, 1972, p. 14).

3. For this somewhat dubious "encounter", see G. Walter, *Robespierre*, 2 vols., Paris 1961, II, 138; and G. Lenotre, *Robespierre et la "Mère de Dieu"*, Paris, 1926, p. 107.

4. Cit. Walter II, 34.

5. J. I. Schulim, "The youthful Robespierre and his ambivalence towards the Ancien Régime," *Eighteenth Century Studies* (Berkeley, California), v, v, 1971–2, 398–420.

6. J. Massin, *Robespierre*, Paris, 1956, p. 18.

7. J. M. Thompson, *Robespierre*, 2 vols., Oxford, 1968, I, 50–1.

8. Thompson, I, 59.

9. *The Correspondence of William Augustus Miles 1789–1817*, 2 vols., London, 1890, I, 245.

10. M. Bouloiseau, *Robespierre*, Paris, 1965, pp. 18–19.

11. Bouloiseau, pp. 22–3.

12. For a fuller discussion of this point, see pp. 155–78.

13. P. Caron, *Les Massacres de septembre*, Paris, 1935.

14. But see A. Patrick, *The Men of the First Republic*, Baltimore, 1973. Dr Patrick, having closely examined the voting lists for the main debates, disputes the traditional view, as presented here, of the relative strengths of the party groups between September 1792 and June 1793.

15. A. Soboul, *The Parisian Sans-Culottes and the French Revolution*, Oxford, 1964.

16. For a fuller account of this "war on the factions" see pp. 172–78.

17. For two very different accounts and interpretations of this incident, see G. Lenotre and A. Mathiez, "New Evidence about Catherine Théot,"

in *The Fall of Robespierre*, New York, 1927; and, for further discussion of Robespierre's religious views, see pp. 122–26.

18. See Arne Ording, *Le bureau de police du Comité de Salut public*, Oslo, 1930.

19. Massin, p. 257; Walter, *Robespierre*, 2 vols., Paris, 1961, II, 138–40; Gallo, p. 298.

PART II – THE CHANGING IMAGE

1. See the bibliographies of Robespierre in J. M. Thompson, *Robespierre*, 2 vols., Oxford, 1935, XV–LV; G. Walter, *Robespierre*, 2 vols., Paris, 1961, II, 400–524; W. Markov, ed., *Maximilien Robespierre 1758–1794*, Berlin (G.D.R.), 1958, pp. 573–98; and A. Soboul, ed., *Actes du Colloque Robespierre*, Paris, 1966, *passim*.

2. See the 93 volumes of economic documents published by the Commission de Recherche et de Publication des Documents relatifs à la Vie économique de la Révolution (founded by Jaurès in 1903) between 1905 and 1929; and also the 10 volumes of *Oeuvres de Maximilien Robespierre*, published by the Société des Etudes Robespierristes, much of it under the supervision of G. Lefebvre, between 1916 and 1967.

3. Thompson, I, xxiv.

4. Des Essarts, *Les crimes de Robespierre et de ses principaux complices*, 3 vols., Paris, 1797, I, 126.

5. *Actes du Colloque Robespierre* (hereafter cited as *Colloque*), p. 19.

6. *The History of Robespierre Political and Personal . . .* , London, 1794.

7. H. M. Williams, *Memories of the Reign of Robespierre*, 3 vols., London, 1795, I, 192–3.

8. J. A. Adolphus, *Biographical Memoirs of the French Revolution*, 2 vols., London, 1799, II, 365, 391, 407, 415, 423, 425, 433, 443.

9. G. Walter, II, 370.

10. *Journal of the Private Life and Conversations of the Emperor Napoleon at Saint Helena by the Count de las Cases*, 2 vols., London, 1823, I, 345–7; G. Rudé, ed., *Robespierre*, New Jersey, 1967, pp. 128–30.

11. See S. Mellon, *The Political Uses of History*, Palo Alto, California, 1959, *passim*.

12. G. de Staël, *Considerations on the principal events of the French Revolution*, 3 vols., London, 1818, I, 14; F. A. M. Mignet, *History of the French Revolution from 1789 to 1815*, Everyman ed., London, 1915, p. 1.

13. A. Thiers, *The History of the French Revolution*, London, n. d. p. 421; Mignet, p. 218.

14. De Staël, pp. 143–4; Thiers, pp. 472–3.

15. Paganel, *Essai historique et critique sur la Révolution française*, Paris, 1810; cited by J. Godechot, in *Colloque*, p. 171.

16. See Godechot, *Colloque*, pp. 171–3.

17. *Mémoires de Levasseur de la Sarthe*, Paris, 1828; cit. L. Jacob, ed., *Robespierre vu par ses contemporains*, Paris, 1938, pp. 155–7.

18. Jacob, p. 201.

19. F. Buonarroti, *Observations sur Maximilien Robespierre*, Paris, 1837; cit. Jacob, pp. 215–19.

20. See Walter, II, 173–6.

21. See Thompson, II, xxix; and Godechot, *Colloque*, pp. 174–5.

22. L. Blanc, *Histoire de la Révolution*, 12 vols., Paris, 1847–62; cit. Walter, II, 183–5.

23. See A. Z. Manfred, "Robespierre dans l'historiographie russe et soviétique", in *Colloque*, pp. 241, 249.

24. See I. Diòszegi, in *Colloque*, pp. 266–7.

25. J. B. O'Brien, *A Dissertation and Elegy on the Life and Death of Maximilien Robespierre*, London, 1859, pp. 31–2; and *The Life and Character of Maximilien Robespierre*, London, 1837, p. 15.

26. A. Cornu, "Karl Marx' Stellung zur französischen Revolution und zu Robespierre (1843–1845)", in Markov, ed., pp. 553–71.

27. See H. Ben-Israel, *English Historians on the French Revolution*, Cambridge, 1968, pp. 120–1.

28. G. Buechner, *Danton's Death*, James Maxwell, trans., San Francisco, 1961, p. 18.

29. T. Carlyle, *The French Revolution*, 2 vols., London, 1955 edn., II, 79, 334.

30. A. de Lamartine, *Histoire des Girondins*, 8 vols., Paris, 1847–8; cit. Walter, II, 177–80.

31. J. Michelet, *Histoire de la Révolution française*, 7 vols., Paris, 1847–53; cit. Walter, II, 181–2.

32. See Ben-Israel, pp. 275 ff.

33. A. Alison, *History of Europe during the French Revolution*, 2 vols., London, 1833, II, 304–6.

34. J. W. Croker, "Robespierre", in *Essays on the Early Period of the French Revolution*, London, 1857, pp. 299–430.

35. W. Smyth, *Lectures on the History of the French Revolution*, 2nd edn., 2 vols., London, 1855, II, 352–6.

36. Ben-Israel, pp. 171, 154–7.

Notes

37. G. H. Lewes, *The Life of Maximilien Robespierre, with Extracts from Unpublished Correspondence*, London, 1849, pp. 4, 388–91.

38. Walter, II, 374.

39. From a MS of June 1857, in *Annales historiques de la Révolution française*, no. 179, Jan.–March 1965.

40. E. Hamel, *Histoire de Robespierre*, 3 vols., Paris, 1865; *Colloque*, pp. 179–80.

41. E. Quinet, *La Révolution*, 2 vols., Paris, 1865; cit. Godechot, *Colloque*, p. 180.

42. H. Taine, *Les origines de la France contemporaine. La Révolution*, 3 vols., 1876, I, 231–72.

43. Cit. Godechot, *Colloque*, pp. 181–2.

44. F. V. A. Aulard, *The French Revolution. A Political History 1789–1804*, 4 vols., London, 1910, III, 85–91.

45. Ben-Israel, p. 235.

46. H. Belloc, *The French Revolution*, London, 1966, pp. 40–43.

47. Lord Acton, *Lectures on the French Revolution*, London, 1910, pp. 226–7, 284, 299–300.

48. Jaurès, *La petite République*, 23 May 1899; cit. Rebèrioux, in *Colloque*, p. 191.

49. Jaurès, Critical Introduction to the *Socialist History*; cit. F. Stern, ed., *The Varieties of History*, New York, 1956, p. 160.

50. Jaurès, *Histoire socialiste*, 8 vols., Paris, 1922, VIII, 261.

51. A. Mathiez, *The Fall of Robespierre and other Essays*, London, 1927, p. 95.

52. A. Mathiez, *The French Revolution*, New York, 1927; *Colloque*, pp. 185–6.

53. Walter, I, 7–8.

54. R. Korngold, *Robespierre and the Fourth Estate*, New York, 1941, pp. vii–x, xv, 325 ff.

55. Thompson, II, 277–80.

56. R. Rolland, *Robespierre*, Paris, 1939, pp. 314–15; cit. Walter, II, 378–9.

57. Walter, II, 379–80.

58. J. Massin, *Robespierre*, Paris, 1956, p. 7.

59. N. H. Webster, *The French Revolution: A Study in Democracy*, London, 1920, pp. 422–34, 490–7.

60. P. Gaxotte, *La Révolution française*, Paris, 1928.

61. J. L. Talmon, *The Origins of Totalitarian Democracy*, London, 1952, p. 253.

62. A. France, *Les dieux ont soif*, Paris, 1912; Walter, II, 378.

63. J. Anouilh, *Pauvre Bitos*, Paris, 1956.

64. R. S. Ward, *Maximilien Robespierre: A Study in Deterioration*, London, 1934, pp. 4, 232.

65. M. Gallo, *Robespierre the Incorruptible: A Psycho-Biography*, New York, 1971, esp. pp. 12–26, 298–9.

66. Walter, II, 374.

67. P. Kropotkin, *The Great French Revolution*, New York, 1929, p. 550.

68. D. Guérin, *La lutte de classes sous la Ière république: bourgeois et "bras-nus" (1793–1797)*, 2 vols., Paris, 1946.

69. K. Marx and F. Engels, *Selected Correspondence*, Moscow, 1965, pp. 405–7 (letter of 4 December 1889).

70. V. I. Lenin, *Collected Works*, . . . vols., London, II, 277.

71. Manfred, in *Colloque*, pp. 247–8.

72. A. Z. Manfred, "La Nature du pouvoir jacobin", *La Pensée*, April 1970, pp. 62–3.

73. See contributions on Germany and Hungary in *Colloque*, pp. 251–8, 265–75.

74. G. Lefebvre, *La Grande Peur de 1789*, Paris, 1932; "Foules révolutionnaires", in *Etudes sur la Révolution française*, Paris, 1954, pp. 68–89.

75. A. Soboul, *Les sans-culottes parisiens en l'an II: mouvement populaire et gouvernement révolutionnaire, 2 juin–9 thermidor an II*, Paris, 1958.

76. R. C. Cobb, *Les armées révolutionnaires: instrument de la Terreur dans les départements, avril 1793–floréal an II*, 2 vols., Paris, 1961, 1963.

77. G. Lefebvre, "Sur Danton", in *Etudes sur la Révolution française*, pp. 25–66.

78. For examples, see R. C. Cobb, *The Police and the People: French Popular Protest 1789–1820*, Oxford, 1973, pp. xviii, 91, 133, 169, 172, 181.

79. For unsuccessful attempts made in 1958 to win some mark of public recognition of Robespierre's historical role, see "Le bicentenaire de Robespierre" in Walter, II, 380–7. Of course, the fact that this was also the year of the Gaullist Generals' *coup* in Algeria may have had something to do with it.

Notes

PART III – THE IDEOLOGUE
CHAPTER I

1. See A. Cobban, "The Fundamental Ideas of Robespierre", in *Aspects of the French Revolution*, London, 1971, p. 138.

2. Cobban, p. 139.

3. J. McDonald, *Rousseau and the French Revolution*, London, 1965, pp. 171-2; G. McNeil, "Robespierre, Rousseau and Representation", in *Ideas in History*, ed. L. Gottschalk, Durham, North Carolina, 1965, p. 143.

4. J. M. Thompson, *Robespierre*, 2 vols., Oxford, 1968, I, 181.

5. G. Walter, *Robespierre*, II, 138; G. Lenotre, *Robespierre et la "Mère de Dieu"*, Paris, 1926, p. 107.

6. Cobban, pp. 152, 158.

7. See, e.g. J. Lanfrey (1879): "C'est le Contrat social fait homme"; cit. J. Godechot in *Actes du Colloques Robespierre*, ed. A. Soboul, Paris, 1966, p. 181.

8. *Oeuvres de Maximilien Robespierre* (hereafter cited as *Oeuvres*), X, Paris, 1930-67, 196.

9. McNeil, p. 137; McDonald, p. 143.

10. Cited by A. Soboul in an unpublished lecture to the Inter-university Centre for European Studies, Montreal, in November 1973. I am grateful to Professor Soboul for allowing me to quote from this manuscript.

11. *Oeuvres*, VII, 161-6 (all translations from Robespierre are, unless otherwise indicated, by the author).

12. *Oeuvres*, VII, 265.

13. *Oeuvres*, VI, 168.

14. *Oeuvres*, VII, 347-8.

15. Walter, II, 42.

16. Cobban, p. 147.

17. McNeil, pp. 149-50, 153.

18. *Correspondance de Maximilien et Augustin Robespierre*, G. Michon, ed., Paris, 1926; cit. McNeil, p. 141.

19. See p. 23.

20. Cit. Walter, II, 36-7 (my translation).

21. *Oeuvres*, VII, 207-15.

22. *Oeuvres*, IX, 500-1.

23. *Oeuvres*, X, 356.

24. M. Bouloiseau, *Robespierre*, Paris, 1965, pp. 42-3; Walter, II, 41-2.

25. *Oeuvres*, VII, 312–18.

26. *Oeuvres*, VII, 646–51.

27. *Oeuvres*, VII, 752–3.

28. Walter, II, 55–65.

29. For the above, see Walter, II, 44–65; Thompson, II, 39–64; *Oeuvres*, IX, 457–71, 495–510.

30. E. Hamel, *Histoire de Robespierre*, 3 vols., Paris, 1865, I, 175; cit. Cobban, "The Political Ideas of Maximilien Robespierre during the Period of the Convention", in *Aspects . . .* , p. 160.

31. See, e.g., J. L. Talmon, *The Origins of Totalitarian Democracy*, London, 1952, pp. 122 ff; and A. Goodwin, *The French Revolution*, London, 1958, pp. 156–7.

32. Thompson, II, 277. Cobban's view is broadly similar, though he writes that Robespierre's new policies "implied a fundamental change of principle"; but he insists that his democratic ideals and quest for political liberty remained unchanged (Cobban, pp. 161, 189).

33. See R. R. Palmer, *Twelve Who Ruled: The Year of the Terror in the French Revolution*, Princeton, 1941, chaps. 6–9.

34. Thompson, II, 6–8; Cobban, p. 161; Walter, II, 278; *Oeuvres*, IX, 310–11, 317.

35. See J. Massin, *Robespierre*, Paris, 1956, pp. 188–90 (my translation).

36. Talmon, pp. 63, 122 ff. Professor Talmon, however, considers the Jacobin dictatorship to have been "an improvisation" that "came into existence by stages, and not in accordance with a blue-print" (p. 122).

37. *Rapport sur les principes du gouvernement révolutionnaire fait au nom du Comité de Salut public par Maximilien Robespierre*, Paris, 1793; *Oeuvres*, IX, 273–82.

38. Walter, II, 91.

39. Walter, II, 91–119.

40. A. Mathiez, *Etudes sur Robespierre*, Paris, 1958, p. 87.

41. Massin, pp. 136–7.

42. Walter, II, 85–6.

43. *Sur les principes de morale politique qui doivent guider la Convention nationale dans l'administration intérieure de la République*, Paris, 1794; *Oeuvres*, X, 350–66.

44. *Oeuvres*, X, 121.

45. *Oeuvres*, X, 352–3 (my italics).

46. *Oeuvres*, X, 109–13, 165–6, 286–7, 419, 533–5.

47. Arch. Nat , AF, II, 47, plaq. 368, fo. 37.

48 See Cobban, p. 173–4.

49. Cobban, p. 175.

Notes

50. *Oeuvres*, X, 35.
51. *Oeuvres*, VIII, 234–5.
52. Cit. Cobban, p. 177 (my translation).
53. Cit. Cobban, p. 178 (my translation).
54. *Oeuvres*, X, 195–7. See M. Bouloiseau: "Le Dieu de Robespierre, c'est donc celui du peuple" (p. 101).
55. *Oeuvres*, X, 361, 363.
56. See Mathiez, pp. 162–5.
57. *Oeuvres*, X, 458–9, 462–4.
58. *Oeuvres*, X, 566–76.
59. J. Michelet, *Histoire de la Révolution française*, 2-vol. edn., Paris, 1939, II, 1148 (my translation).

CHAPTER 2

1. G. Lefebvre, "Sur la pensée politique de Robespierre," in *Etudes sur la Révolution française*, Paris, 1954, pp. 95–8.
2. *Oeuvres*, VI, 481–3; VII, 135–8.
3. J. Massin, *Robespierre*, Paris, 1956, p. 46.
4. Massin, pp. 109–10 (my translation).
5. *Sur les subsistances*, Paris, 1792; *Oeuvres*, IX, 106–20 (my italics).
6. *Oeuvres*, IX, 274–6, 286–8.
7. *Oeuvres*, IX, 459–63.
8. G. Rudé, "La section des Champs Elysées et l'indemnité des quarante sous," shortly to appear in *Annales hist. de la Révolution française*.
9. *Le Moniteur (Réimpression)*, XIX, 565.
10. A. Z. Manfred, "La nature du pouvoir jacobin", *La Pensée*, no. 150, April 1970, p. 71.
11. R. B. Rose, "The French Revolution and the Grain Supply," *Bulletin of the John Rylands Library* XXXIX (1) (Sept. 1956), 171–87; Rudé, *The Crowd in History*, New York/London, 1964, pp. 120–1.
12. *Oeuvres*, X, 45.
13. *Oeuvres*, X, 19.
14. *Oeuvres*, X, 554.
15. For a critical comment, see C. L. R. James, *The Black Jacobins*, New York, 1963, pp. 140–2.
16. Cit. A. Soboul, in public lecture at Montreal, Nov. 1973 (see chap. I, n. 10, above).
17. A. Mathiez, *La Révolution française*, III, 41, 148; cit. Soboul, "Robespierre and the Popular Movement of 1793–4", *Past and Present*,

May 1954, p. 65; and A. Soboul, *Les sans-culottes parisiens en l'an II*, Paris, 1958, p. 715, n. 114.

18. A. Soboul, "Robespierre and the Popular Movement of 1793–4", in *Past and Present*, May 1954, p. 65; *Les sans-culottes parisiens*, pp. 708–17.

19. R. R. Palmer, *Twelve Who Ruled: The Year of the Terror in the French Revolution*, Princeton, 1941, pp. 284–7, 312–15.

20. Lefebvre, *Etudes*, p. 97 (my translation).

21. F. Braesch, "Un essai de statistique de la population ouvrière de Paris vers 1791," *La Révolution française*, LXIII (1912), 289–321.

22. There were exceptions: François Robert, for example, of the Cordeliers Club, who gave support to the striking journeymen carpenters in May–June 1791; and Marat, on occasion, as when he opened the columns of *L'Ami du peuple* to workers' correspondence at this time. (See G. Rudé, *The Crowd and the French Revolution*, London, 1959, p. 85.)

23. J. M. Thompson, *Robespierre*, 2 vols., Oxford, 1968, II, 53.

24. See A. Aulard, *Recueil des actes du Comité de salut public*, 26 vols., Paris, 1889–1923, esp. vols. VI–XIV; Rudé, "Die Arbeiter und die Revolutionsregierung", in *Maximilien Robespierre 1758–1794*, W. Markov, ed., Berlin (G.D.R.), 1958, pp. 301–2. See also Palmer, pp. 240–3.

25. See Rudé and Soboul, "Le maximum des salaires parisiens et le 9 thermidor," *Ann. hist. de la Rév. franc.* no. 134, 1954, pp. 1–22.

26. Cit. Rose, *The Enragés: Socialists of the French Revolution*, Sydney, 1965, p. 89.

27. *Oeuvres*, IX, 588–9, 593–4, 600–3, 606; X, 52–3, 59–60.

28. *Oeuvres*, X, 93–5.

29. *Oeuvres*, X, 114–15.

30. *Le Moniteur (Réimpression)*, XIX, 631.

31. Arch. Nat., F^{1c} III, Seine (report of 29 March 1794).

32. *Oeuvres*, X, 384.

33. M. Deslandres, *Histoire constitutionnelle de la France de 1789 à 1870*, Paris, 1932, I, 268; cit. Thompson, II, 52.

34. *Le Défenseur de la Constitution*, June 1792; cit. Massin, p. 112 (Massin's italics; my translation).

35. *Oeuvres*, IX, 459.

PART IV – THE PRACTITIONER OF REVOLUTION
CHAPTER I

1. J. M. Thompson, *Robespierre*, 2 vols., Oxford, 1968, II, 279. For Jaurès' contrary view that Robespierre was a political realist who "kept

himself abreast of every detail of revolutionary activity", see p. 78.

2. *Oeuvres*, VII, 220.

3. See J. Massin, *Robespierre*, Paris, 1956, p. 65; G. Walter, *Robespierre*, 2 vols., Paris, 1961, II, 35–6.

4. For these events, see Massin, pp. 64–6; and A. Mathiez, *Le Club des Cordeliers pendant la crise de Varennes et le massacre du Champ de Mars*, Paris, 1910.

5. Massin, p. 64 (my translation).

6. *Oeuvres*, IX, 410–11, 424.

7. *Oeuvres*, X, 352.

8. *Oeuvres*, VIII, 47–52, 58–64.

9. Thompson, II, 54.

10. *Oeuvres*, X, 167–84.

11. *Oeuvres*, X, 572.

12. For much of the above, see G. Michon, *Robespierre et la guerre révolutionnaire 1791–1792*, Paris, 1937.

13. *Oeuvres*, VII, 432–7 (my italics).

14. *Oeuvres*, IX, 129–30 (my italics).

15. *Oeuvres*, X, 274.

16. *Oeuvres*, X, 357–9 (my italics).

17. *Oeuvres*, X, 133–6, 370–1.

18. *Oeuvres*, X, 354 (my italics).

19. *L'Ami du Peuple*, 3 May 1792 (my italics).

20. For Marat's very different reaction to this event, see pp. 208–9.

21. My presentation of this episode closely follows Massin's (pp. 120–3).

22. *Réponse de Maximilien Robespierre à l'accusation de J.-B. Louvet*, Paris, 1972; *Oeuvres*, IX, 79–100, esp. 88–94 (my italics).

23. *Oeuvres*, IX, 278–9.

24. See G. Lefebvre, *La Révolution française*, Paris, 1951, pp. 333, 338–41.

25. *Oeuvres*, IX, 370–1.

26. *Oeuvres*, IX, 376–412, 413–17.

27. *Oeuvres*, IX, 526.

28. *Oeuvres*, X, 248.

29. *Oeuvres*, X, 219–24, 253–5.

30. *Oeuvres*, X, 275–6.

31. *Oeuvres*, X, 359–64.

32. *Oeuvres*, X, 374.

33. For useful accounts of the "war on the factions" see Massin, pp. 216–45; and R. R. Palmer, *Twelve Who Ruled: The Year of the Terror in*

the French Revolution, Princeton, 1941, esp. pp. 110–29, 280–304.

34. Massin, p. 253 (my translation).

1. For a presentation of this theme, see G. Rudé, *The Crowd in the French Revolution*, Oxford, 1959.

2. *Oeuvres*, VIII, 90–1 (my italics).

3. *Oeuvres*, VI, 39.

4. *Oeuvres*, VI, 227–8, 239–44.

5. See Rudé, pp. 80–94.

6. P. Caron, *Les massacres de septembre*, Paris, 1935.

7. *Oeuvres*, IX, 180–1.

8. *Oeuvres*, IX, 545.

9. *L'Ami du peuple*, 12 June 1791.

10. Arch. Nat. F^7 4622, plaq. 1, fo. 141.

11. *Oeuvres*, IX, 275, 287.

12. *Oeuvres*, IX, 94–5.

13. *Oeuvres*, IX, 110.

14. For much of what follows, see A. Soboul, *Les sans-culottes parisiens en l'an II*, Paris, 1958, and its abbreviated English version, *The Parisian Sans-Culottes and the French Revolution, 1793-4*, Oxford, 1964; also (by the same author), "Robespierre and the Popular Movement of 1793-4", *Past and Present*, May 1954, pp. 54–70.

15. D. Guérin, *La lutte de classes sous la IIère République: bourgeois et "bras nus" (1793-1797)*, 2 vols., Paris, 1946, I, II. Closely related is Guérin's view that "in 1793, bourgeois revolution and the embryo of proletarian revolution overlap" (I, 17).

16. Soboul, *Sans-culottes parisiens*, pp. 444–5; P. Sainte-Claire Deville, *La Commune de l'an II*, Paris, 1946, pp. 361–79.

17. Soboul, "Robespierre and the Popular Movement," p. 59.

18. *Oeuvres*, X, 352–3.

19. *Oeuvres*, X, 165–6, 286. See also his speech of 31 March 1794 (*Oeuvres*, X, 419–20).

20. Arch. Nat. AF^{II} 47, plaqs. 365–6.

21. A. Aulard, *Paris pendant la réaction thermidorienne*, 5 vols., Paris, 1898–1902, I, II; R. C. Cobb, "Une 'coalition' des garçons brossiers de la section des Lombards," *Ann. hist. Rév. franç.*, no. 130, 1953, pp. 67–70.

22. Cit. Soboul, *Sans-culottes parisiens*, p. 315 (my translation).

Notes

CHAPTER 3

1. J. M. Thompson, *Robespierre*, 2 vols., Oxford, 1968, II, 278–80.
2. See A. Z. Manfred, "La nature du pouvoir jacobin", *La Pensée*, April 1970, pp. 75–6; E. Aarons, *Lenin's Theories on Revolution*. Sydney, 1970, p. 11.
3. L. Jacob, ed., *Robespierre vu par ses contemporains*, Paris, 1938, pp. 145–9 (my translation).
4. J. Jaurès, *Histoire socialiste*, 8 vols., Paris, 1922; cit. M. Bouloiseau, *Robespierre*, Paris, 1965, p. 23.
5. Figures from Bouloiseau, pp. 18–25.
6. *Oeuvres*, x, 354 (my italics).
7. F. Buonarroti, *Observations sur Maximilien Robespierre*, 1837; cit. Jacob, pp. 215–19.
8. G. Winstanley, *A New Year's Gift for the Parliament and Army*, 1649; cit. Christopher Hill, ed., *Winstanley. The law of Freedom and other Writings*, London, 1973, pp. 161–2.
9. Aarons, p. 71.
10. Jacob, pp. 82–3.
11. *Oeuvres*, x, 356.
12. Hill, p. 67.
13. Aarons, pp. 83–5.
14. *Oeuvres*, x, 361.
15. V. I. Lenin and J. Stalin, *The Russian Revolution*, London, 1938, p. 207 (my italics).
16. Lenin, *Selected Works*, IX, 298–9; cit. Stalin, *Foundations of Leninism*, London, 1942, p. 91 (my italics).
17. *Tribun du peuple*, 5 Nov. 1795.
18. *The Correspondence of William Augustus Miles*, 2 vols., London, 1890, II, 175–8 (letter of 22 June 1794).
19. Cit. Jacob, p. 146. In fact, as we have seen, Robespierre only came to live at the Duplays' two years after the Revolution began, in the summer of 1791.
20. Jacob, pp. 166, 191.
21. *Mémoires de Levasseur de la Sarthe*, Paris, 1828; cit. Jacob pp. 155–7.
22. *Oeuvres*, x, 357, 546–8.
23. Jacob, p. 219.
24. Jacob, pp. 88, 201.
25. J. Massin, *Robespierre*, Paris, 1956, p. 66.

26. *L'Ami du Peuple*, 3 May 1792 (my translation).

27. *Oeuvres*, x, 550.

28. Manfred, p. 78.

29. C. L. R. James, *The Black Jacobins*, New York, 1963, pp. 76–7, 141–2, 178.

30. James, Preface to 1938 edition, p. x.

INDEX

Acton, Lord, historian, 66, 75, 76, 82
Adolphus, John A., historian, 58, 85
"agrarian law" (*loi agraire*), 151-2, 189
Alison, Sir Archibald, historian, 67
Alsace, 26
Amar, André, 48
Anouilh, Jean, playwright, 85
Appel à la nation artésienne, 17, 130
"aristocratic revolt", 16-17
Armées révolutionnaires 37, 40, 44, 90, 110, 112
Arras (Artois), 14-17, 25, 67, 82, 85, 95, 101, 129, 130
Artois, Comte d', 19
assignats, 34, 36, 39, 46, 138, 145, 204
August Decrees, 20, 131, 137
Aulard, Alphonse, historian, 22, 56, 68, 70, 73-4, 77, 78, 80, 89, 91, 207
"Austrian Committee", 28
Avignon, 23, 25, 102

Babeuf, Gracchus, 61, 84, 89, 96, 143, 204, 211, 212
Bailly, Jean-Sylvain, 117
Barère, Bertrand, 38, 46, 50, 51, 61, 69, 106, 115, 119-20, 147, 150, 183, 207
Barnave, Pierre-Joseph, 21, 77, 117
Barras, Paul-Jean, 50, 52
Barruel, Abbé, author, 83
Bastille, 19, 135, 170, 179, 180, 184
Belgium, 34, 48, 161, 203
Belloc, Hilaire, biographer, 74-5
Billaud-Varenne, Jean-Nicolas, 27, 32, 38, 43, 50, 60, 61, 129, 142, 149
Blanc, Louis, historian, 62-3, 67, 70
Blanqui, Auguste, 86, 208
Boissy d'Anglas, François-Antoine, 143, 152
Bonaparte, Napoleon, 38, 52, 58, 68, 71, 75, 196, 197, 205

Bordeaux, 38, 50, 111, 206
Bouillé, Comte de, 23, 24
Bouloiseau, Marc, historian, 11
Breton Club, 18, 24; *see also* Jacobins
Brinton, Crane, historian, 80
Brissot de Warville, Jacques-Pierre, 27, 28, 29-30, 117, 159, 161, 163, 171, 180, 183, 185, 205
Brissotins, 20, 32, 131, 157; *see also* Girondins
Brougham, Henry, political essayist, 69, 72
Brunswick, Duke of, 28, 29-30
Buchez and Roux, editors, 56, 62
Buechner, George, playwright, 45, 64-5, 66, 67, 84
Buonarroti, Filippo, 61, 63, 201, 206-7
Burke, Edmund, political essayist, 59, 68, 83

cahiers de doléances, 101, 138
Cambacérès, Jean-Jacques, 58, 60, 68, 75
Cambon, Pierre-Joseph, 143, 152, 211
Carlyle, Thomas, 22, 38, 65
Carnot, Lazare, 16, 38, 49-50, 115, 197
Carrier, Jean-Baptiste, 40, 50, 60, 80, 175, 206
Champ de Mars, 24-5, 48, 157-8, 168, 181-2, 183, 188, 191, 202, 209, 210
Chaumette, Anaxagoras, 37, 38, 42, 43, 185-6, 191, 192
Cloots, Anacharsis, 161, 162, 172, 173, 174, 175
Cobb, Richard, historian, 90, 91, 112
Collot d'Herbois, Jean-Marie, 32, 38, 39, 43, 47, 50, 60, 67, 142, 145-6, 149, 175, 206
comités révolutionnaires 44, 52, 110, 114, 191-2

249

Index

Index

Index

Index